DISNEY | SQUARE ENIX

KINGDOM HEARTS
CHAIN OF MEMORIES

2

Adapted by
Shiro Amano

TOKYOPOP®

HAMBURG // LONDON // LOS ANGELES // TOKYO

Kingdom Hearts Chain of Memories Volume 2
Created by Shiro Amano

Associate Editor - Peter Ahlstrom
Retouch and Lettering - Kimie Kim
Cover Layout - James Lee

Editor - Bryce P. Coleman
Digital Imaging Manager - Chris Buford
Pre-Production Supervisor - Erika Terriquez
Art Director - Anne Marie Horne
Production Manager - Elisabeth Brizzi
Managing Editor - Vy Nguyen
VP of Production - Ron Klamert
Editor-in-Chief - Rob Tokar
Publisher - Mike Kiley
President and C.O.O. - John Parker
C.E.O. and Chief Creative Officer - Stuart Levy

A  Manga

TOKYOPOP Inc.
5900 Wilshire Blvd. Suite 2000
Los Angeles, CA 90036

E-mail: info@TOKYOPOP.com
Come visit us online at www.TOKYOPOP.com

ISBN: 978-1-4278-0445-7

First TOKYOPOP printing: February 2007
10 9 8 7 6 5 4 3 2 1
Printed in the USA

KINGDOM HEARTS
CHAIN OF MEMORIES

Disney SQUARE ENIX

KINGDOM HEARTS CHAIN OF MEMORIES

2

Sora

A boy chosen by the Keyblade—the key for saving the world. In search of his missing friend Riku, Sora continues his journey to return to his Destiny Islands home.

Goofy

Together with Sora and Donald, he is searching for the missing King Mickey. His trademark phrases are "A-hyuck" and "Gawrsh."

Donald Duck

Sora's comrade in the journey. He's a master magician, but once he gets bent out of shape...

CHARACTER & STORY

Sora lives peacefully on the Destiny Islands with his friends Riku and Kairi until they are whisked away to separate worlds in the middle of a mysterious storm. While searching for Riku and Kairi, Sora receives the Keyblade, which he uses to fight the Heartless monsters who are trying to steal people's hearts and to infiltrate the heart of all worlds, Kingdom Hearts. He also meets Donald and Goofy, who are searching for their missing King, Mickey, and they join together to search for their lost friends.

After journeying through numerous worlds, they at last find their friends and discover that a wise man named Ansem created the Heartless and became corrupted in his search for power. Riku, who also has been tempted by darkness, joins with Mickey to close the door to Kingdom Hearts from the inside as Sora closes it from the outside, and Ansem is defeated.

Kairi makes it back home safe, but Sora finds himself parted from her again. As he, Donald, and Goofy renew their search for Riku and the King, they come across the mysterious Castle Oblivion and a hooded figure who cryptically says, "Ahead lies something you need, but to claim it, you must lose something dear," and "In this place, to find is to lose...and to lose is to find." As Sora & co. progress through the castle, they find that they are steadily losing their memories! Riku also awakens in the castle's depths to find that he is not as rid of Ansem and the darkness as he had hoped. The shadowy members of Organization XIII who run the castle also seem to have their own sinister plans for Sora and Riku, plans involving a young girl with a sketchbook...

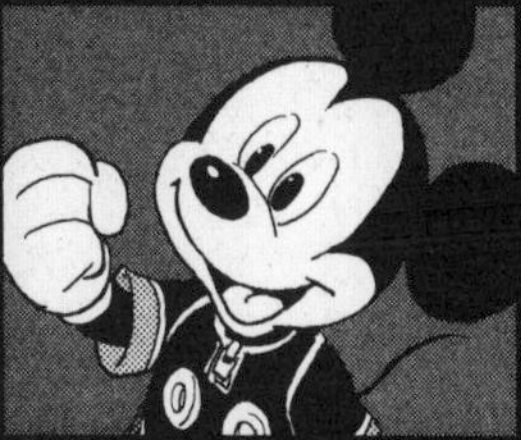

King [Mickey]

King of Disney Castle. He is missing together with Riku.

Naminé

A mysterious girl who is quietly drawing pictures alone in one of the castle rooms.

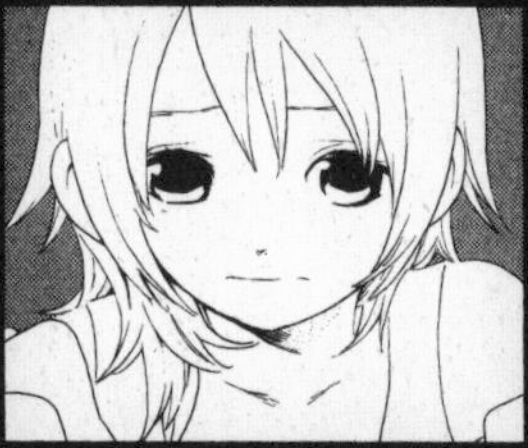

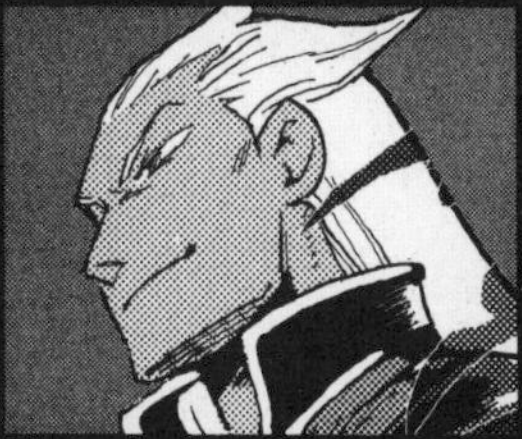

Ansem

The "Seeker of Darkness" who hid in Riku's heart to control him.

Kairi

Sora's childhood friend. She's waiting on the island for Sora to return.

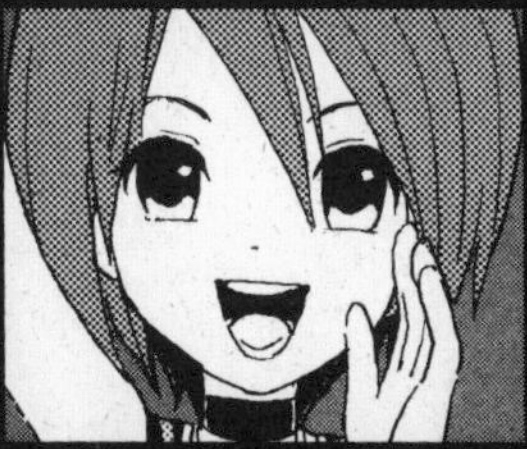

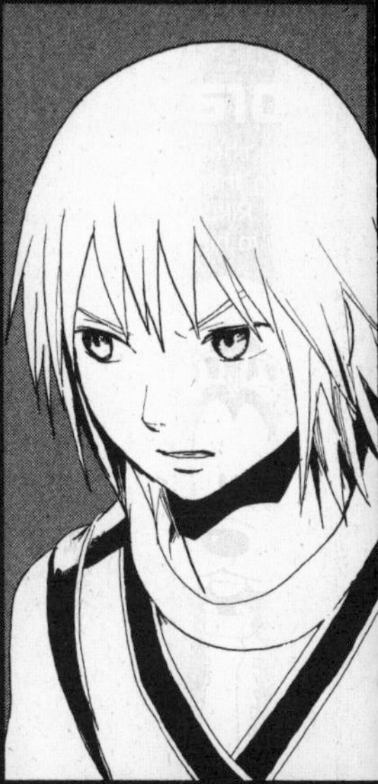

Riku

Sora's best friend. He closes the door from the inside together with the King, and gets left behind in the world of darkness.

Organization XIII Members

The members of this mysterious organization dress in black robes and search for secrets of the heart...

Underground Members

Zexion

[No. 6 in the Organization]

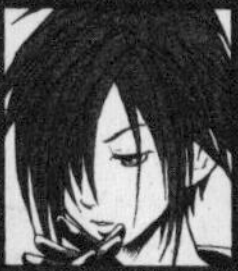

Leader of the Underground Members. Meticulous by nature, the word is that he's a surprisingly domestic type!

Lexaeus

[No. 5 in the Organization]

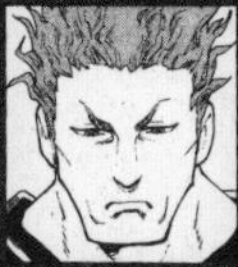

Administers the underground together with Zexion and Vexen. Avid puzzler.

Vexen

[No. 4 in the Organization]

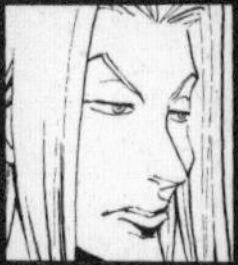

Oldest member of Castle Oblivion. But not necessarily respected by the younger members...

Aboveground Members

Larxene

[No. 12 in the Organization]

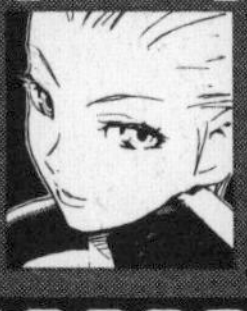

Cold-blooded, temperamental and vicious. Once she flies off the handle, there's no stopping her.

Marluxia

[No. 11 in the Organization]

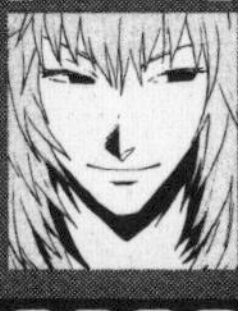

Lord of Castle Oblivion who loves flowers. It seems he's plotting something...

Axel

[No. 8 in the Organization]

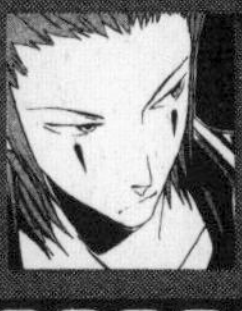

Mysterious individual who appears before Sora from time to time and leaves little bits of advice.

CONTENTS

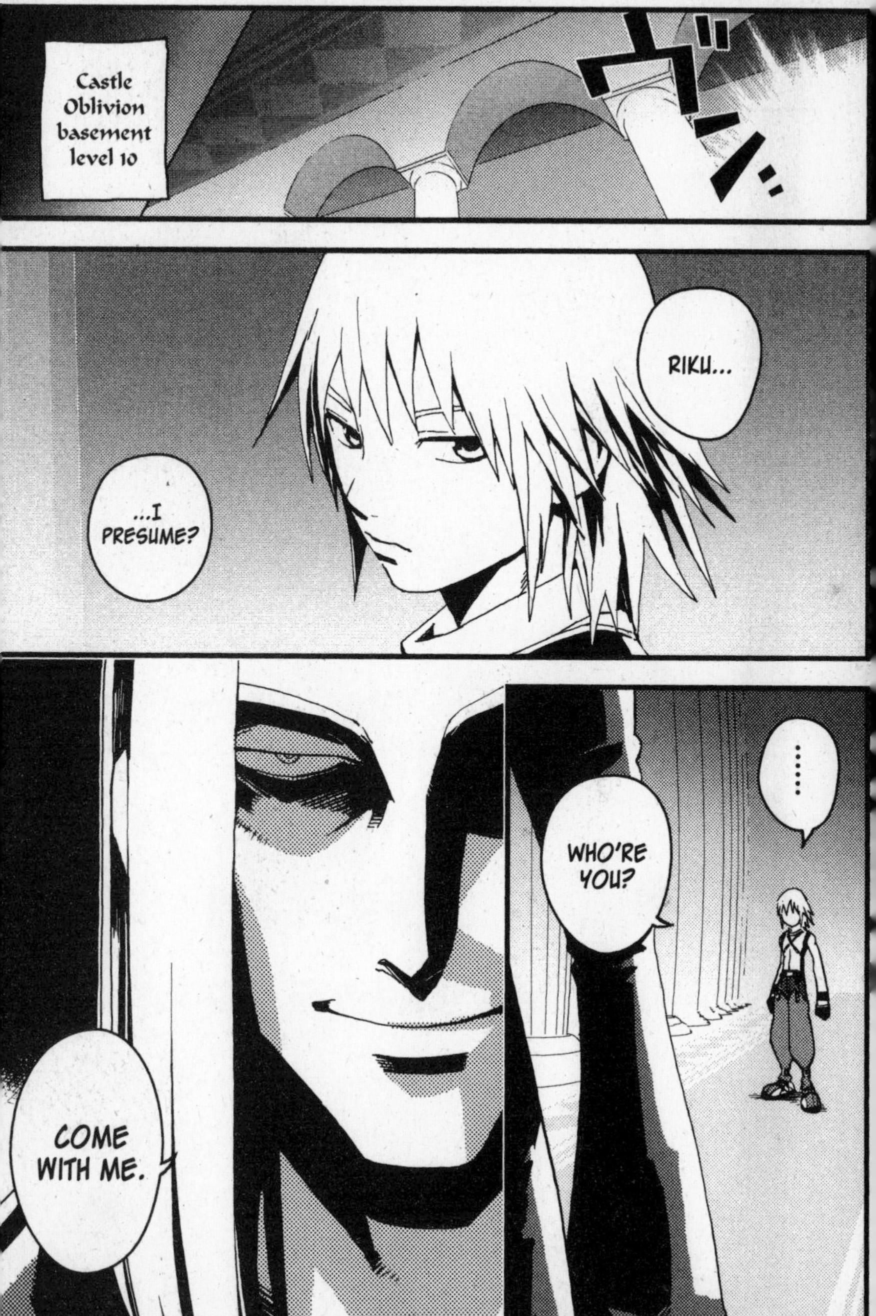
Castle Oblivion basement level 10
RIKU...
...I PRESUME?
......
WHO'RE YOU?
COME WITH ME.

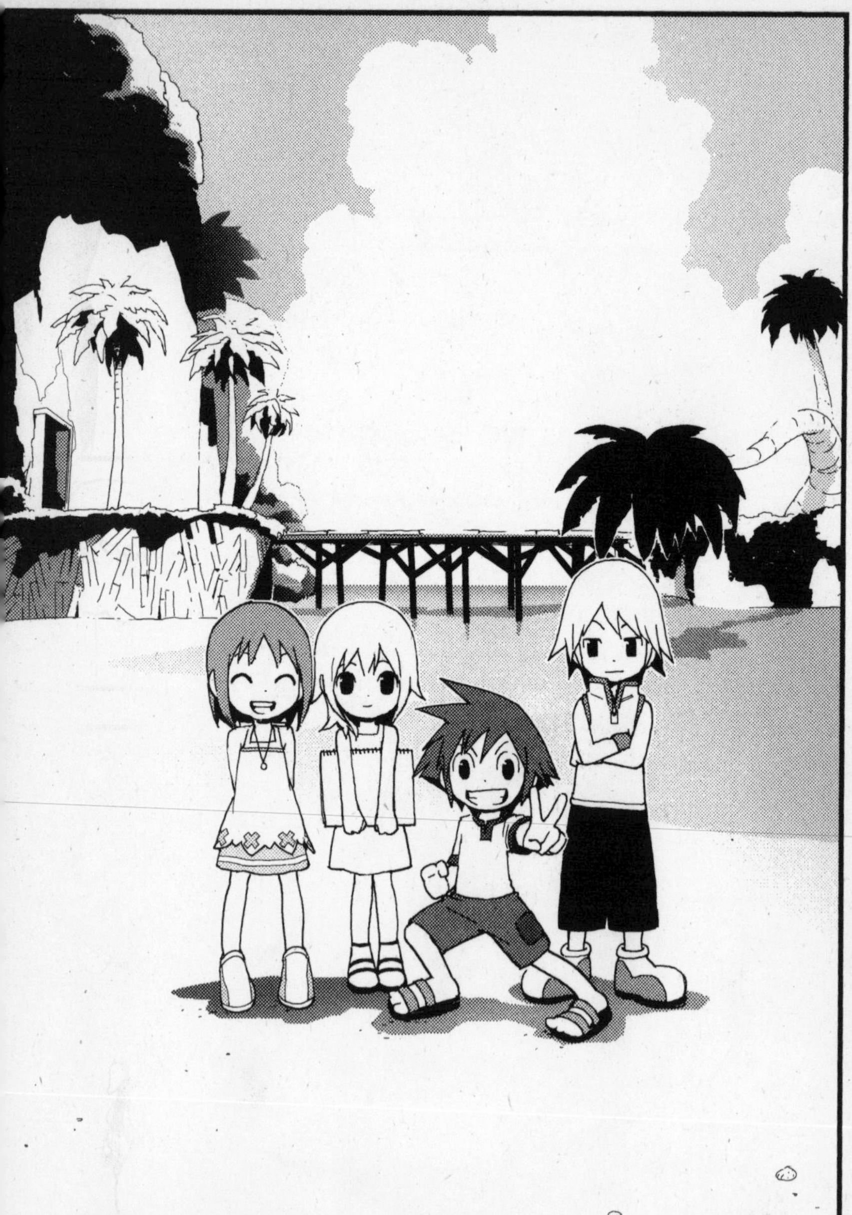

Card 07 Memories

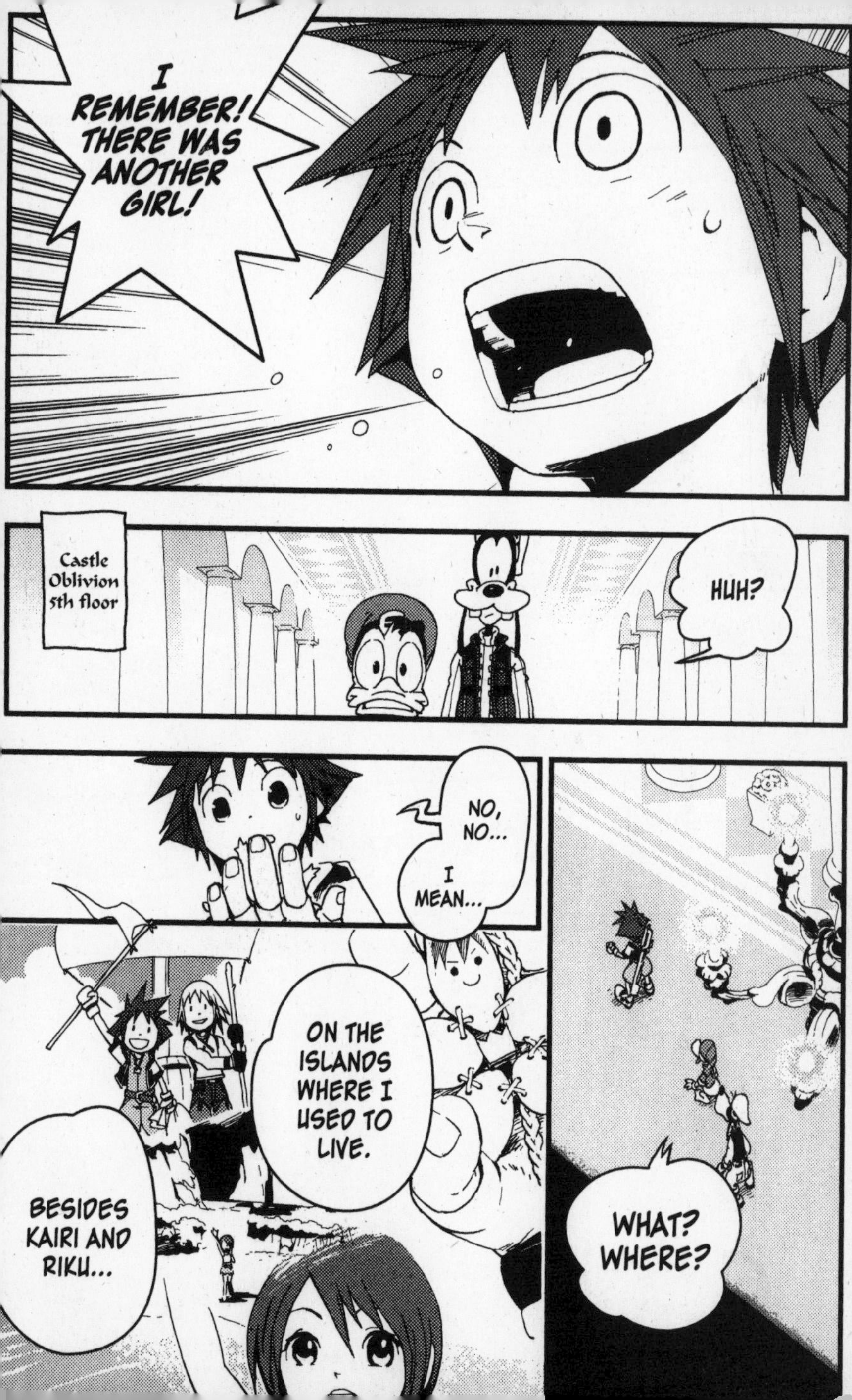
I REMEMBER! THERE WAS ANOTHER GIRL!
HUH?
Castle Oblivion 5th floor
WHAT? WHERE?
NO, NO...
I MEAN...
ON THE ISLANDS WHERE I USED TO LIVE.
BESIDES KAIRI AND RIKU...

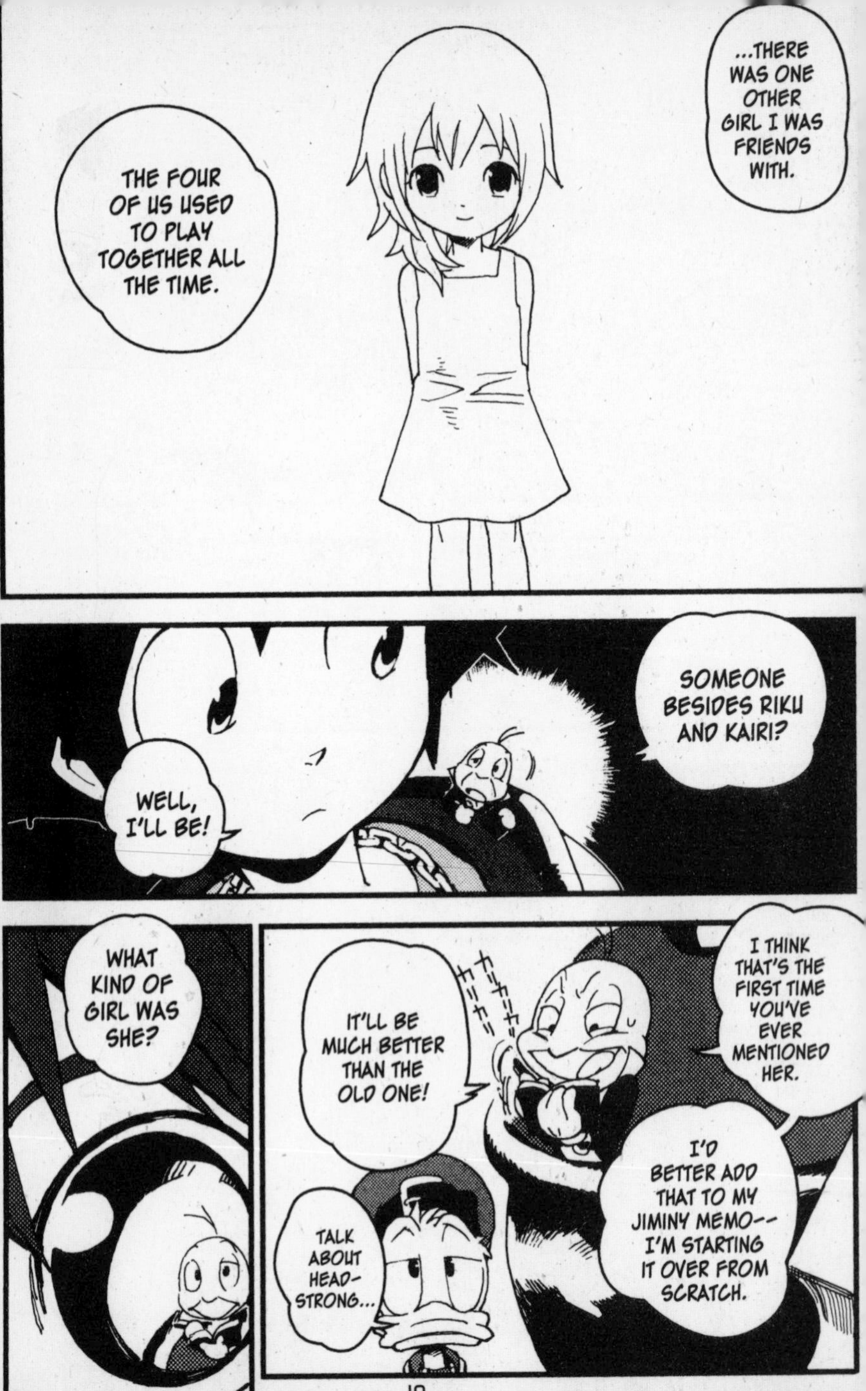
...THERE WAS ONE OTHER GIRL I WAS FRIENDS WITH.
THE FOUR OF US USED TO PLAY TOGETHER ALL THE TIME.
SOMEONE BESIDES RIKU AND KAIRI?
WELL, I'LL BE!
I THINK THAT'S THE FIRST TIME YOU'VE EVER MENTIONED HER.
I'D BETTER ADD THAT TO MY JIMINY MEMO-- I'M STARTING IT OVER FROM SCRATCH.
IT'LL BE MUCH BETTER THAN THE OLD ONE!
TALK ABOUT HEAD-STRONG...
WHAT KIND OF GIRL WAS SHE?

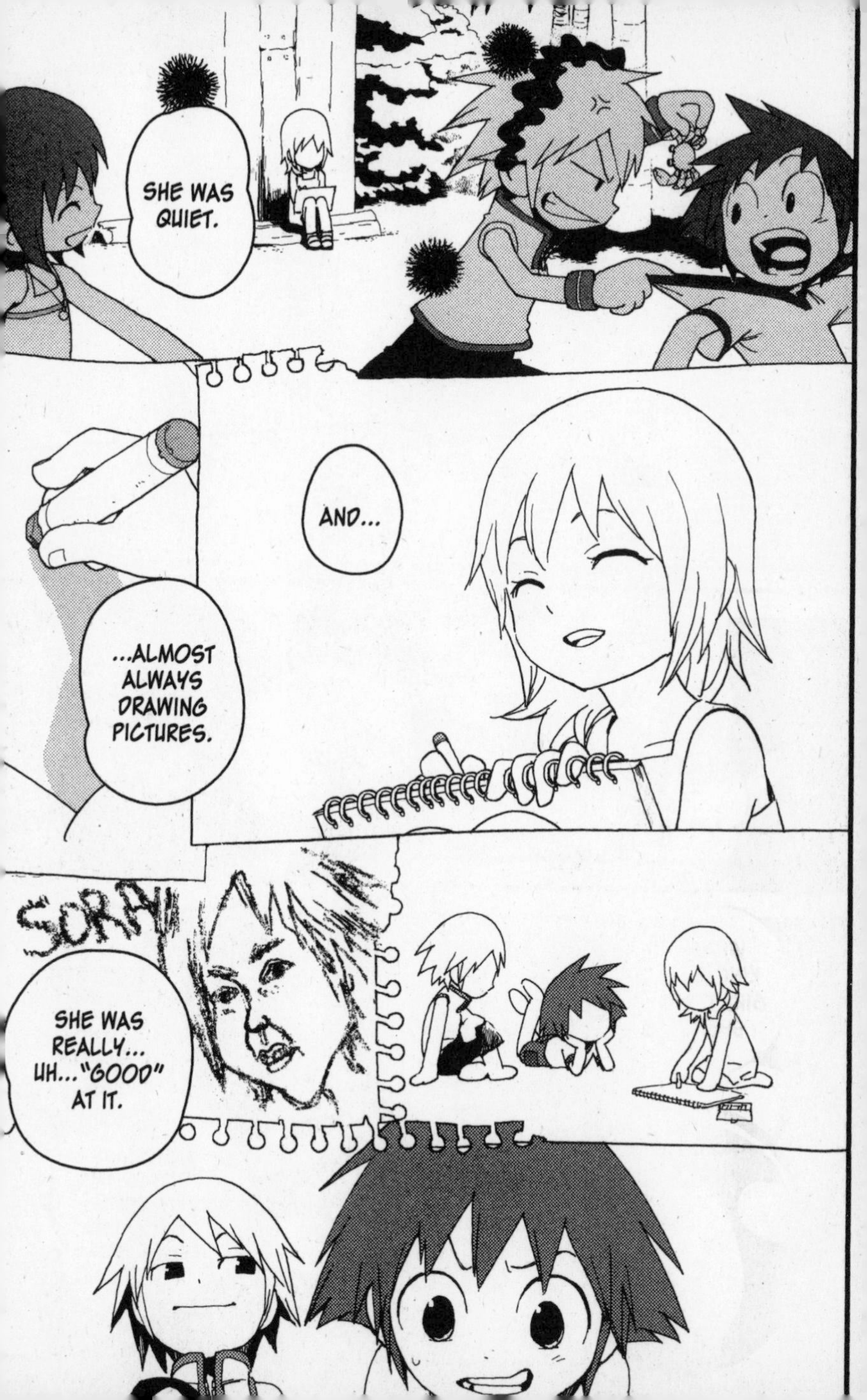

SHE WAS QUIET.
AND...
...ALMOST ALWAYS DRAWING PICTURES.
SORA!!
SHE WAS REALLY... UH..."GOOD" AT IT.

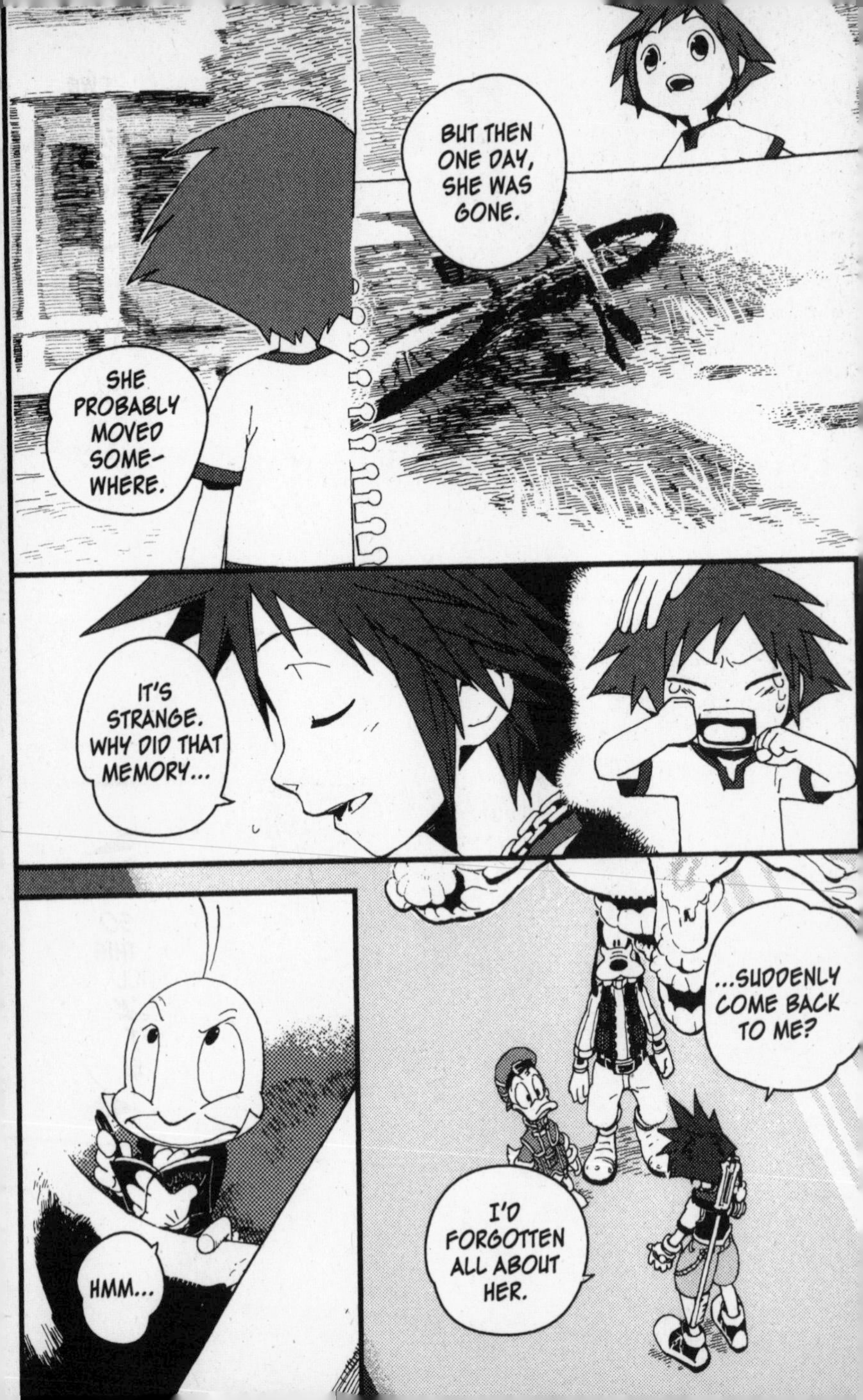
BUT THEN ONE DAY, SHE WAS GONE.
SHE PROBABLY MOVED SOME-WHERE.
IT'S STRANGE. WHY DID THAT MEMORY...
...SUDDENLY COME BACK TO ME?
I'D FORGOTTEN ALL ABOUT HER.
HMM...

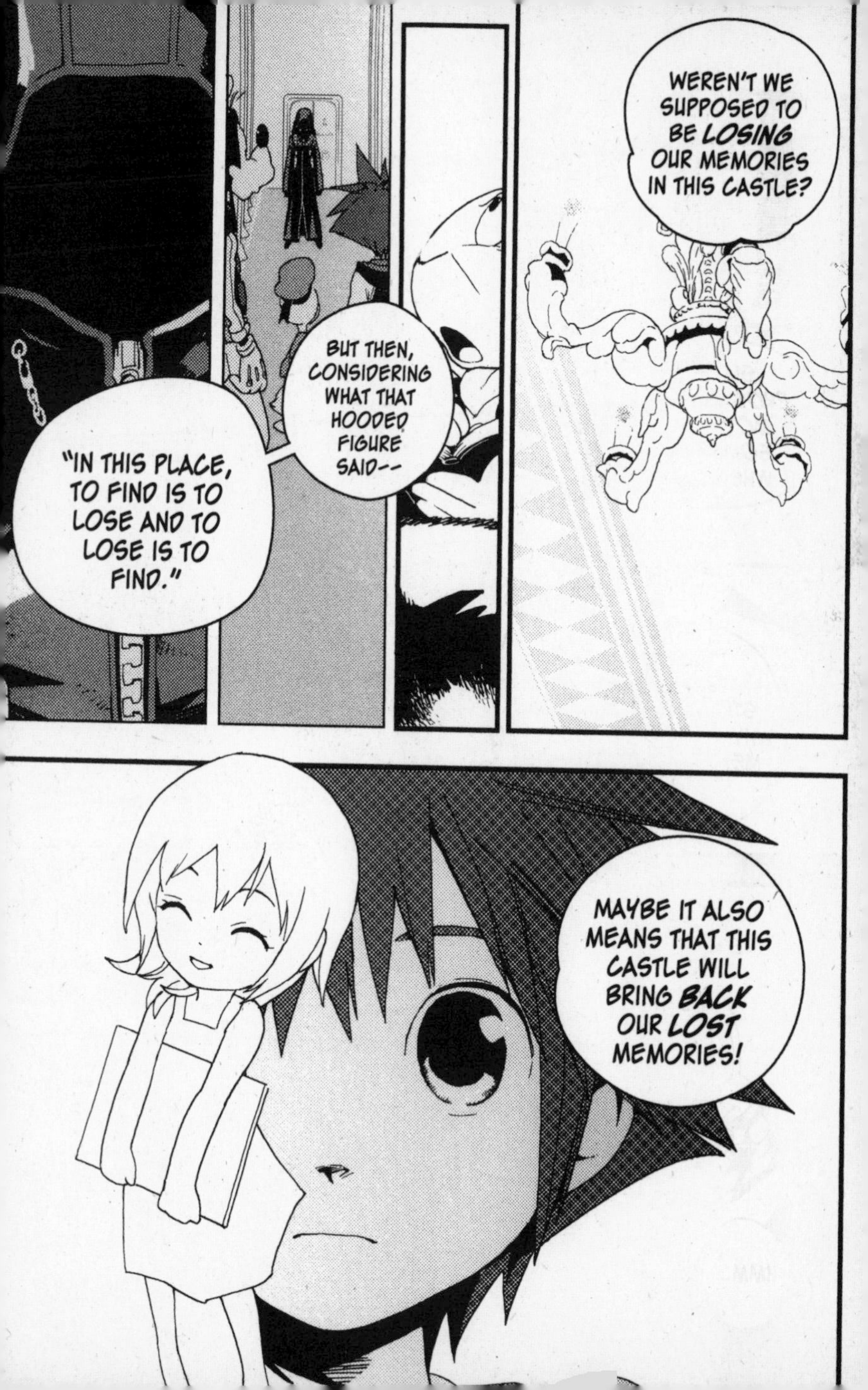
WEREN'T WE SUPPOSED TO BE *LOSING* OUR MEMORIES IN THIS CASTLE?
BUT THEN, CONSIDERING WHAT THAT HOODED FIGURE SAID--
"IN THIS PLACE, TO FIND IS TO LOSE AND TO LOSE IS TO FIND."
MAYBE IT ALSO MEANS THAT THIS CASTLE WILL BRING *BACK* OUR *LOST* MEMORIES!

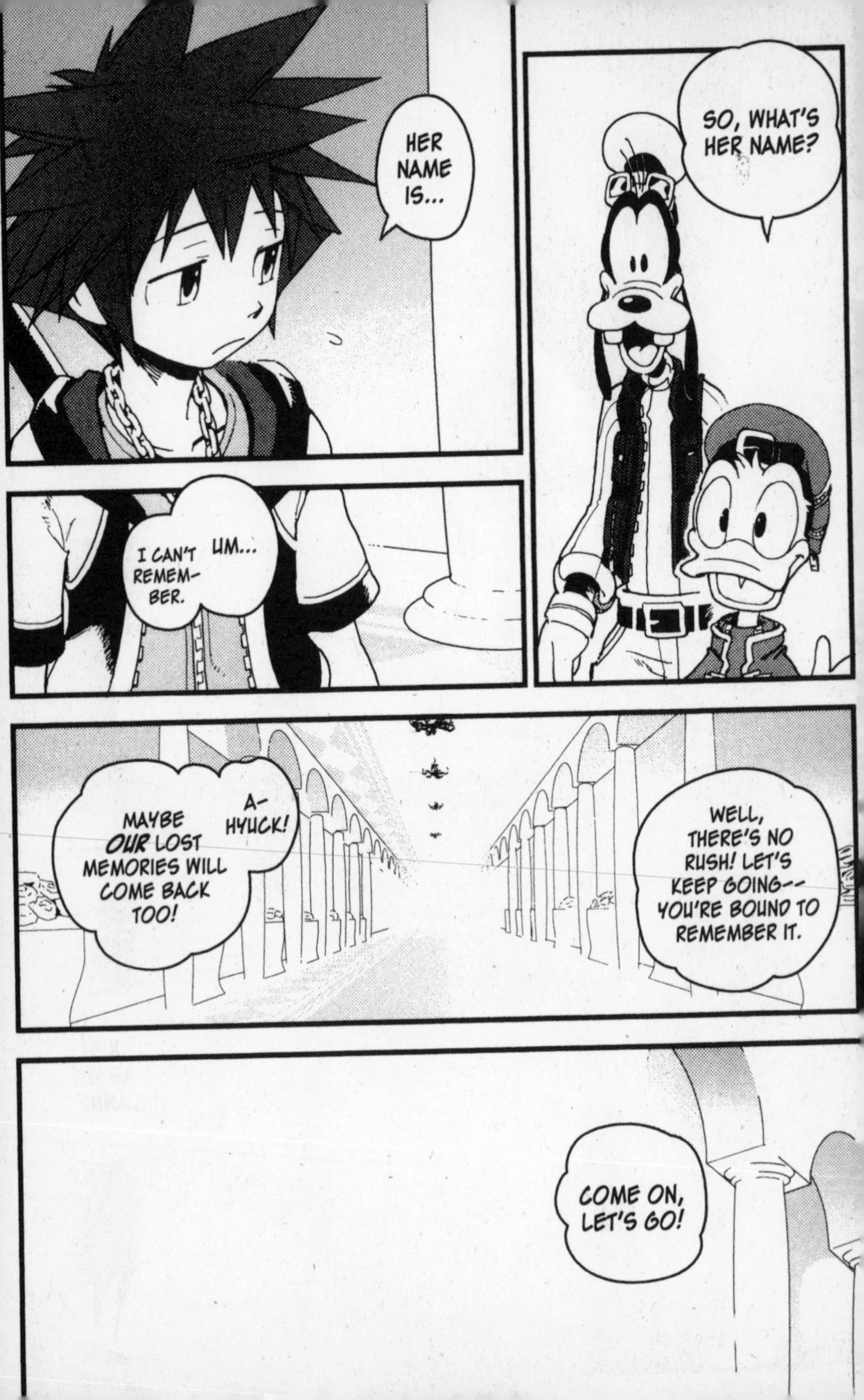
SO, WHAT'S HER NAME?
HER NAME IS...
UM...
I CAN'T REMEMBER.
WELL, THERE'S NO RUSH! LET'S KEEP GOING--YOU'RE BOUND TO REMEMBER IT.
A-HYUCK!
MAYBE OUR LOST MEMORIES WILL COME BACK TOO!
COME ON, LET'S GO!

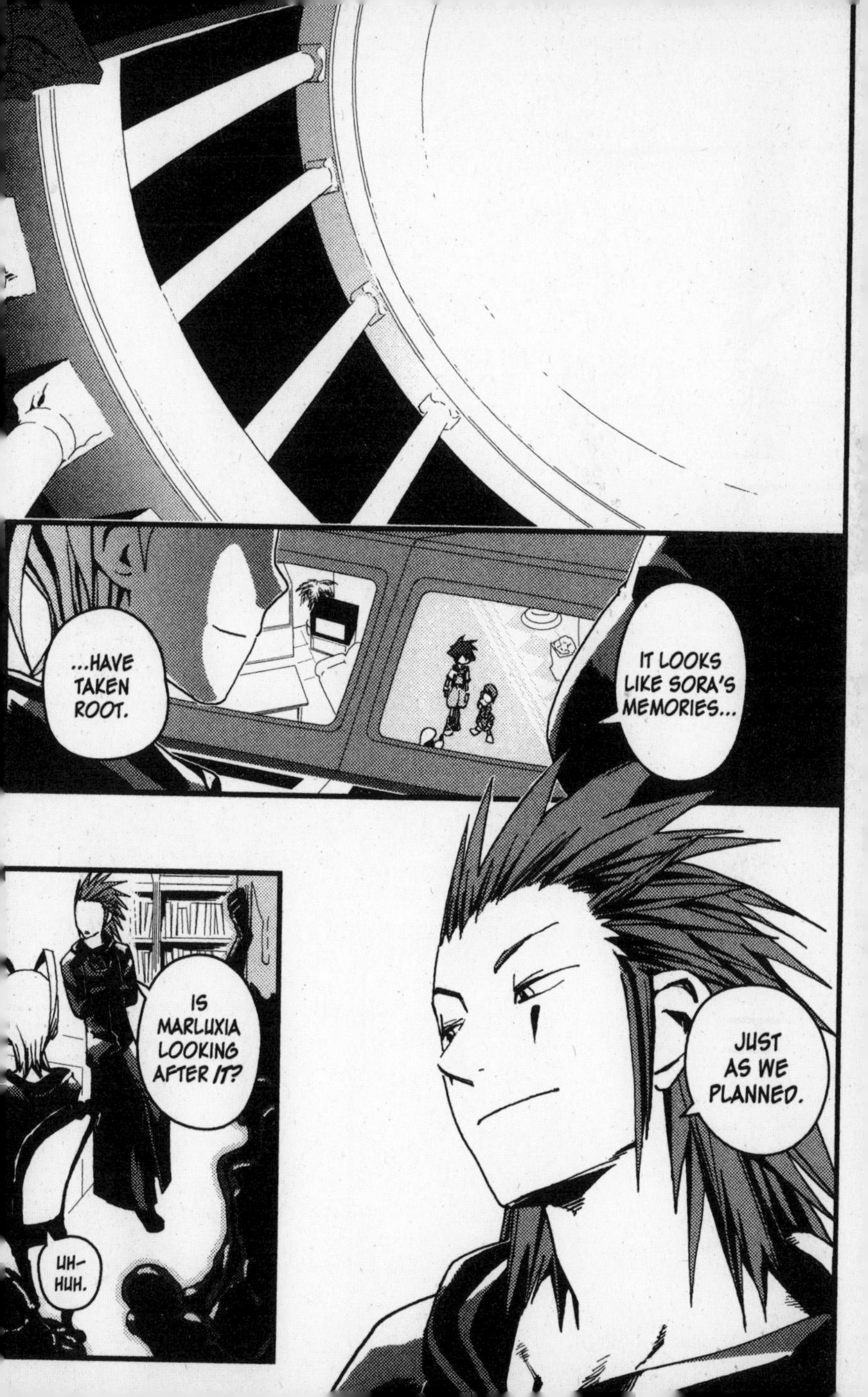
IT LOOKS LIKE SORA'S MEMORIES...
...HAVE TAKEN ROOT.
JUST AS WE PLANNED.
IS MARLUXIA LOOKING AFTER *IT*?
UH-HUH.

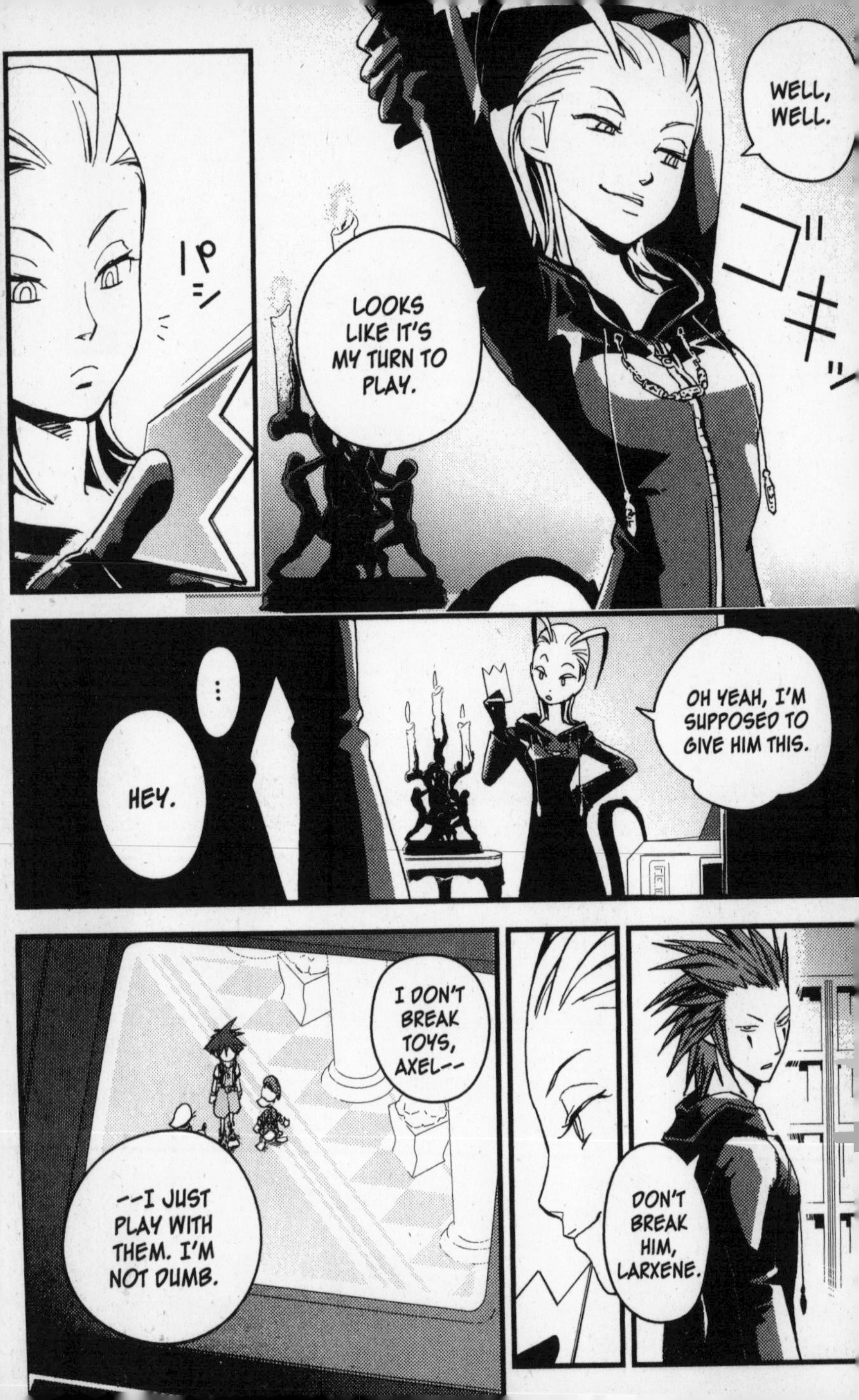
WELL, WELL.
LOOKS LIKE IT'S MY TURN TO PLAY.
OH YEAH, I'M SUPPOSED TO GIVE HIM THIS.
...
HEY.
DON'T BREAK HIM, LARXENE.
I DON'T BREAK TOYS, AXEL--
--I JUST PLAY WITH THEM. I'M NOT DUMB.

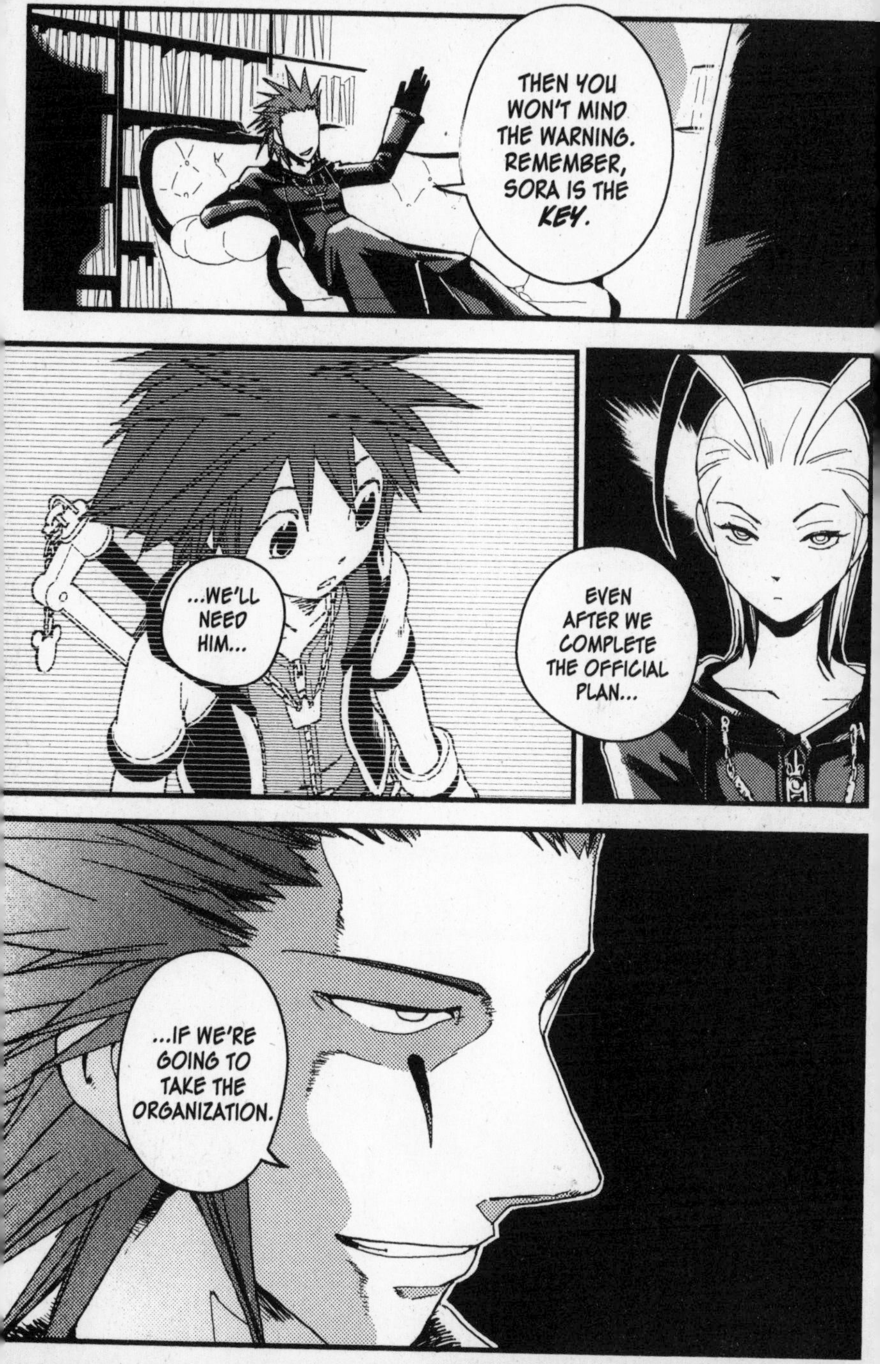
THEN YOU WON'T MIND THE WARNING. REMEMBER, SORA IS THE KEY.
EVEN AFTER WE COMPLETE THE OFFICIAL PLAN...
...WE'LL NEED HIM...
...IF WE'RE GOING TO TAKE THE ORGANIZATION.

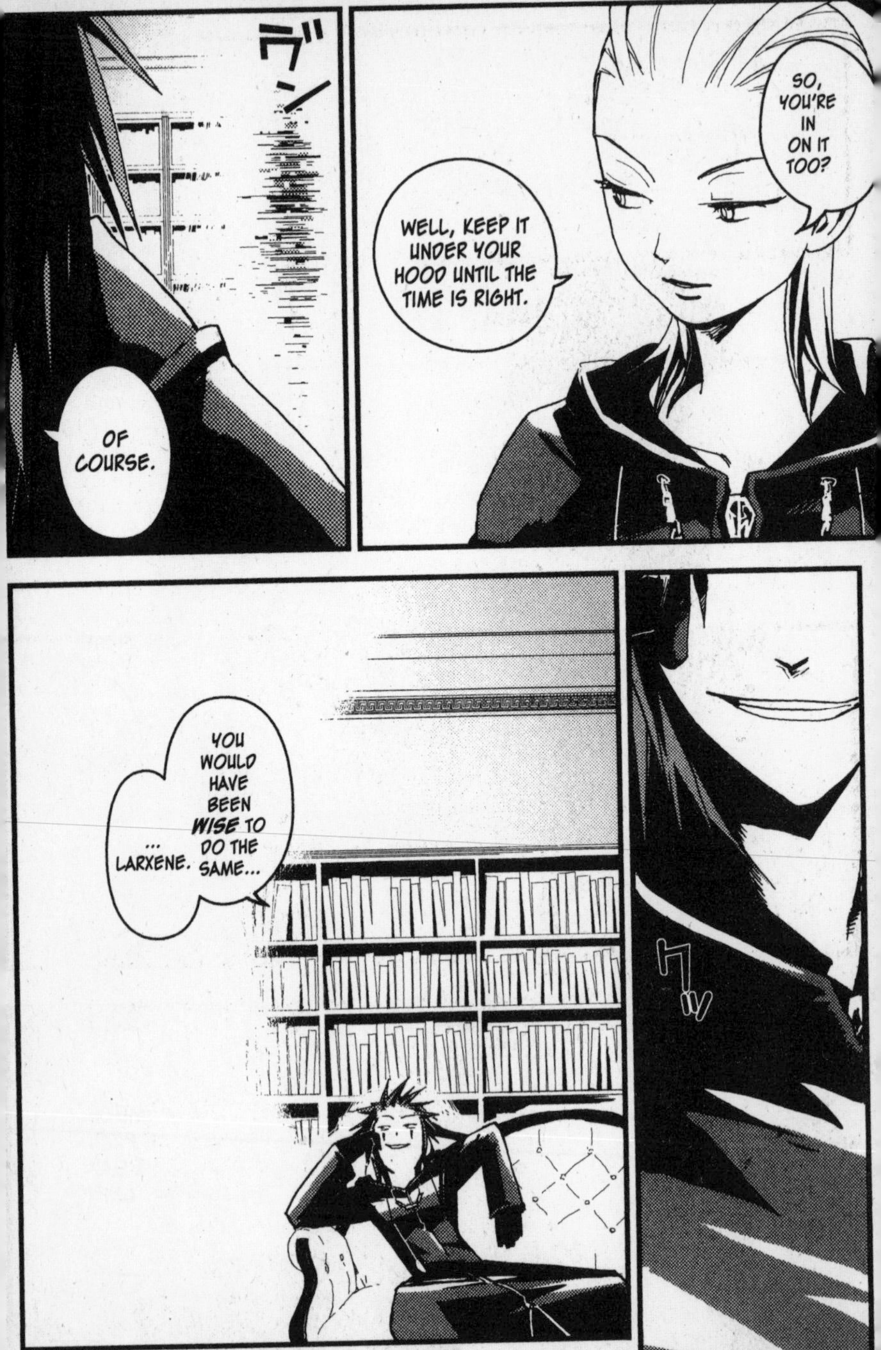
SO, YOU'RE IN ON IT TOO?
WELL, KEEP IT UNDER YOUR HOOD UNTIL THE TIME IS RIGHT.
ヴン
OF COURSE.
YOU WOULD HAVE BEEN *WISE* TO DO THE SAME... ... LARXENE.

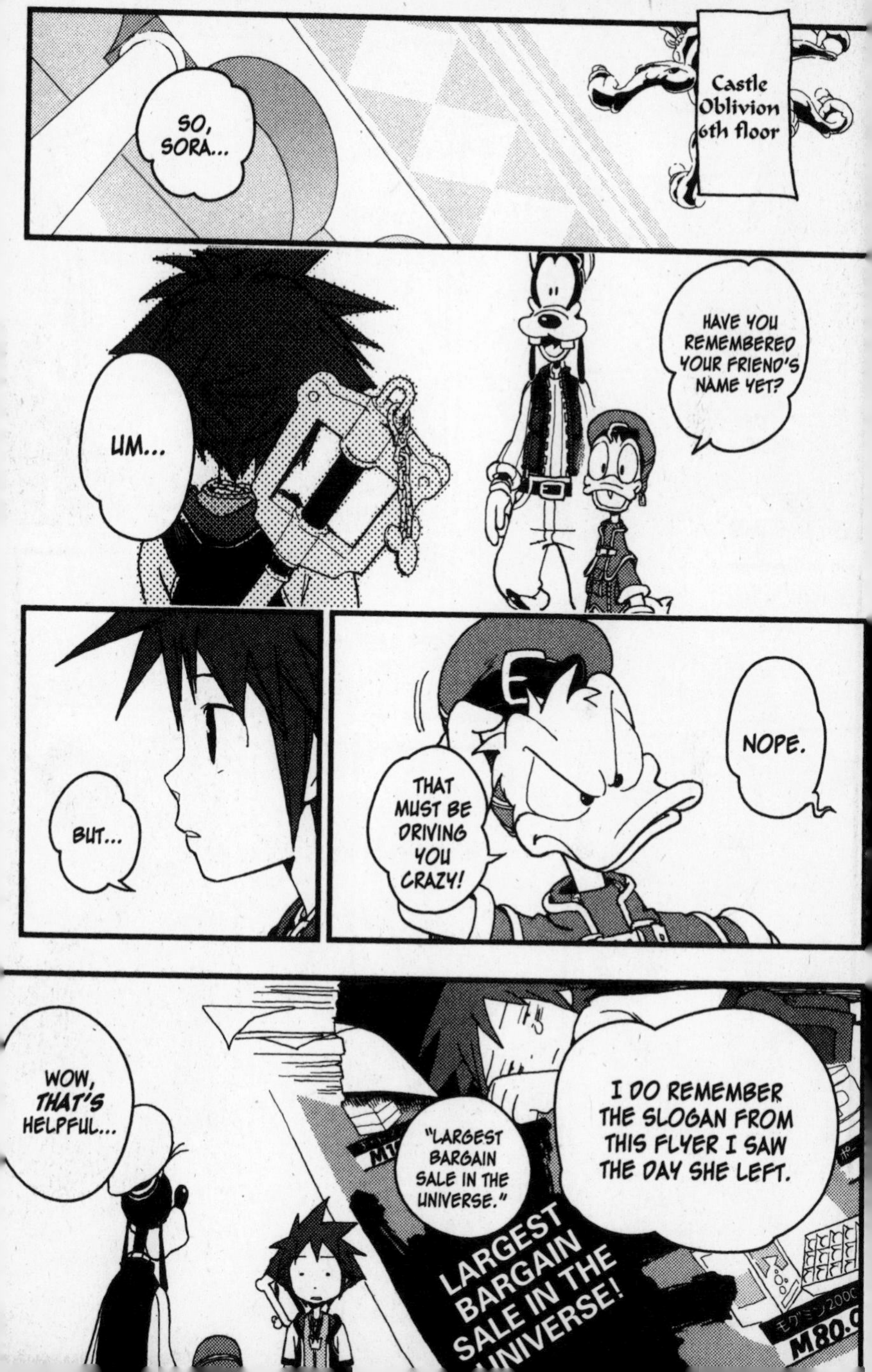
Castle Oblivion 6th floor
SO, SORA...
HAVE YOU REMEMBERED YOUR FRIEND'S NAME YET?
UM...
NOPE.
THAT MUST BE DRIVING YOU CRAZY!
BUT...
I DO REMEMBER THE SLOGAN FROM THIS FLYER I SAW THE DAY SHE LEFT.
"LARGEST BARGAIN SALE IN THE UNIVERSE."
WOW, *THAT'S* HELPFUL...
LARGEST BARGAIN SALE IN THE UNIVERSE!

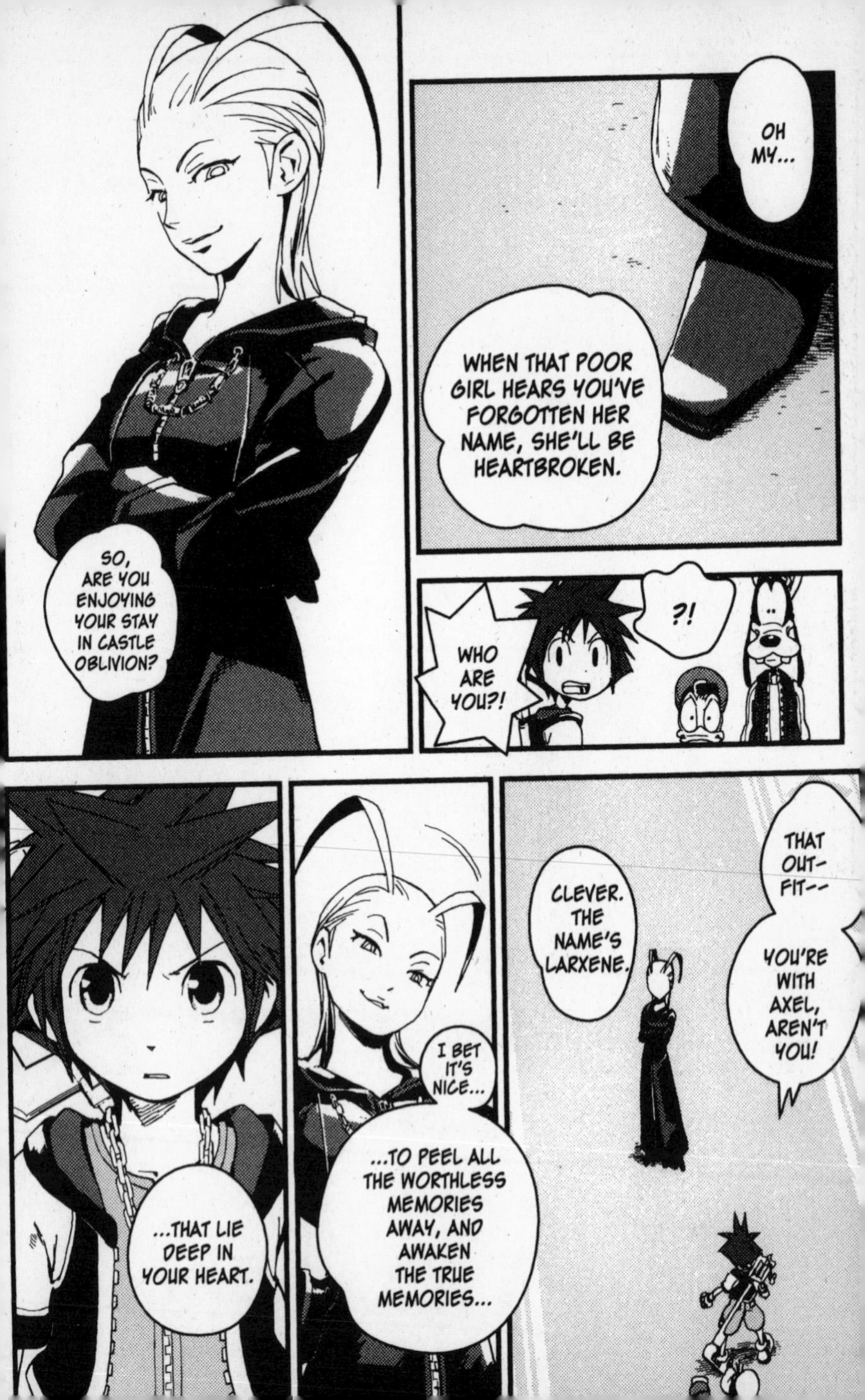
OH MY...
WHEN THAT POOR GIRL HEARS YOU'VE FORGOTTEN HER NAME, SHE'LL BE HEARTBROKEN.
?!
WHO ARE YOU?!
SO, ARE YOU ENJOYING YOUR STAY IN CASTLE OBLIVION?
THAT OUT-FIT--
YOU'RE WITH AXEL, AREN'T YOU!
CLEVER. THE NAME'S LARXENE.
I BET IT'S NICE...
...TO PEEL ALL THE WORTHLESS MEMORIES AWAY, AND AWAKEN THE TRUE MEMORIES...
...THAT LIE DEEP IN YOUR HEART.

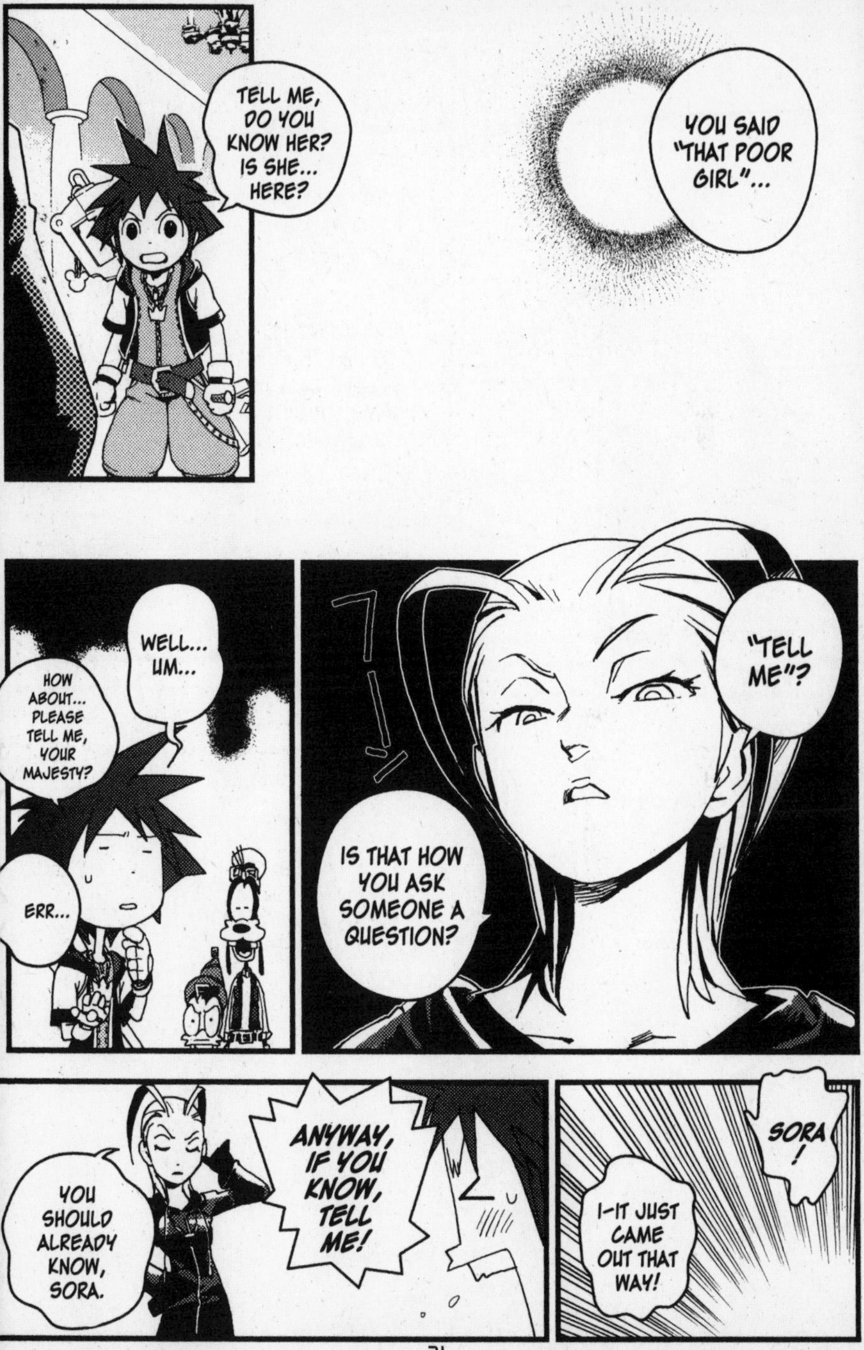
YOU SAID "THAT POOR GIRL"...
TELL ME, DO YOU KNOW HER? IS SHE... HERE?
"TELL ME"?
IS THAT HOW YOU ASK SOMEONE A QUESTION?
WELL... UM...
HOW ABOUT... PLEASE TELL ME, YOUR MAJESTY?
ERR...
SORA!
I-IT JUST CAME OUT THAT WAY!
ANYWAY, IF YOU KNOW, TELL ME!
YOU SHOULD ALREADY KNOW, SORA.

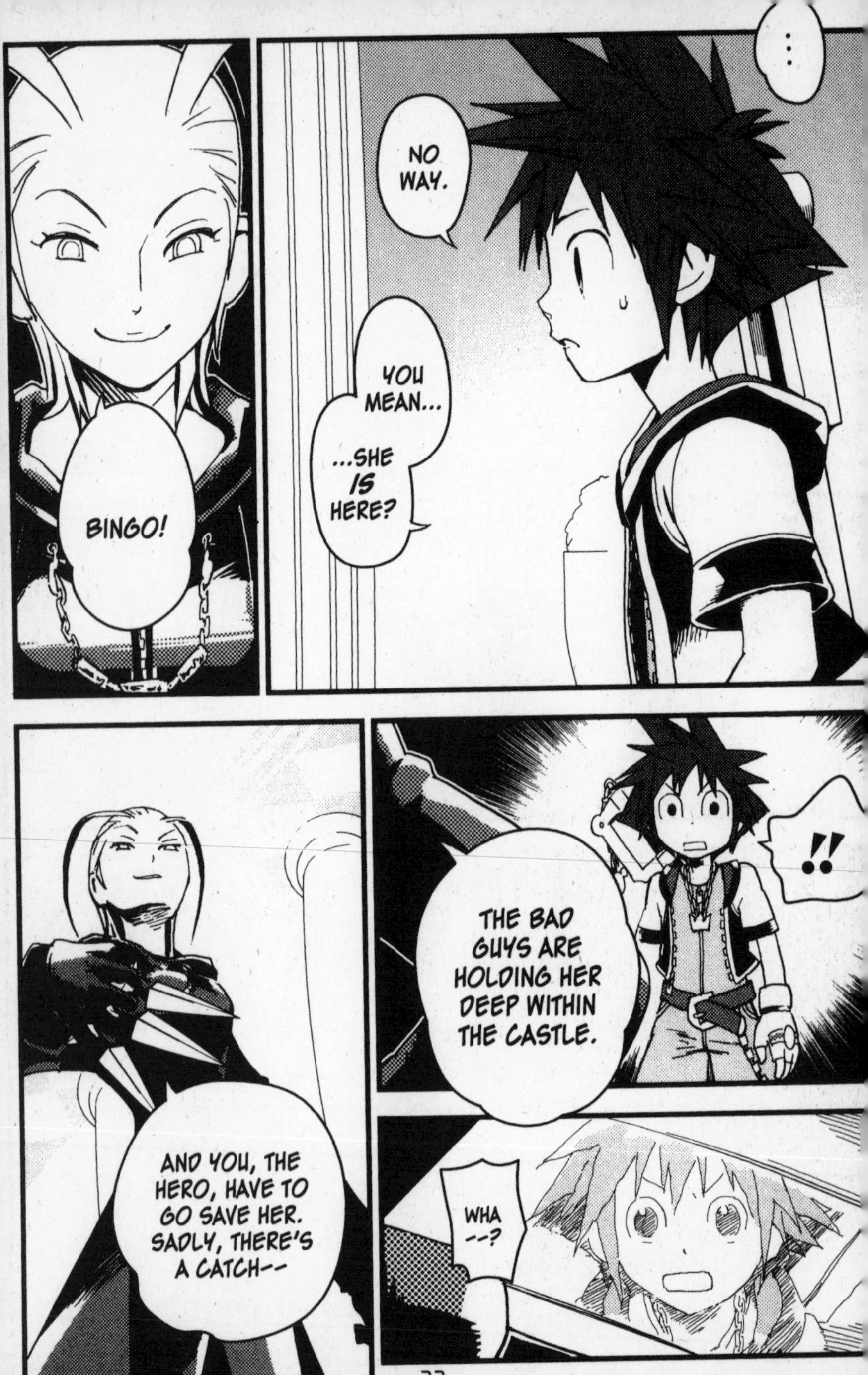
...
NO WAY.
YOU MEAN...
...SHE *IS* HERE?
BINGO!
!!
THE BAD GUYS ARE HOLDING HER DEEP WITHIN THE CASTLE.
WHA--?
AND YOU, THE HERO, HAVE TO GO SAVE HER. SADLY, THERE'S A CATCH--

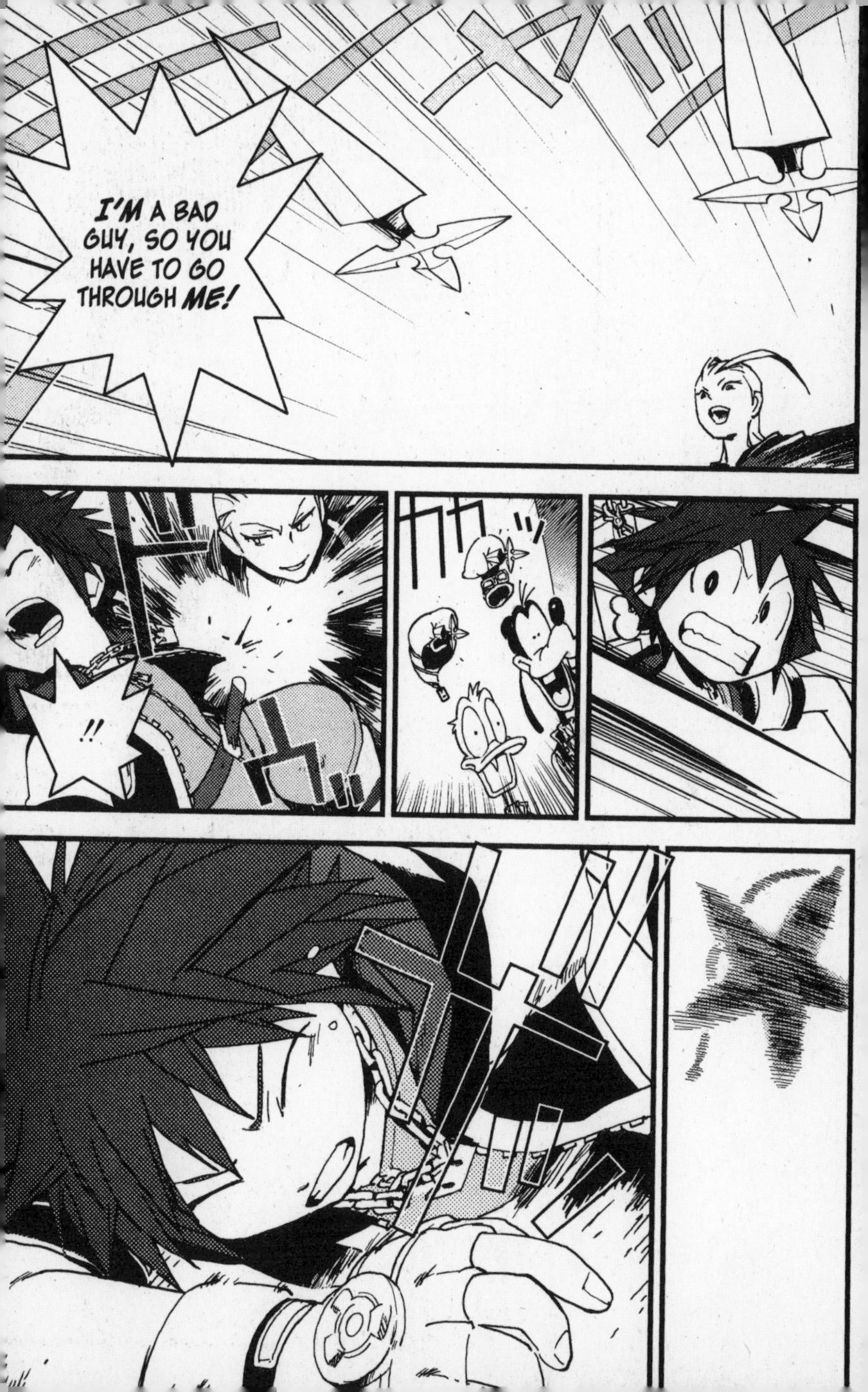
I'M A BAD GUY, SO YOU HAVE TO GO THROUGH ME!
!!

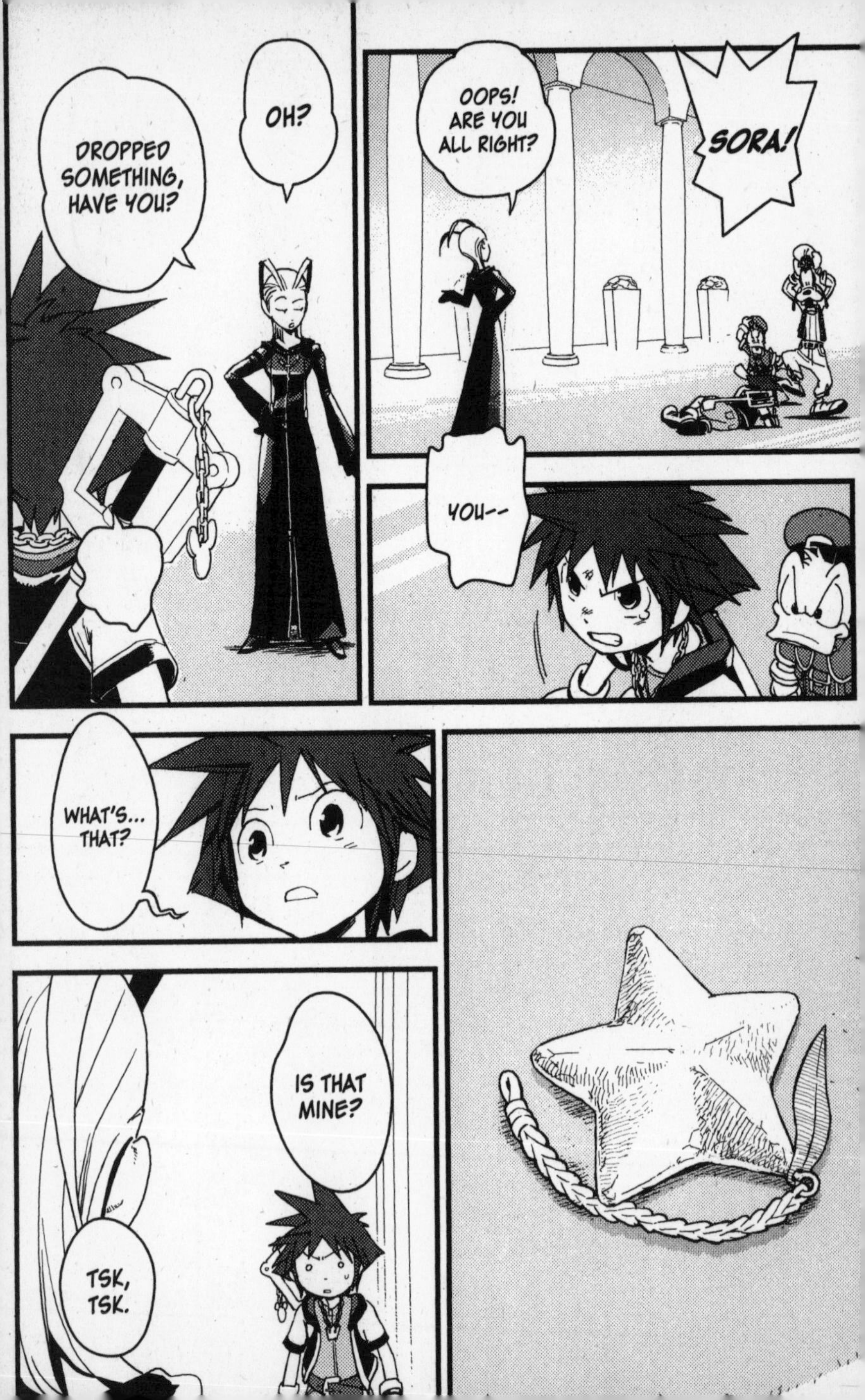
SORA!
OOPS! ARE YOU ALL RIGHT?
YOU--
OH?
DROPPED SOMETHING, HAVE YOU?
WHAT'S... THAT?
IS THAT MINE?
TSK, TSK.

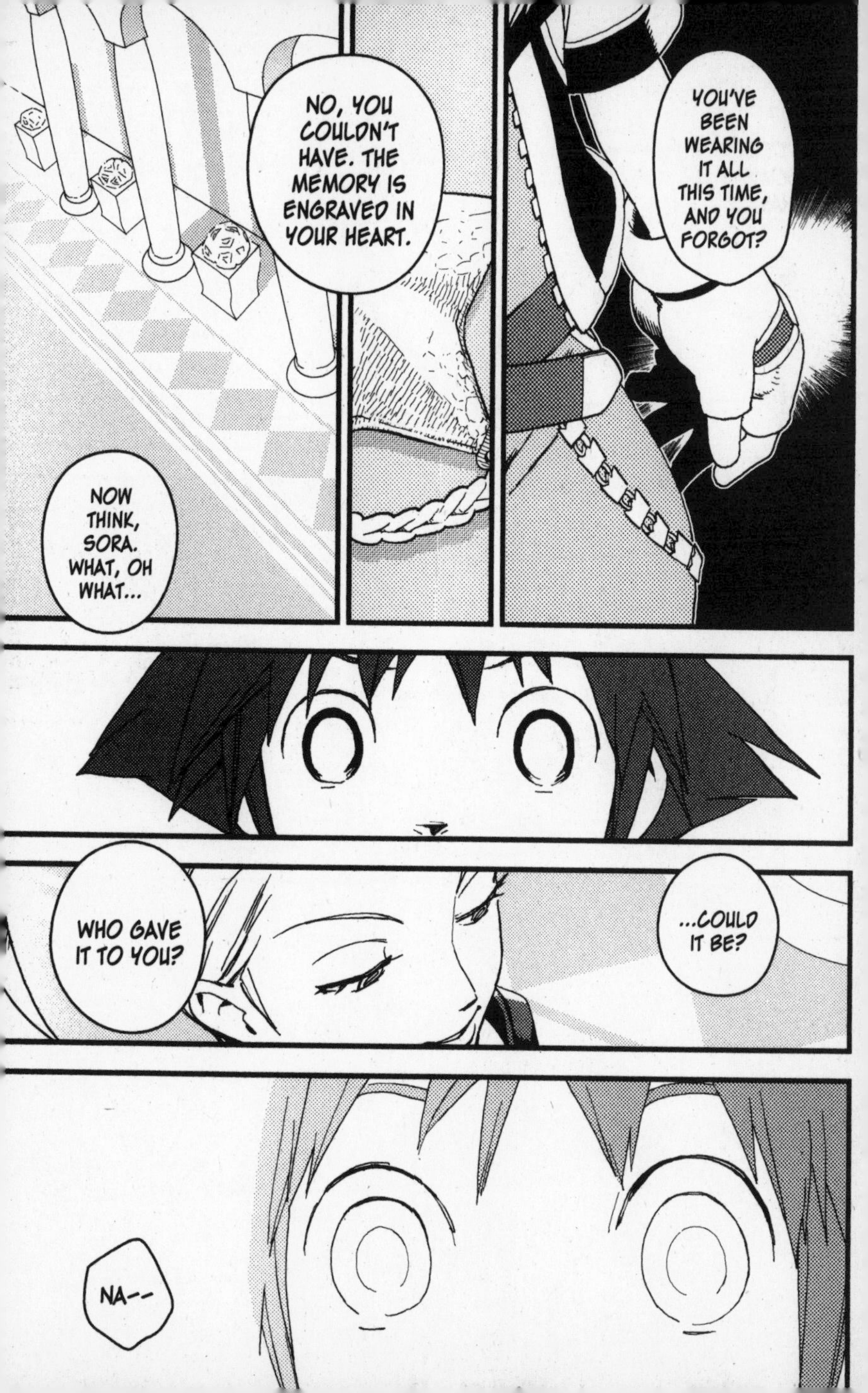
YOU'VE BEEN WEARING IT ALL THIS TIME, AND YOU FORGOT?
NO, YOU COULDN'T HAVE. THE MEMORY IS ENGRAVED IN YOUR HEART.
NOW THINK, SORA. WHAT, OH WHAT...
...COULD IT BE?
WHO GAVE IT TO YOU?
NA--

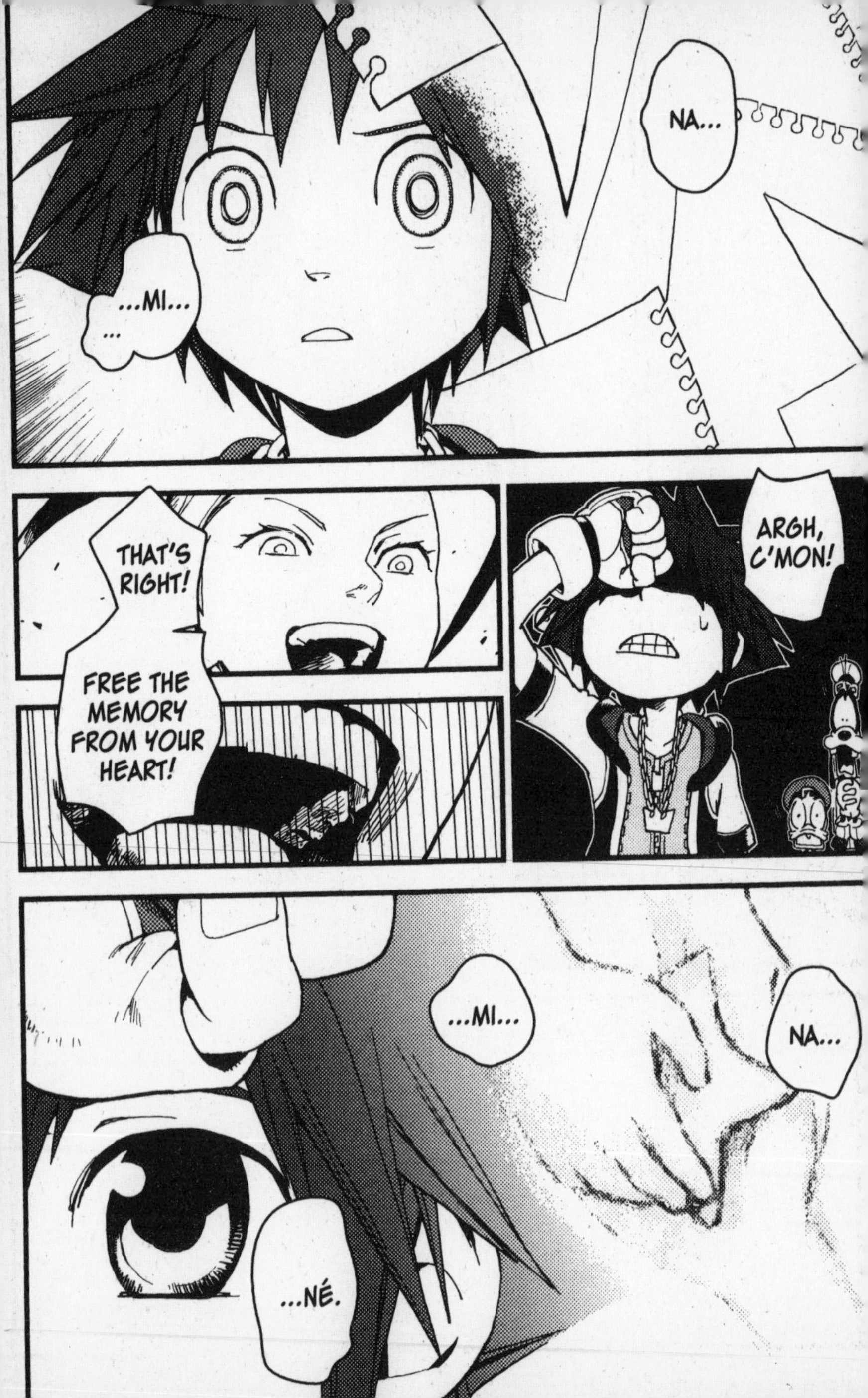
NA...
...MI...
...
ARGH, C'MON!
THAT'S RIGHT!
FREE THE MEMORY FROM YOUR HEART!
NA...
...MI...
...NÉ.

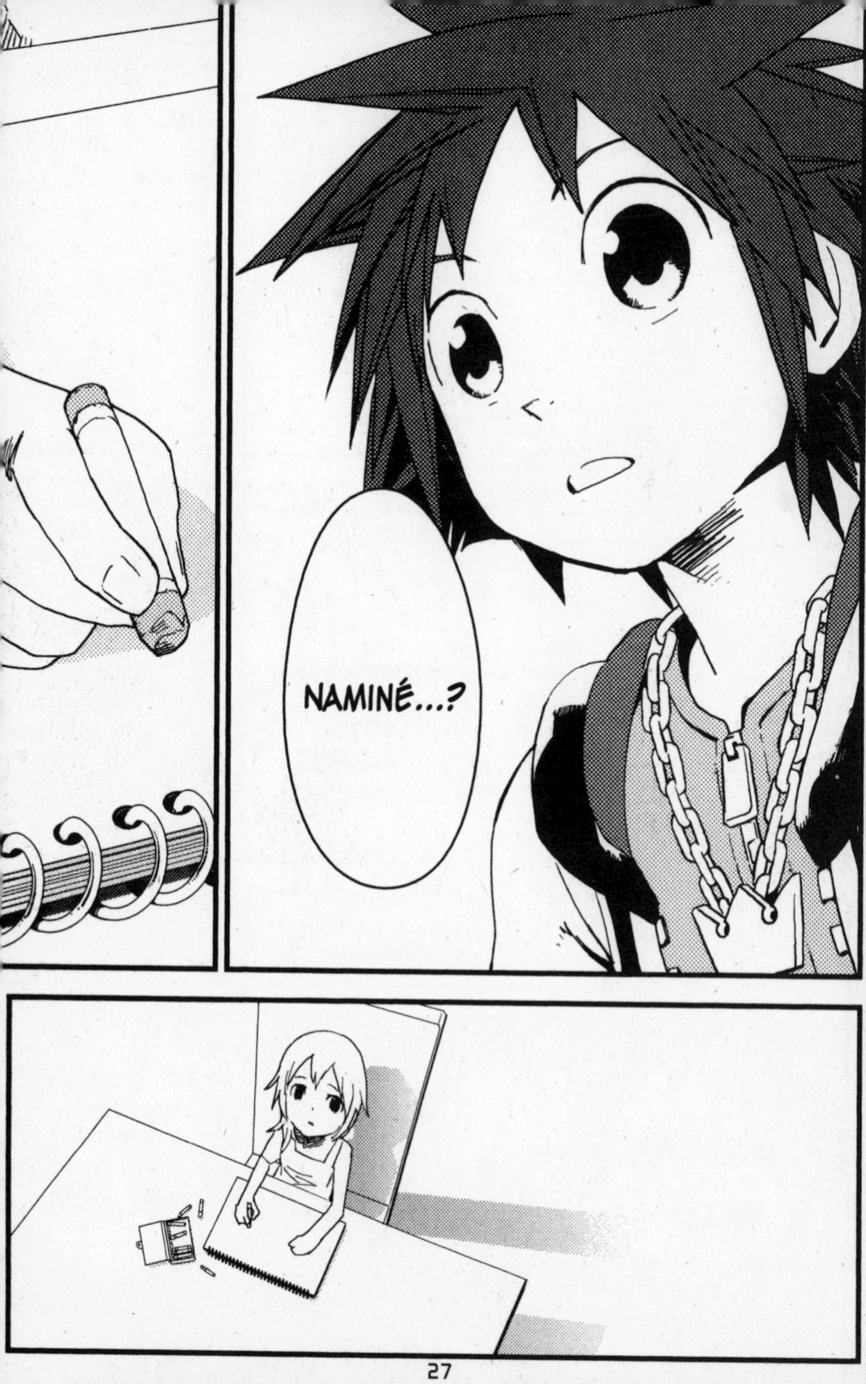
NAMINÉ...?

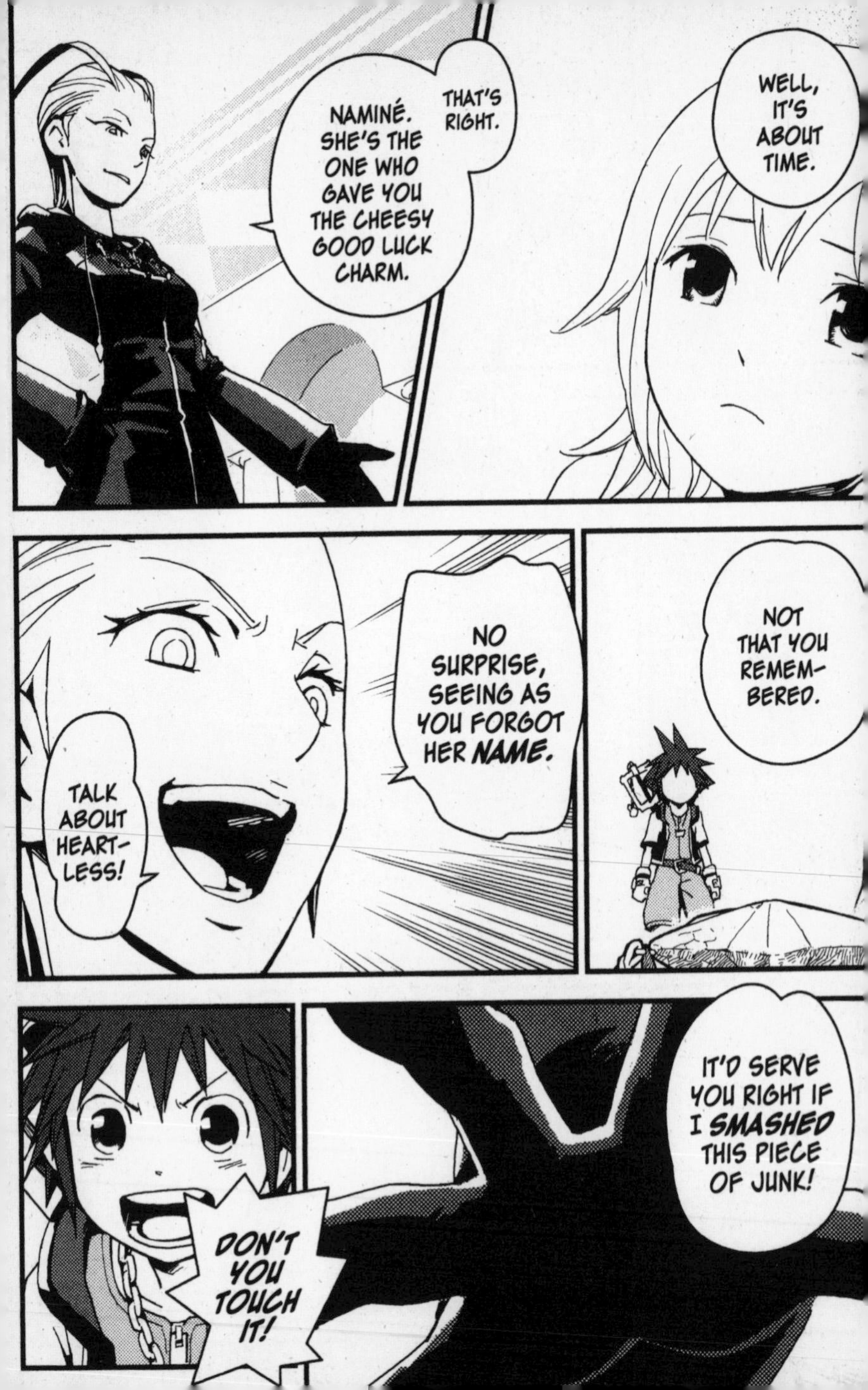
WELL, IT'S ABOUT TIME.
THAT'S RIGHT.
NAMINÉ. SHE'S THE ONE WHO GAVE YOU THE CHEESY GOOD LUCK CHARM.
NOT THAT YOU REMEMBERED.
NO SURPRISE, SEEING AS YOU FORGOT HER **NAME.**
TALK ABOUT HEARTLESS!
IT'D SERVE YOU RIGHT IF I ***SMASHED*** THIS PIECE OF JUNK!
DON'T YOU TOUCH IT!

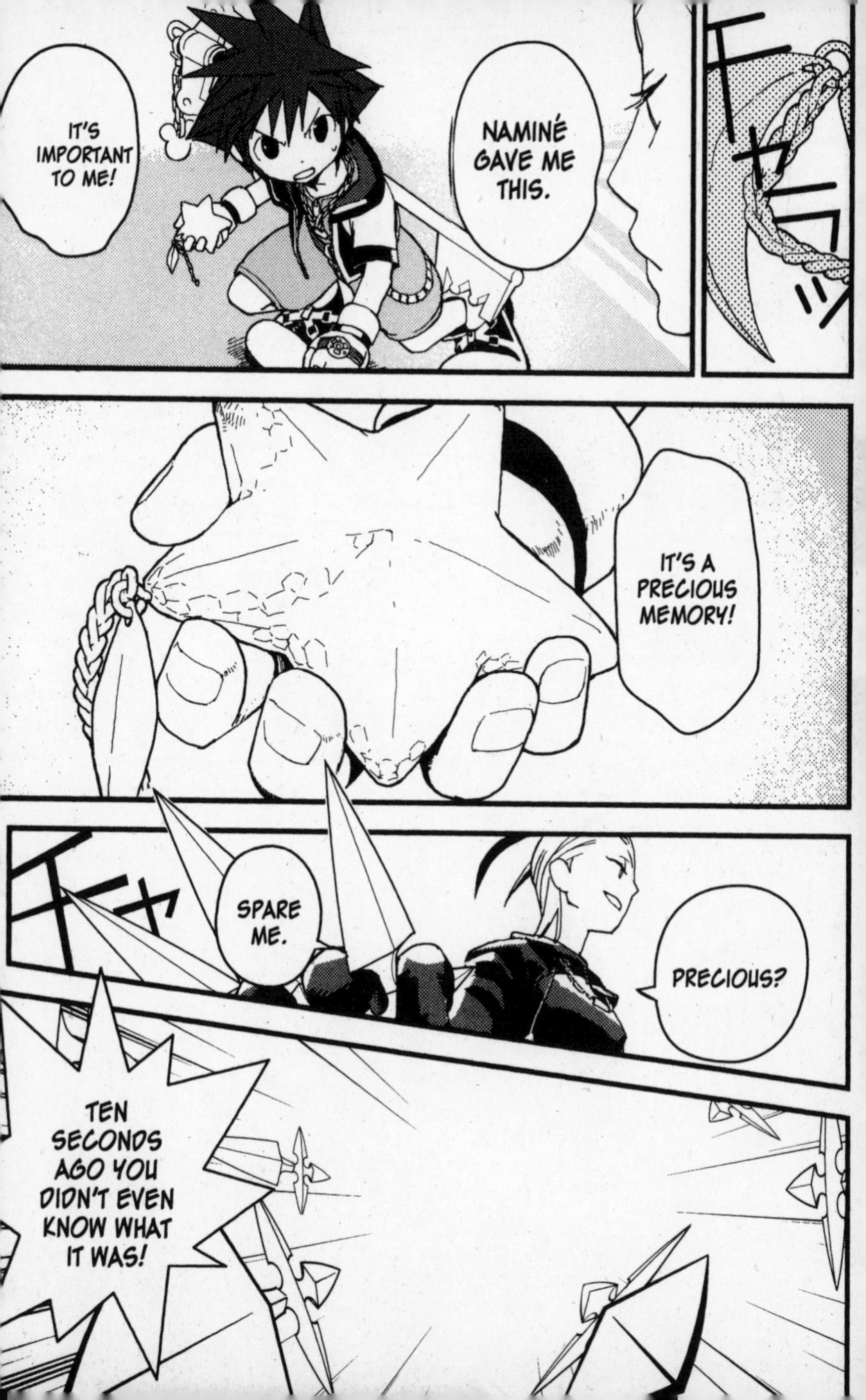
NAMINÉ GAVE ME THIS.
IT'S IMPORTANT TO ME!
IT'S A PRECIOUS MEMORY!
PRECIOUS?
SPARE ME.
TEN SECONDS AGO YOU DIDN'T EVEN KNOW WHAT IT WAS!

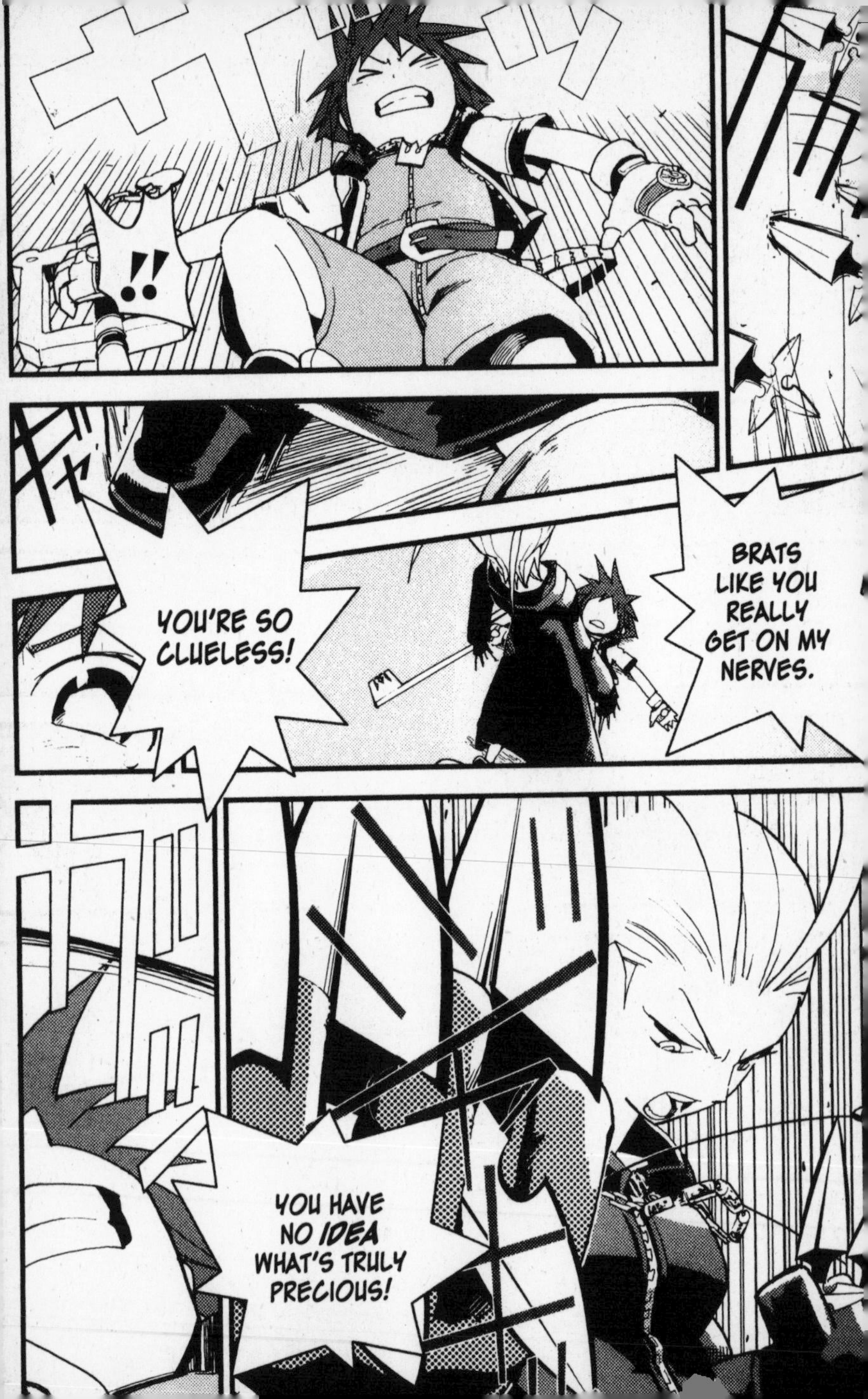
!!
BRATS LIKE YOU REALLY GET ON MY NERVES.
YOU'RE SO CLUELESS!
YOU HAVE NO *IDEA* WHAT'S TRULY PRECIOUS!

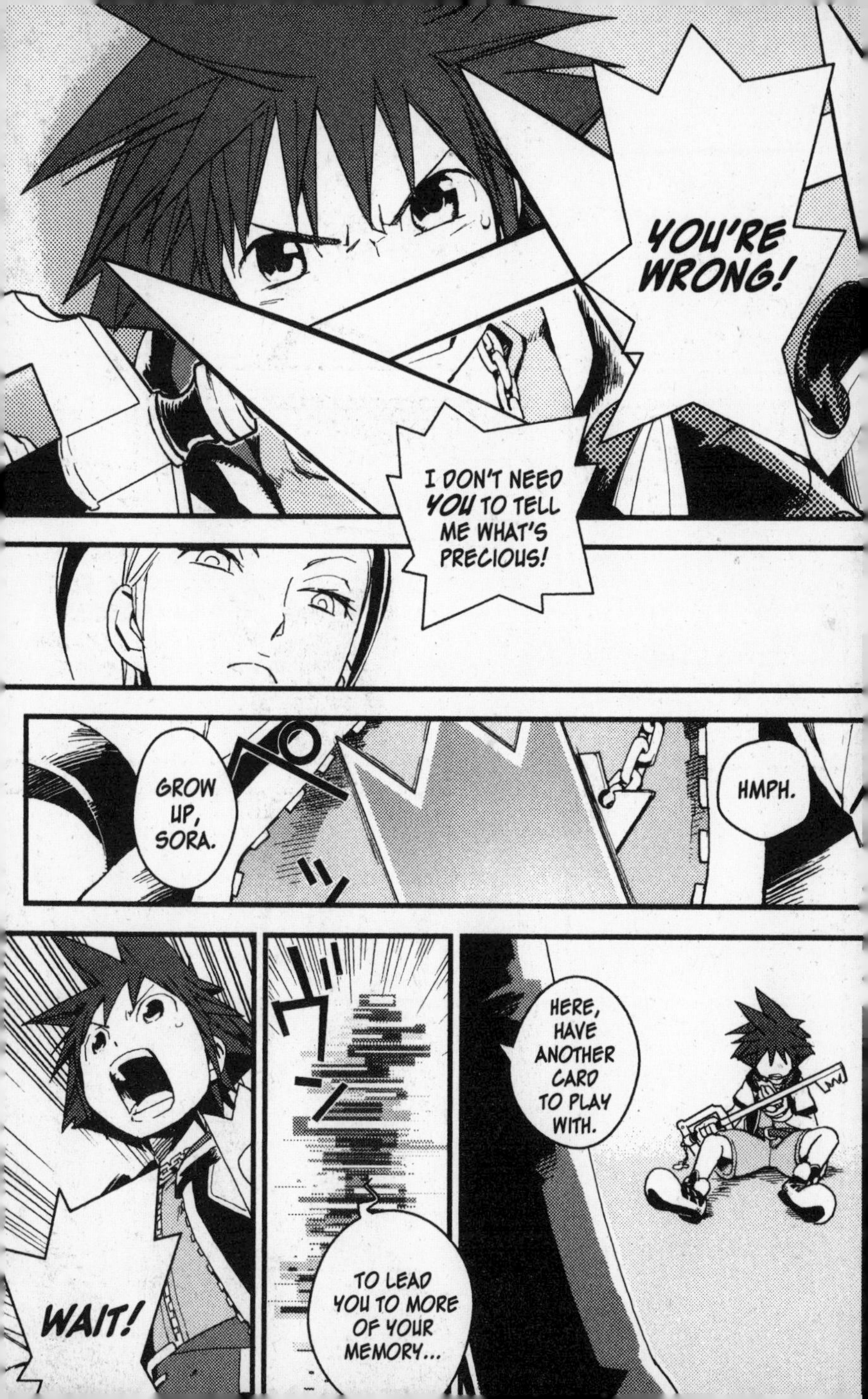
YOU'RE WRONG!
I DON'T NEED YOU TO TELL ME WHAT'S PRECIOUS!
HMPH.
GROW UP, SORA.
HERE, HAVE ANOTHER CARD TO PLAY WITH.
TO LEAD YOU TO MORE OF YOUR MEMORY...
WAIT!

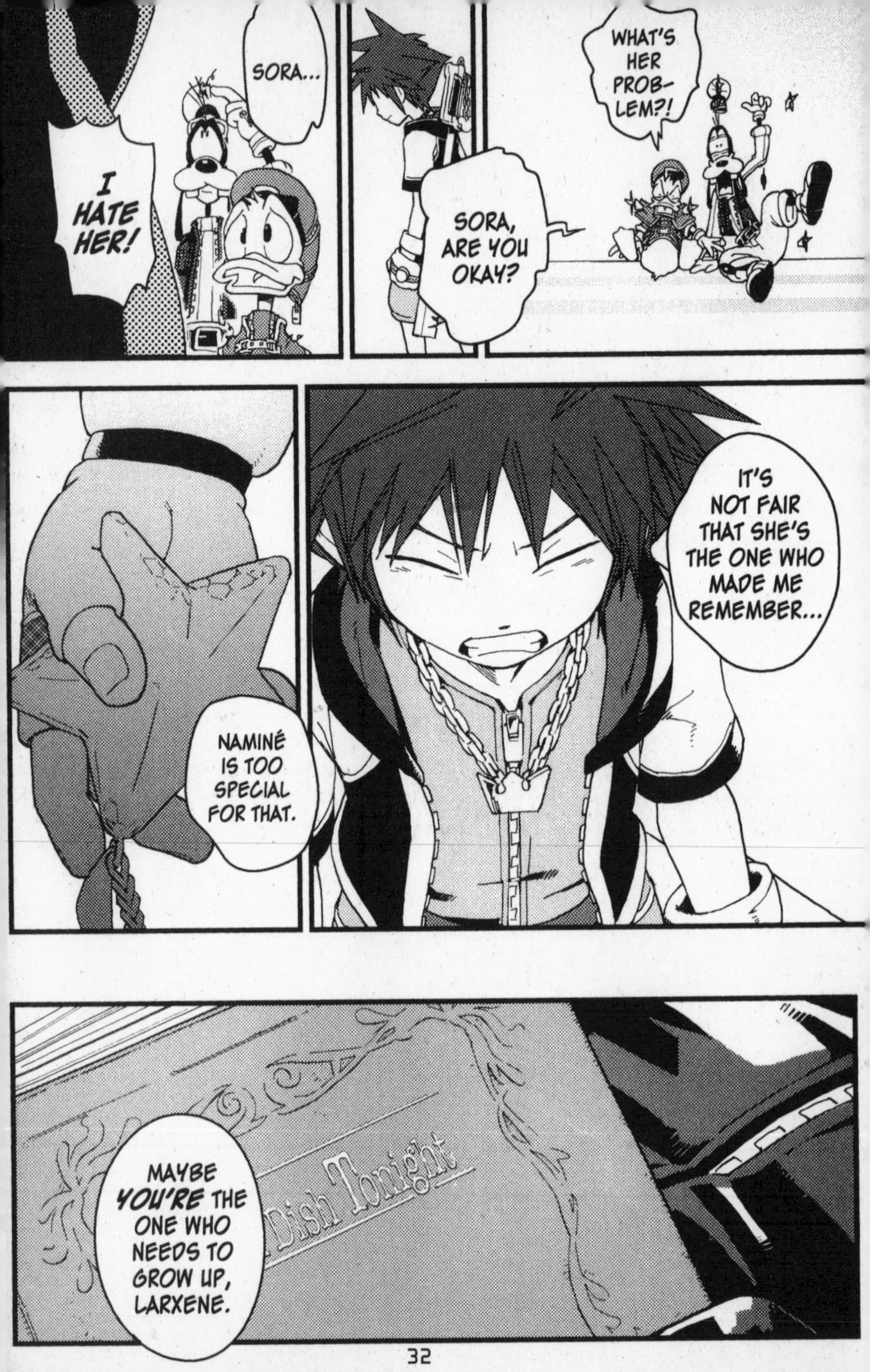

WHAT'S HER PROB-LEM?!
SORA, ARE YOU OKAY?
SORA...
I HATE HER!
IT'S NOT FAIR THAT SHE'S THE ONE WHO MADE ME REMEMBER...
NAMINÉ IS TOO SPECIAL FOR THAT.
Dish Tonight
MAYBE ***YOU'RE*** THE ONE WHO NEEDS TO GROW UP, LARXENE.

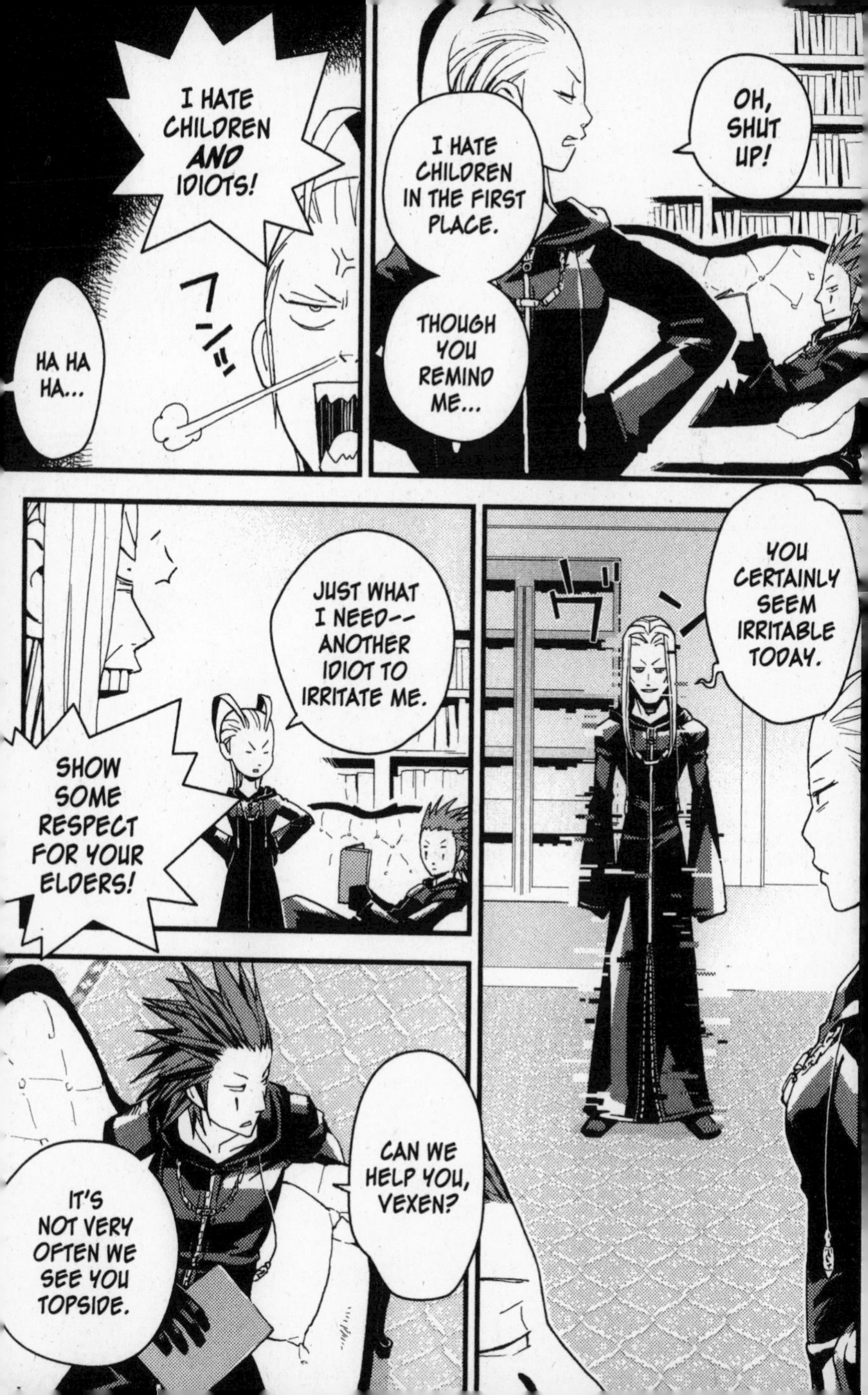
OH, SHUT UP!
I HATE CHILDREN IN THE FIRST PLACE.
THOUGH YOU REMIND ME...
I HATE CHILDREN AND IDIOTS!
HA HA HA...
YOU CERTAINLY SEEM IRRITABLE TODAY.
JUST WHAT I NEED--ANOTHER IDIOT TO IRRITATE ME.
SHOW SOME RESPECT FOR YOUR ELDERS!
CAN WE HELP YOU, VEXEN?
IT'S NOT VERY OFTEN WE SEE YOU TOPSIDE.

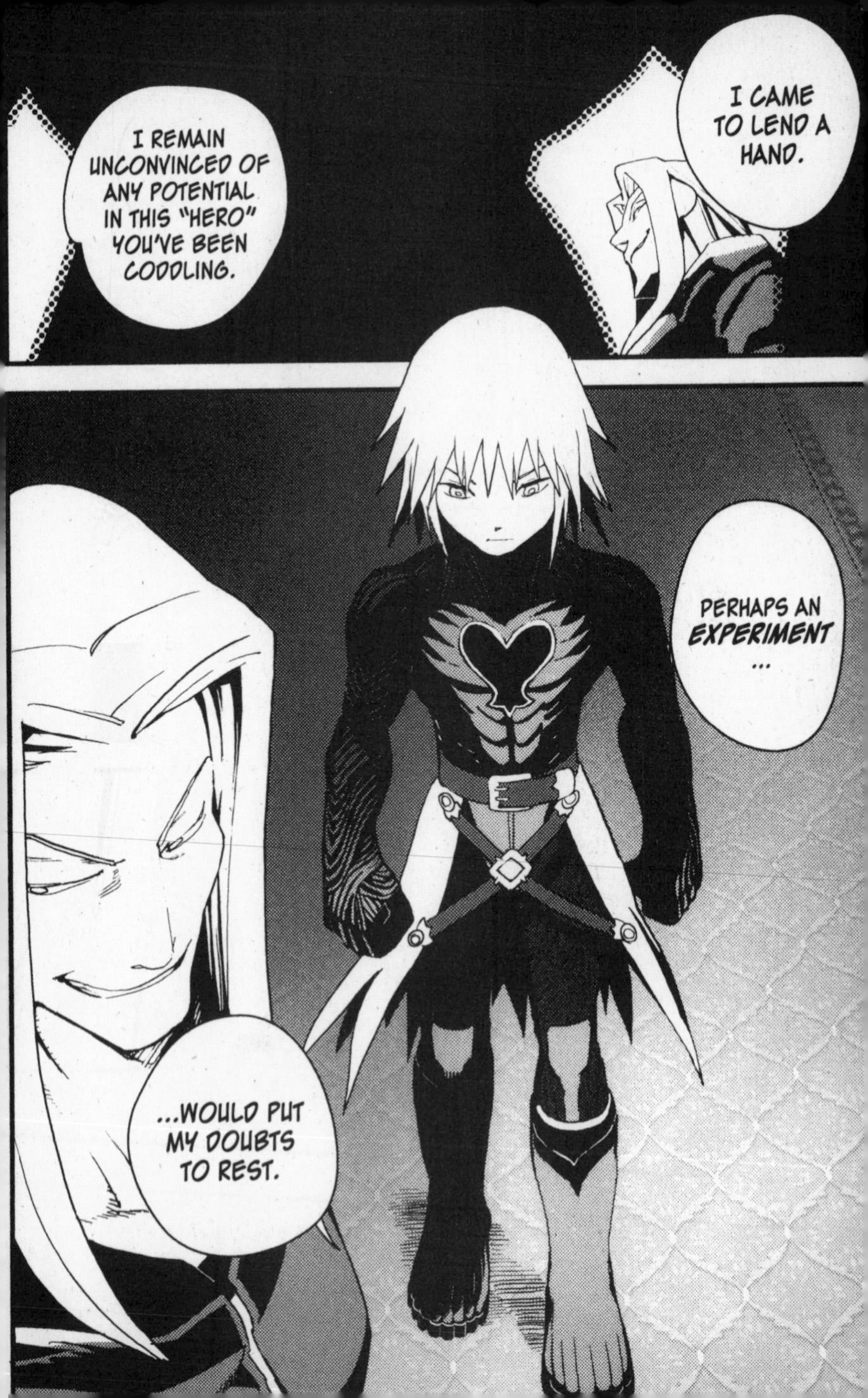
I CAME TO LEND A HAND.
I REMAIN UNCONVINCED OF ANY POTENTIAL IN THIS "HERO" YOU'VE BEEN CODDLING.
PERHAPS AN *EXPERIMENT* ...
...WOULD PUT MY DOUBTS TO REST.

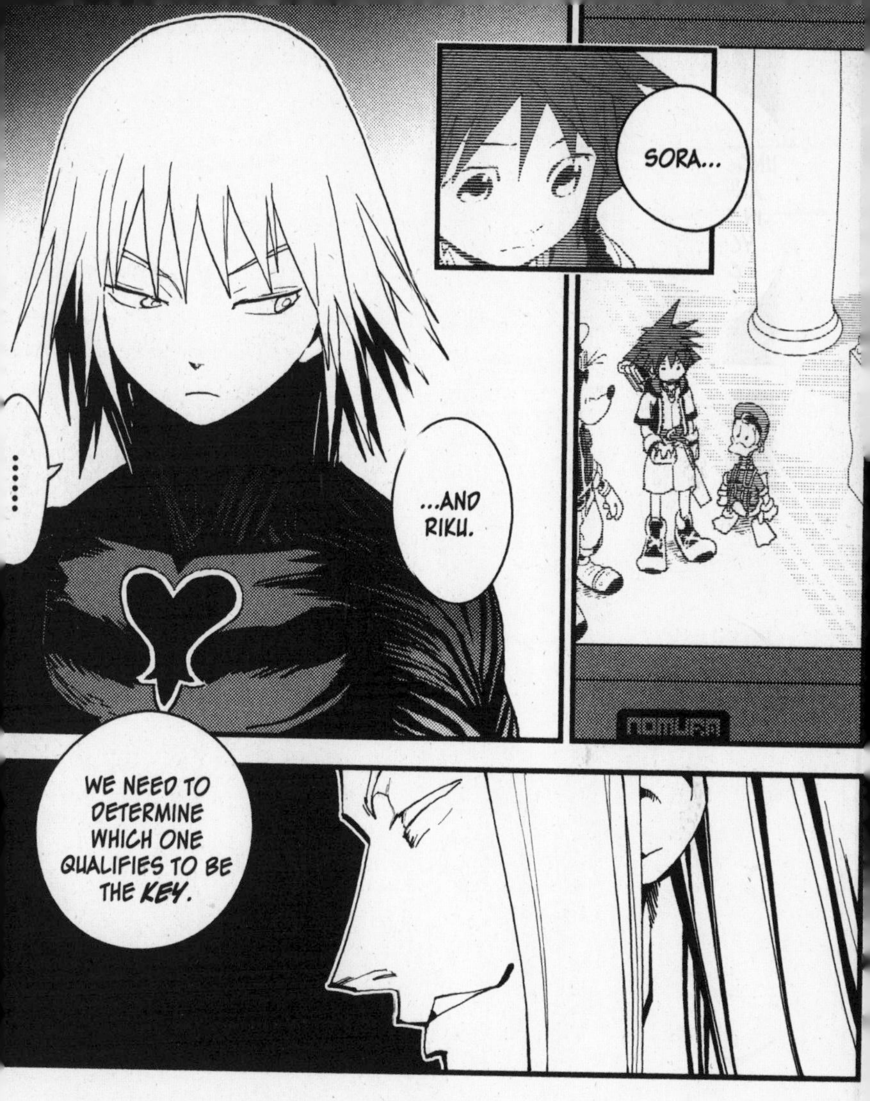
SORA...
NOMURA
...AND RIKU.
......
WE NEED TO DETERMINE WHICH ONE QUALIFIES TO BE THE *KEY*.

Card 08 Promise

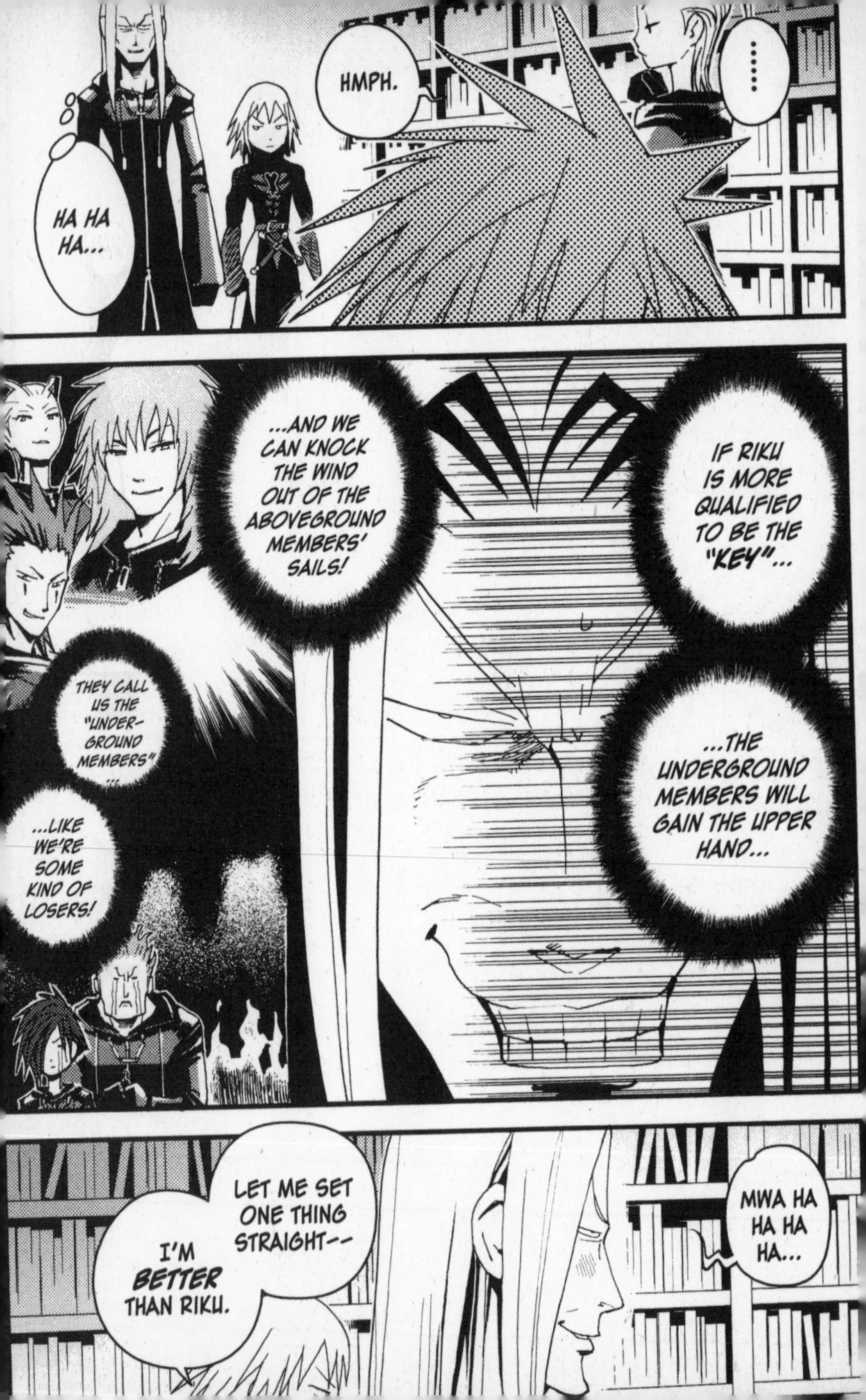
......
HMPH.
HA HA HA...
IF RIKU IS MORE QUALIFIED TO BE THE "KEY"...
...THE UNDERGROUND MEMBERS WILL GAIN THE UPPER HAND...
...AND WE CAN KNOCK THE WIND OUT OF THE ABOVEGROUND MEMBERS' SAILS!
THEY CALL US THE "UNDERGROUND MEMBERS"...
...LIKE WE'RE SOME KIND OF LOSERS!
MWA HA HA HA HA...
LET ME SET ONE THING STRAIGHT--
I'M BETTER THAN RIKU.

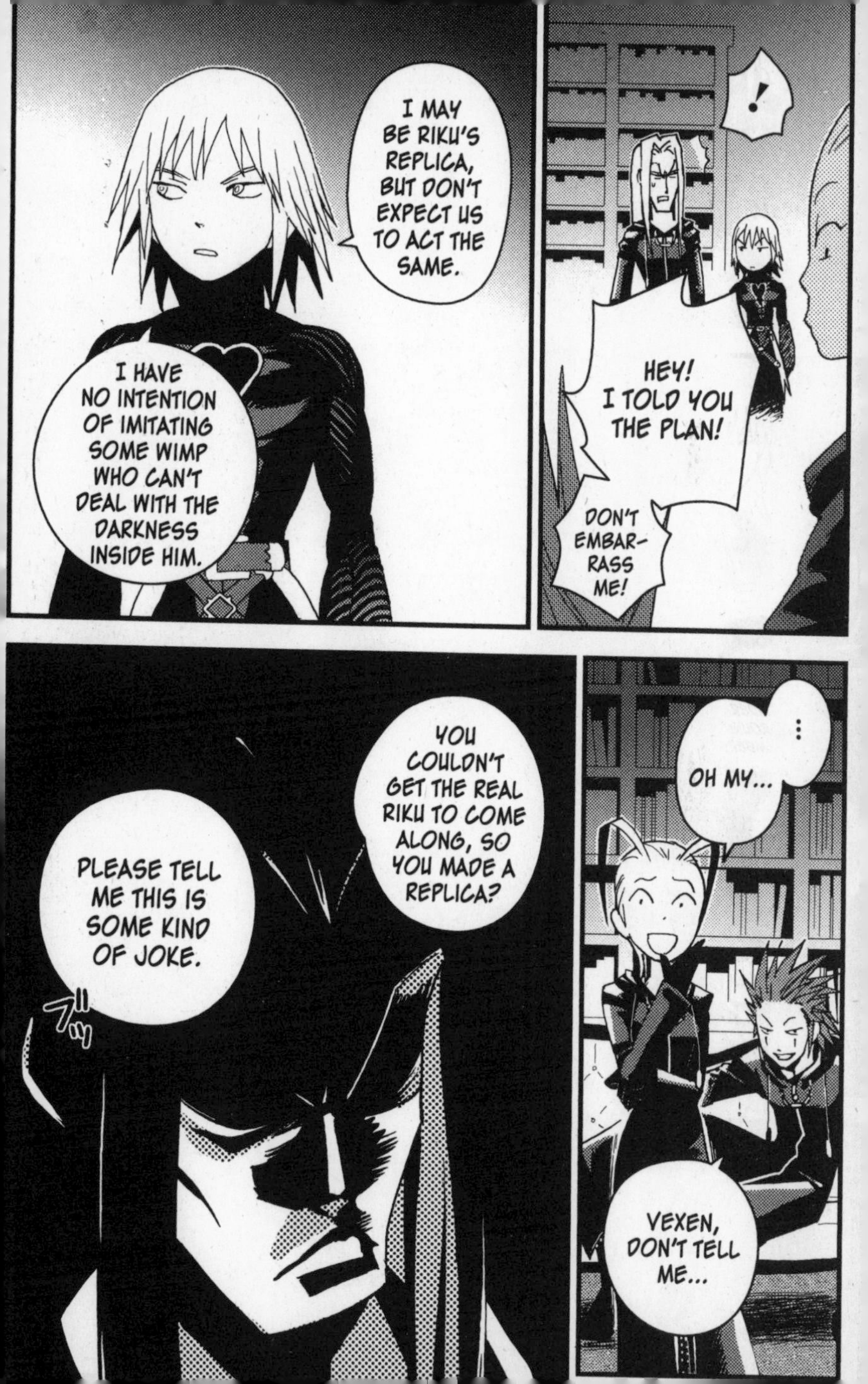
!
HEY! I TOLD YOU THE PLAN!
DON'T EMBARRASS ME!
I MAY BE RIKU'S REPLICA, BUT DON'T EXPECT US TO ACT THE SAME.
I HAVE NO INTENTION OF IMITATING SOME WIMP WHO CAN'T DEAL WITH THE DARKNESS INSIDE HIM.
...
OH MY...
VEXEN, DON'T TELL ME...
YOU COULDN'T GET THE REAL RIKU TO COME ALONG, SO YOU MADE A REPLICA?
PLEASE TELL ME THIS IS SOME KIND OF JOKE.

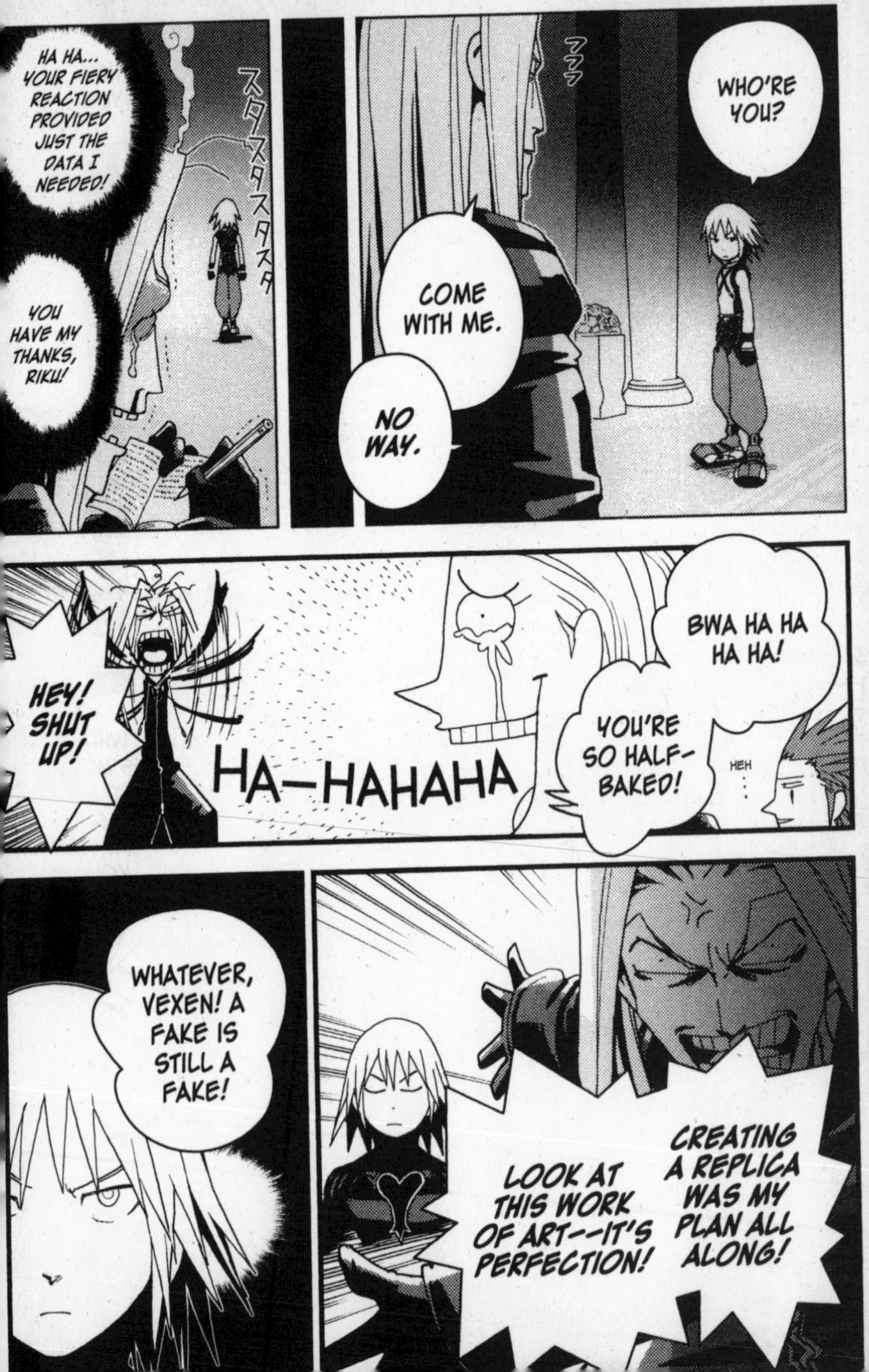
WHO'RE YOU?
COME WITH ME.
NO WAY.
HA HA... YOUR FIERY REACTION PROVIDED JUST THE DATA I NEEDED!
YOU HAVE MY THANKS, RIKU!
BWA HA HA HA HA!
YOU'RE SO HALF-BAKED!
HEH...
HA-HAHAHA
HEY! SHUT UP!
CREATING A REPLICA WAS MY PLAN ALL ALONG!
LOOK AT THIS WORK OF ART--IT'S PERFECTION!
WHATEVER, VEXEN! A FAKE IS STILL A FAKE!

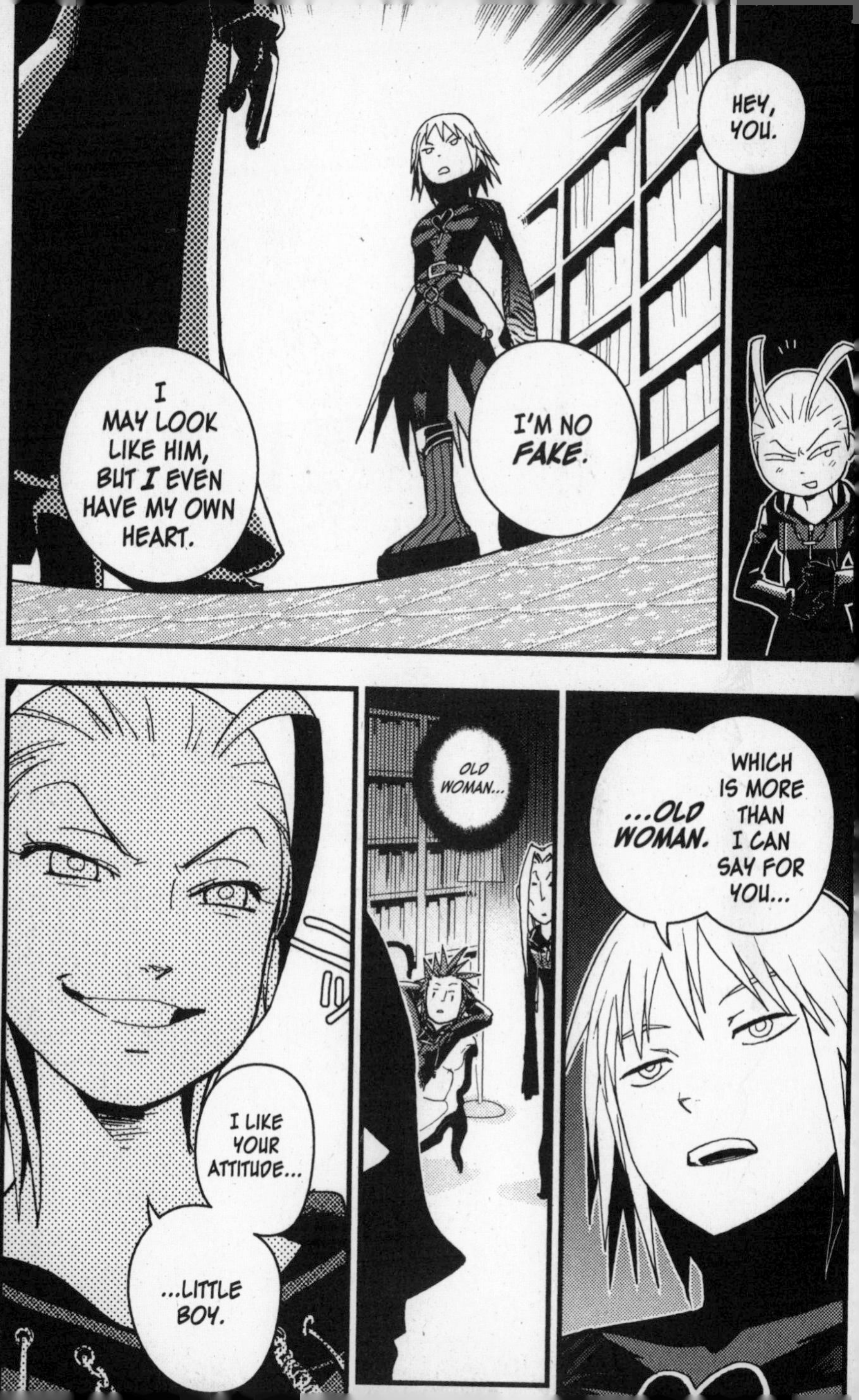
HEY, YOU.
I'M NO FAKE.
I MAY LOOK LIKE HIM, BUT I EVEN HAVE MY OWN HEART.
WHICH IS MORE THAN I CAN SAY FOR YOU...
...OLD WOMAN.
OLD WOMAN...
I LIKE YOUR ATTITUDE...
...LITTLE BOY.

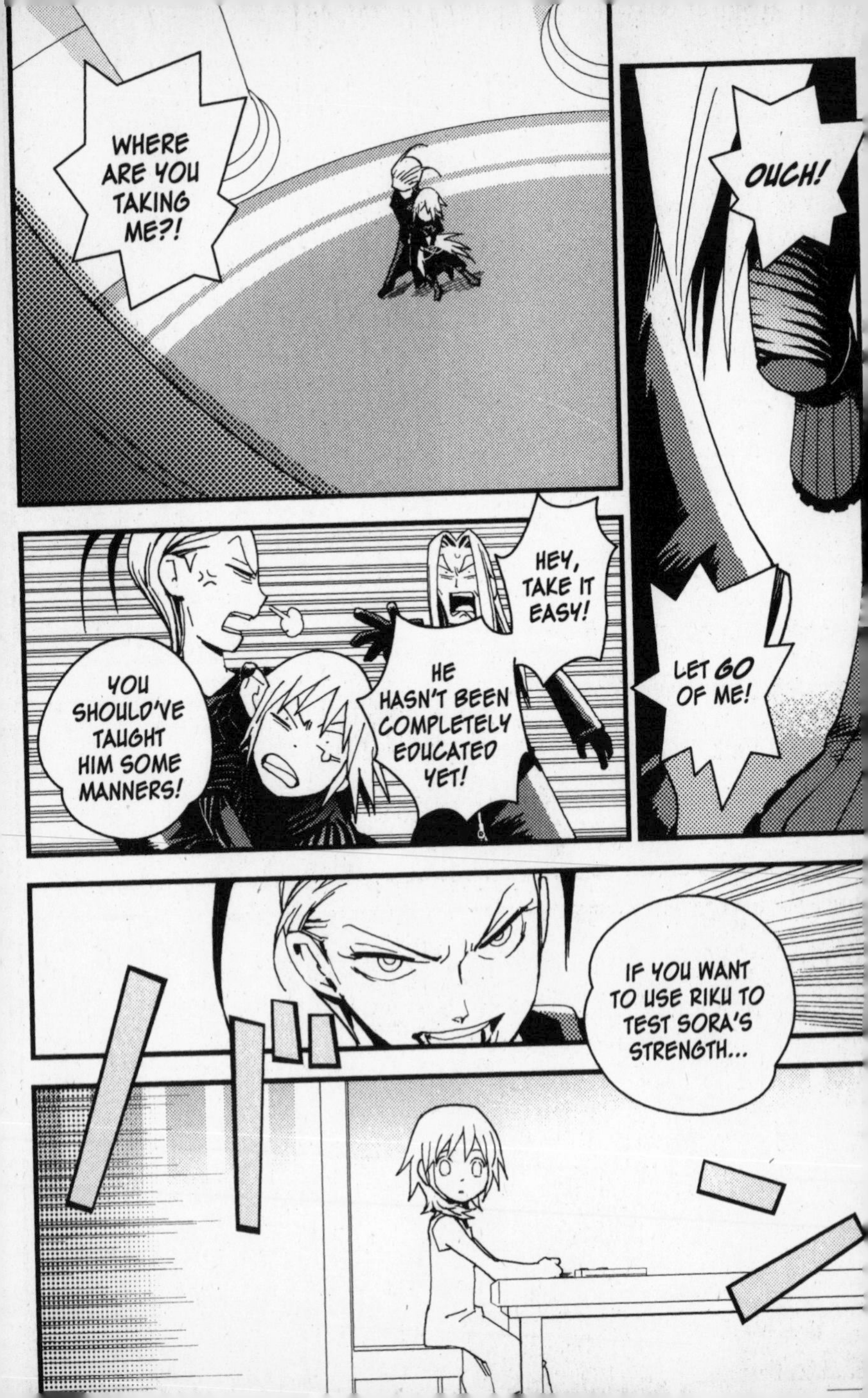
OUCH!
LET GO OF ME!
WHERE ARE YOU TAKING ME?!
HEY, TAKE IT EASY!
HE HASN'T BEEN COMPLETELY EDUCATED YET!
YOU SHOULD'VE TAUGHT HIM SOME MANNERS!
IF YOU WANT TO USE RIKU TO TEST SORA'S STRENGTH...

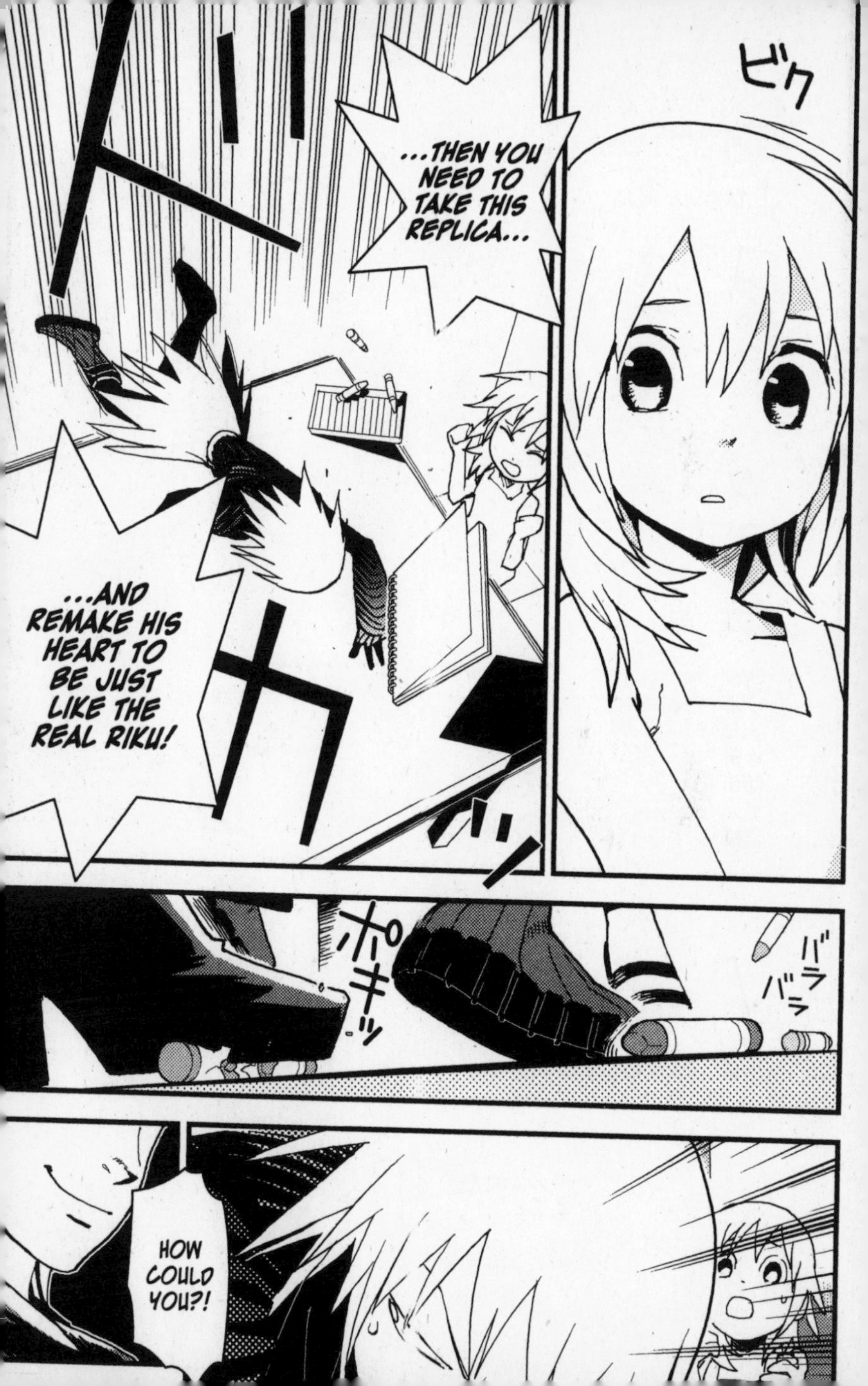
ビク
...THEN YOU NEED TO TAKE THIS REPLICA...
...AND REMAKE HIS HEART TO BE JUST LIKE THE REAL RIKU!
ドカッ
バラバラ
ポキッ
HOW COULD YOU?!

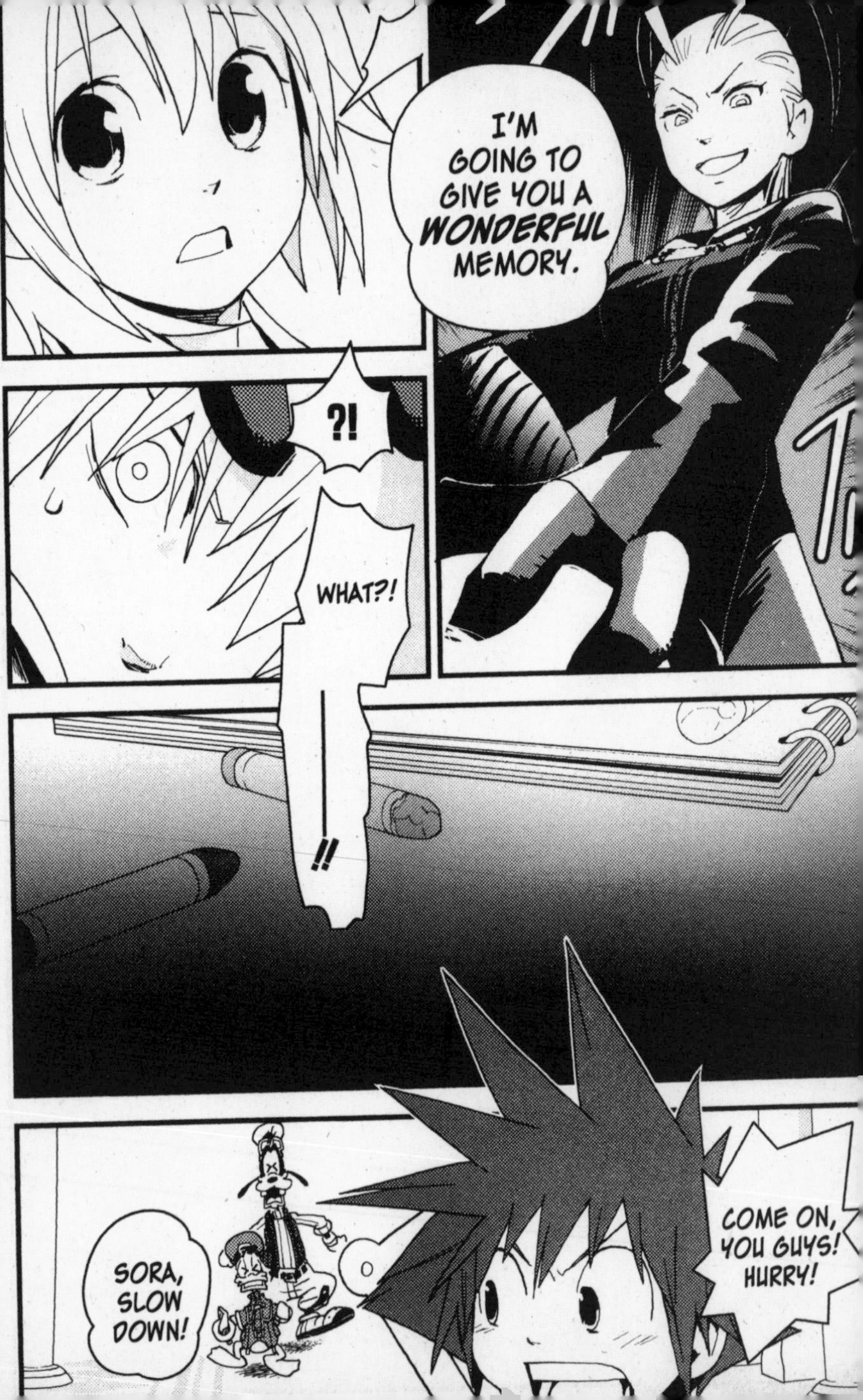
I'M GOING TO GIVE YOU A WONDERFUL MEMORY.
?!
WHAT?!
!!
COME ON, YOU GUYS! HURRY!
SORA, SLOW DOWN!

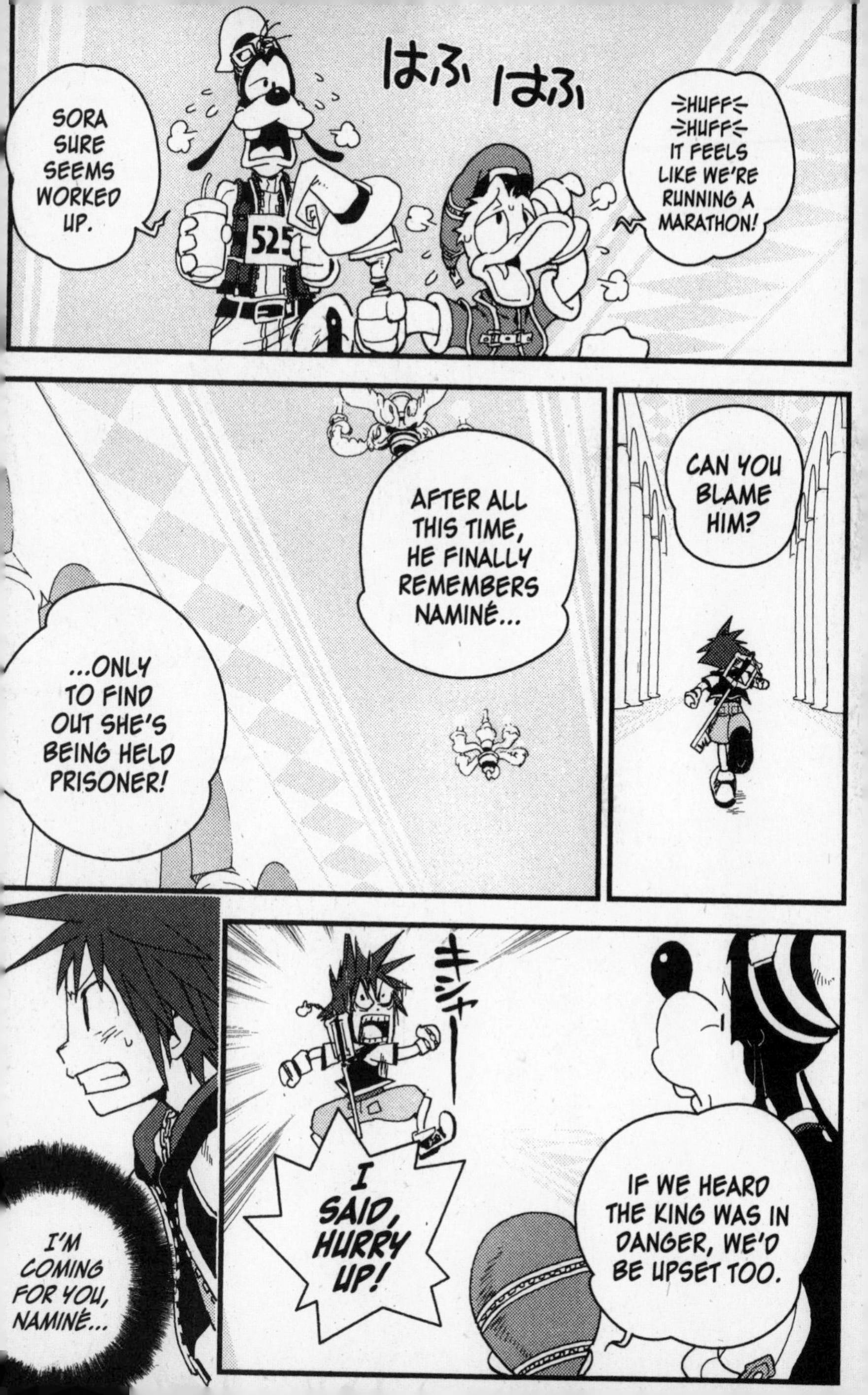
はふ はふ
=HUFF= =HUFF= IT FEELS LIKE WE'RE RUNNING A MARATHON!
SORA SURE SEEMS WORKED UP.
525
CAN YOU BLAME HIM?
AFTER ALL THIS TIME, HE FINALLY REMEMBERS NAMINÉ...
...ONLY TO FIND OUT SHE'S BEING HELD PRISONER!
IF WE HEARD THE KING WAS IN DANGER, WE'D BE UPSET TOO.
キシャー
I SAID, HURRY UP!
I'M COMING FOR YOU, NAMINÉ...

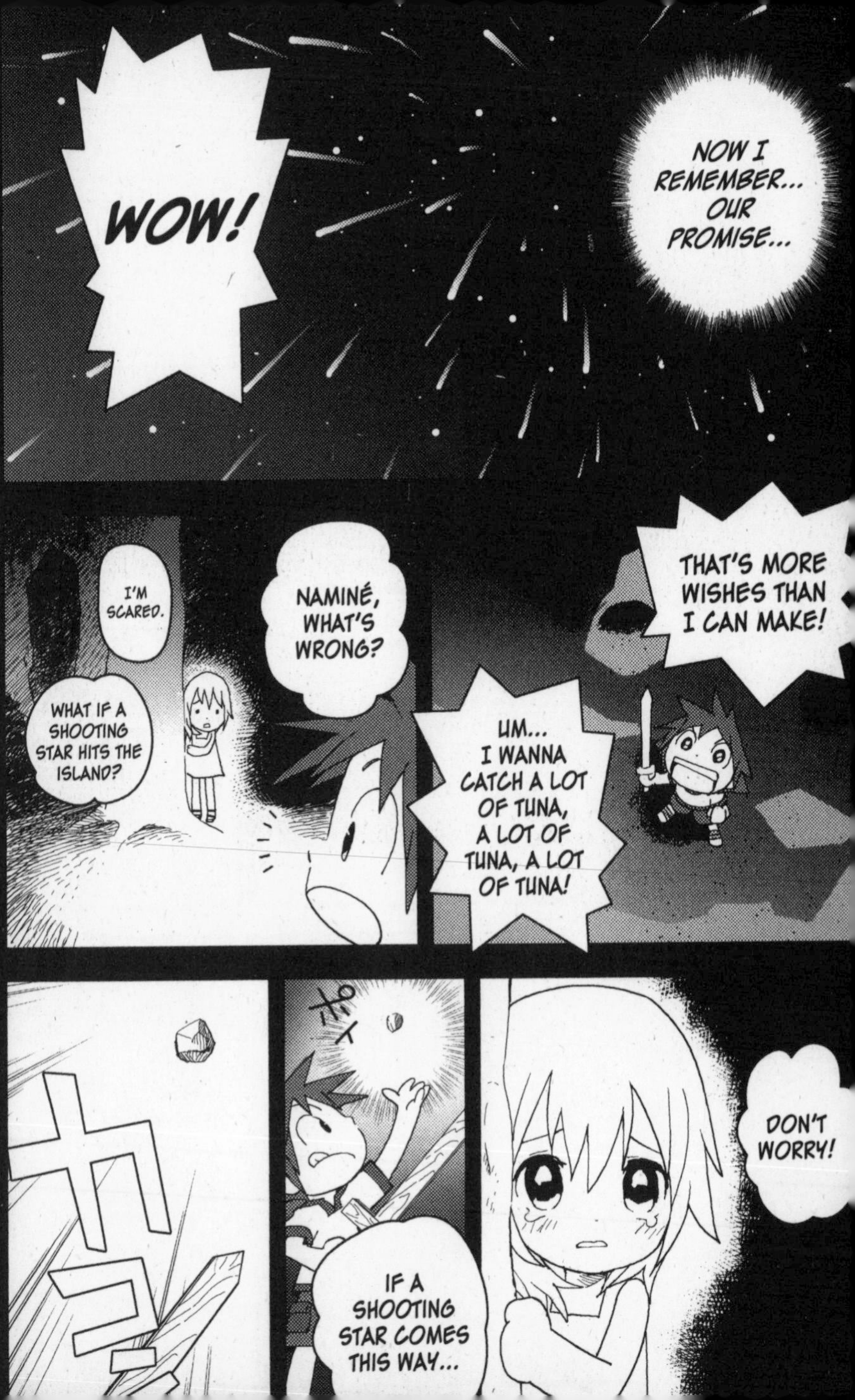
NOW I REMEMBER... OUR PROMISE...
WOW!
THAT'S MORE WISHES THAN I CAN MAKE!
UM... I WANNA CATCH A LOT OF TUNA, A LOT OF TUNA, A LOT OF TUNA!
NAMINÉ, WHAT'S WRONG?
I'M SCARED.
WHAT IF A SHOOTING STAR HITS THE ISLAND?
DON'T WORRY!
IF A SHOOTING STAR COMES THIS WAY...

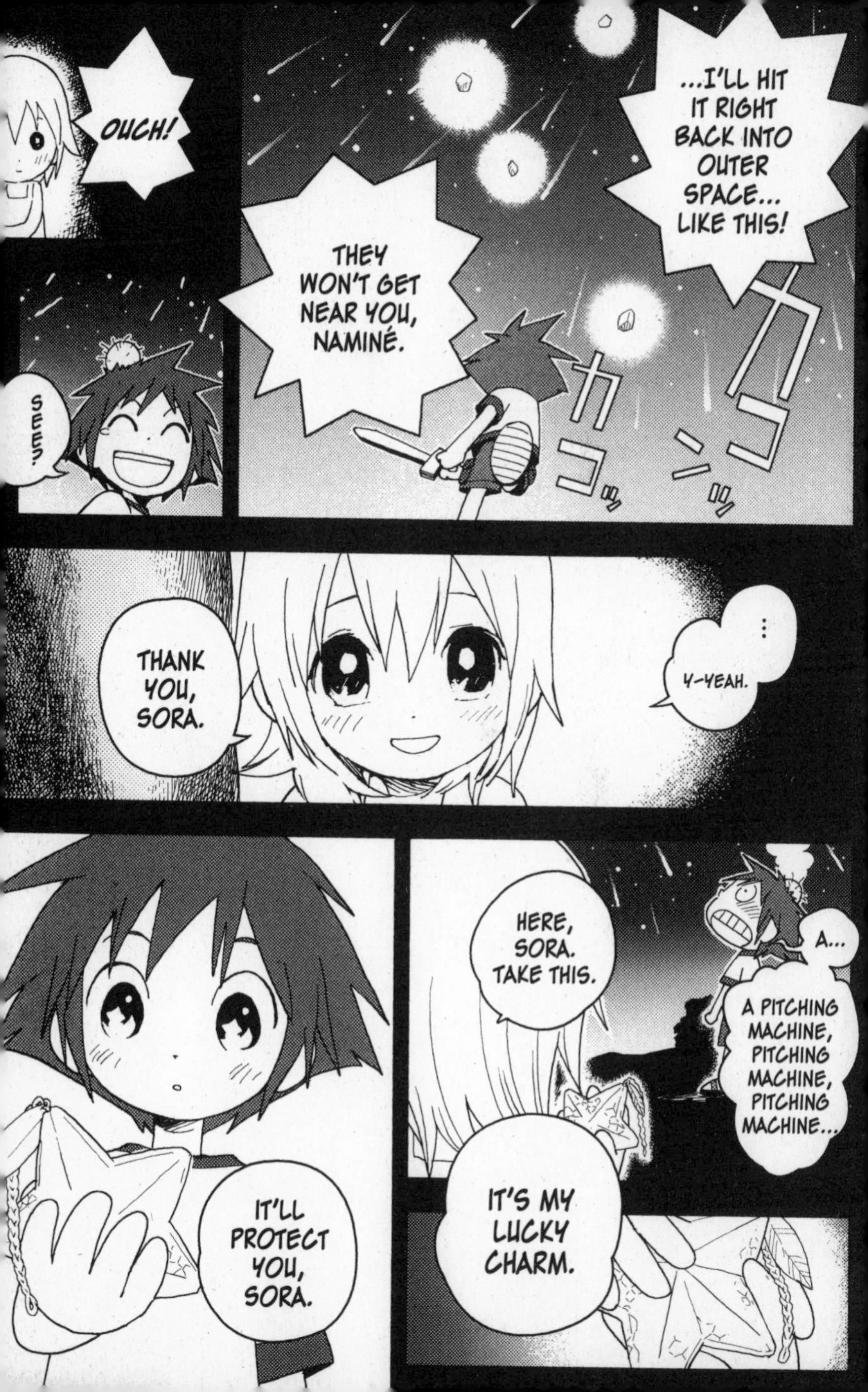
...I'LL HIT IT RIGHT BACK INTO OUTER SPACE... LIKE THIS!
THEY WON'T GET NEAR YOU, NAMINÉ.
OUCH!
SEE?
...
Y-YEAH.
THANK YOU, SORA.
A...
A PITCHING MACHINE, PITCHING MACHINE, PITCHING MACHINE...
HERE, SORA. TAKE THIS.
IT'S MY LUCKY CHARM.
IT'LL PROTECT YOU, SORA.

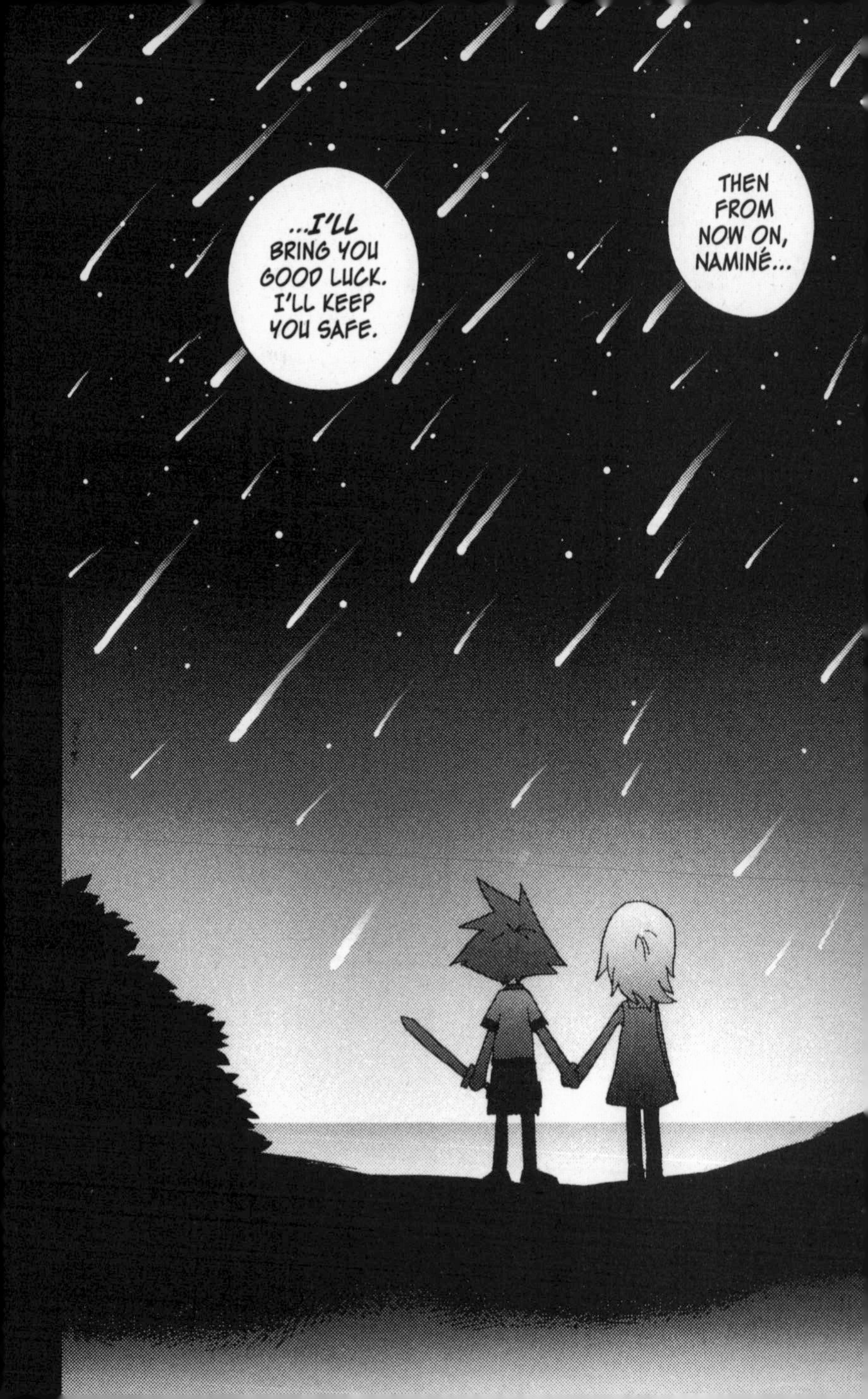
THEN FROM NOW ON, NAMINÉ...
...I'LL BRING YOU GOOD LUCK. I'LL KEEP YOU SAFE.

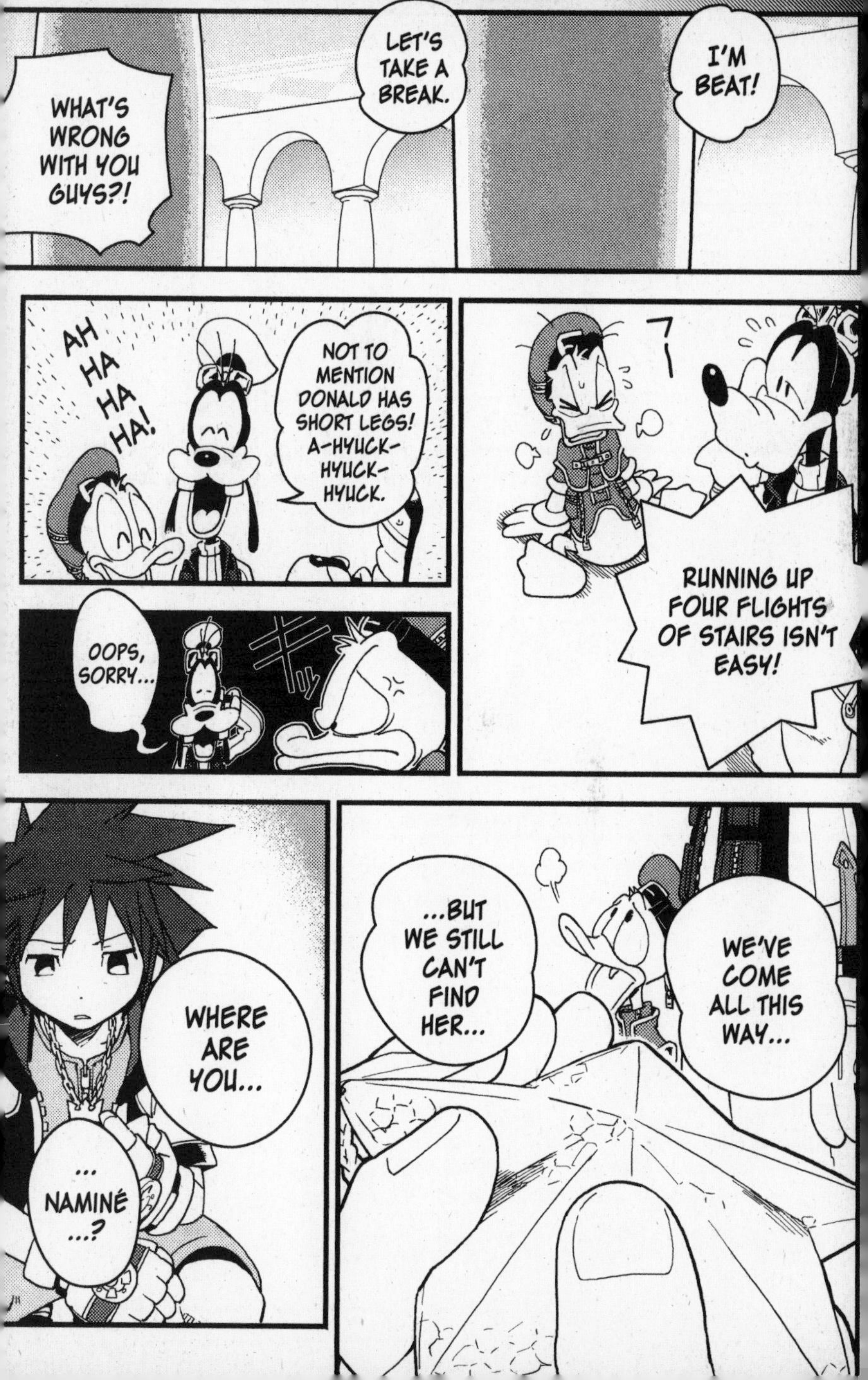
I'M BEAT!
LET'S TAKE A BREAK.
WHAT'S WRONG WITH YOU GUYS?!
RUNNING UP FOUR FLIGHTS OF STAIRS ISN'T EASY!
NOT TO MENTION DONALD HAS SHORT LEGS! A-HYUCK-HYUCK-HYUCK.
AH HA HA HA!
OOPS, SORRY...
WE'VE COME ALL THIS WAY...
...BUT WE STILL CAN'T FIND HER...
WHERE ARE YOU...
... NAMINÉ ...?

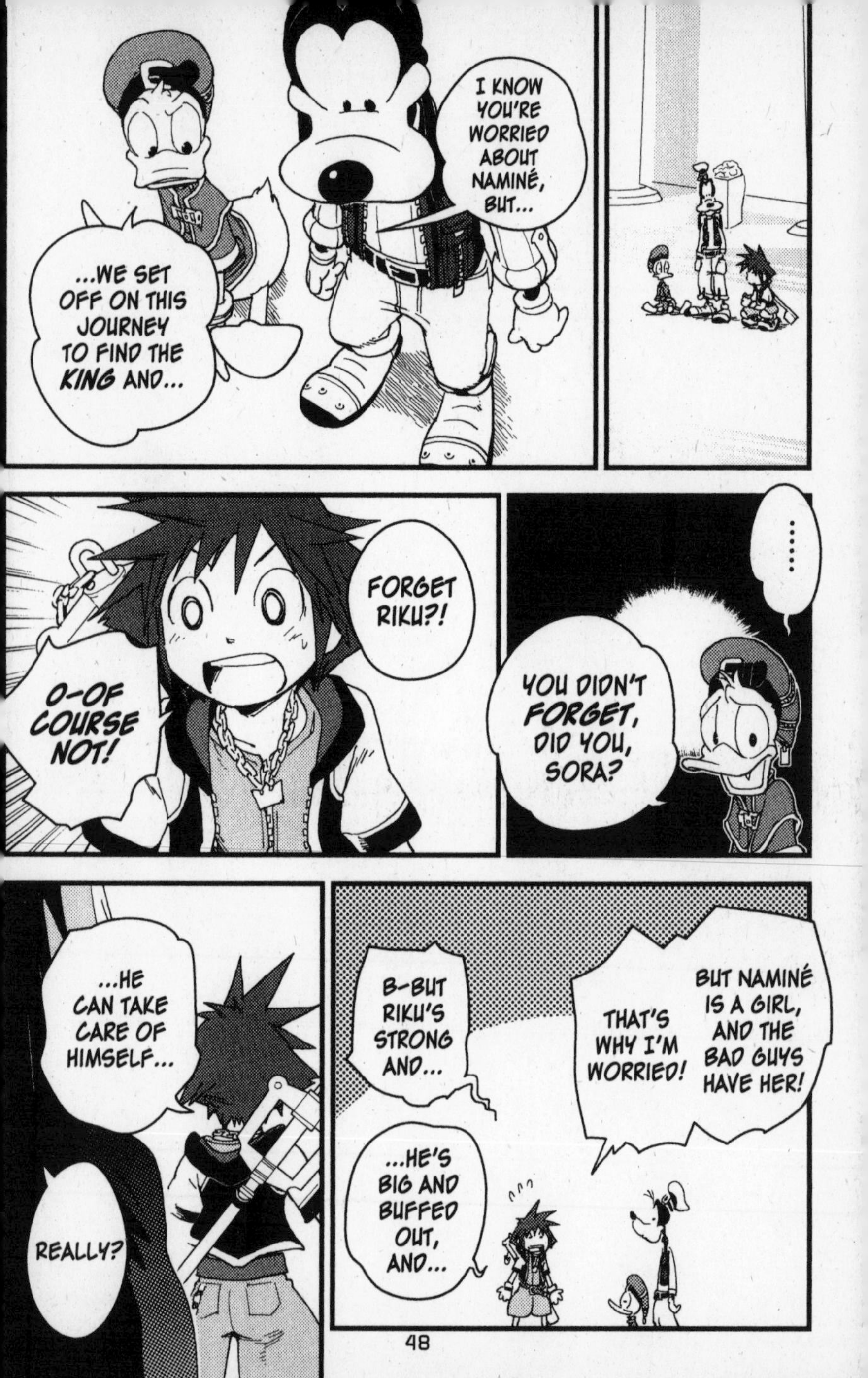
I KNOW YOU'RE WORRIED ABOUT NAMINÉ, BUT...
...WE SET OFF ON THIS JOURNEY TO FIND THE *KING* AND...
......
YOU DIDN'T *FORGET*, DID YOU, SORA?
FORGET RIKU?!
O-OF COURSE NOT!
BUT NAMINÉ IS A GIRL, AND THE BAD GUYS HAVE HER!
THAT'S WHY I'M WORRIED!
B-BUT RIKU'S STRONG AND...
...HE'S BIG AND BUFFED OUT, AND...
...HE CAN TAKE CARE OF HIMSELF...
REALLY?

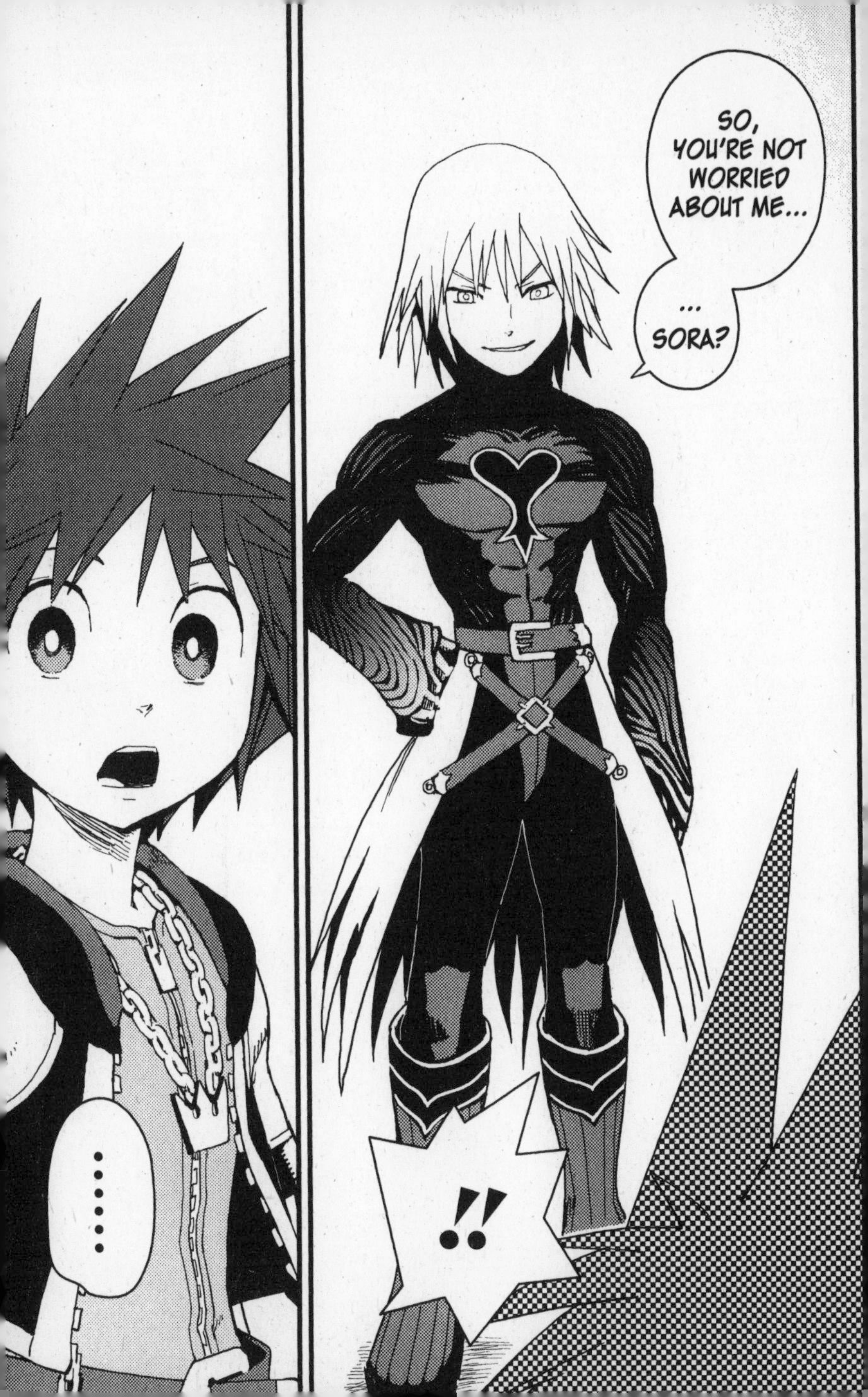
SO, YOU'RE NOT WORRIED ABOUT ME...
... SORA?
!!
......

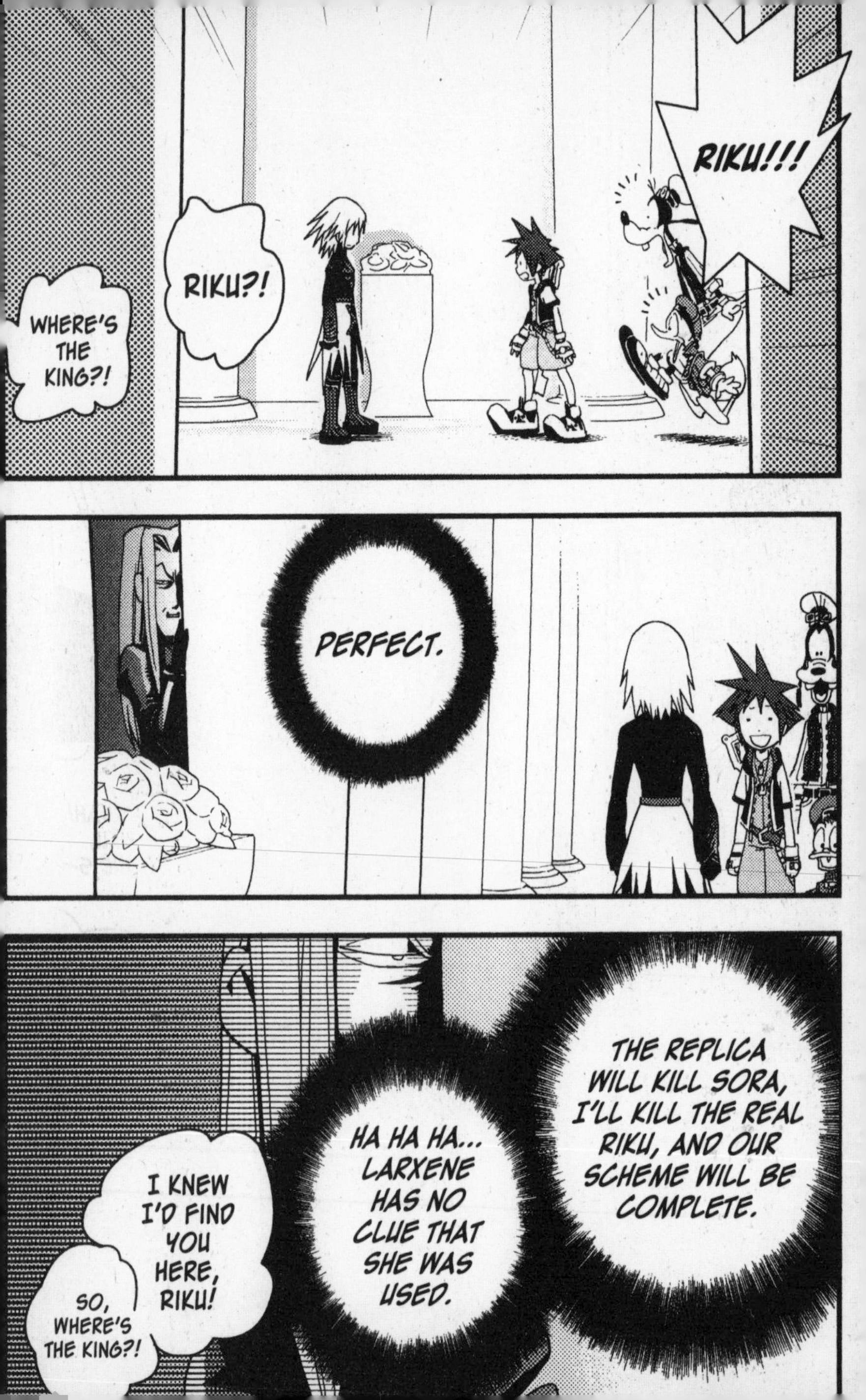
RIKU!!!
RIKU?!
WHERE'S THE KING?!
PERFECT.
THE REPLICA WILL KILL SORA, I'LL KILL THE REAL RIKU, AND OUR SCHEME WILL BE COMPLETE.
HA HA HA... LARXENE HAS NO CLUE THAT SHE WAS USED.
I KNEW I'D FIND YOU HERE, RIKU!
SO, WHERE'S THE KING?!

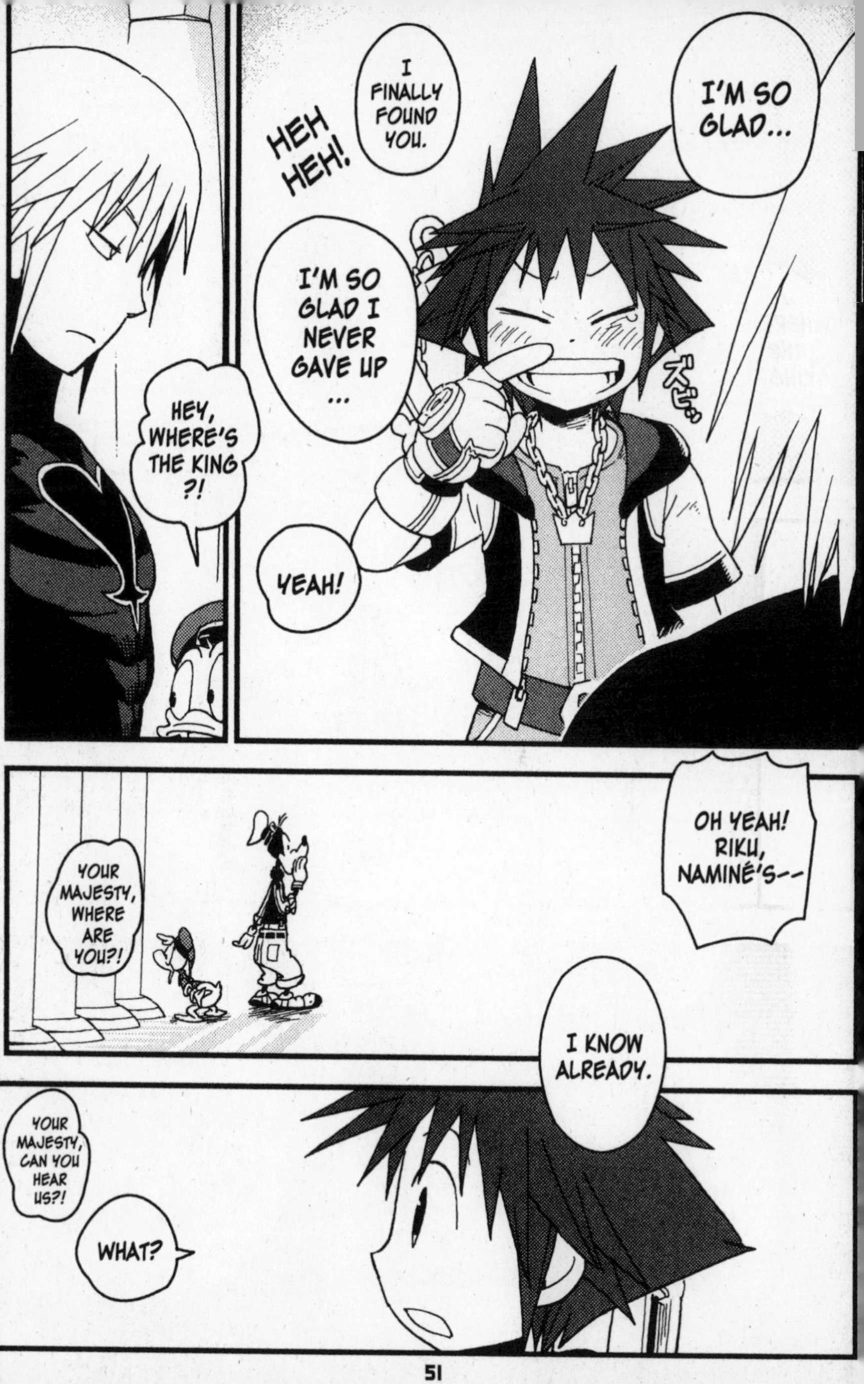
I'M SO GLAD...
I FINALLY FOUND YOU.
HEH HEH!
I'M SO GLAD I NEVER GAVE UP ...
YEAH!
HEY, WHERE'S THE KING ?!
OH YEAH! RIKU, NAMINÉ'S--
YOUR MAJESTY, WHERE ARE YOU?!
I KNOW ALREADY.
YOUR MAJESTY, CAN YOU HEAR US?!
WHAT?

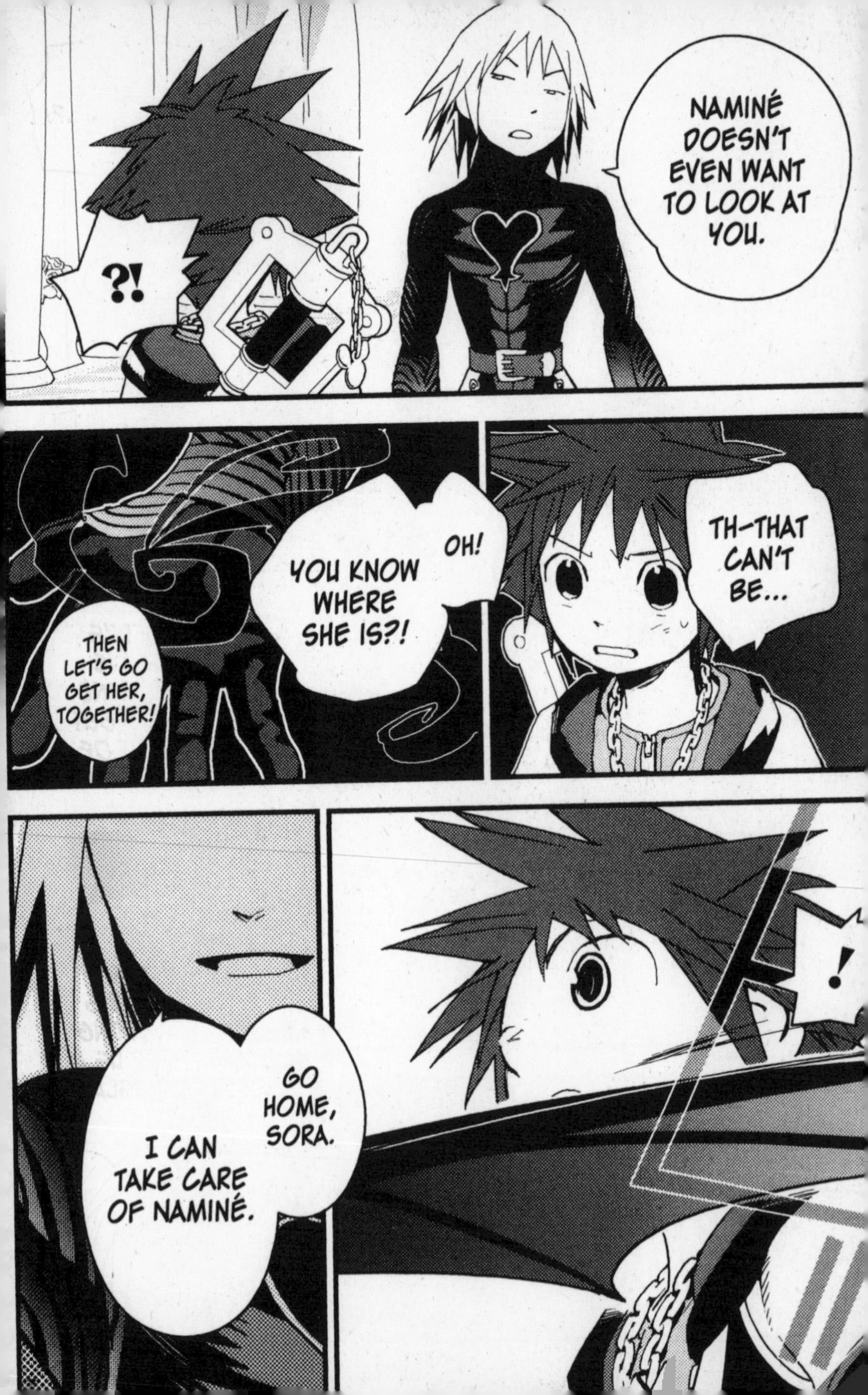
NAMINÉ DOESN'T EVEN WANT TO LOOK AT YOU.
?!
TH-THAT CAN'T BE...
OH!
YOU KNOW WHERE SHE IS?!
THEN LET'S GO GET HER, TOGETHER!
!
GO HOME, SORA.
I CAN TAKE CARE OF NAMINÉ.

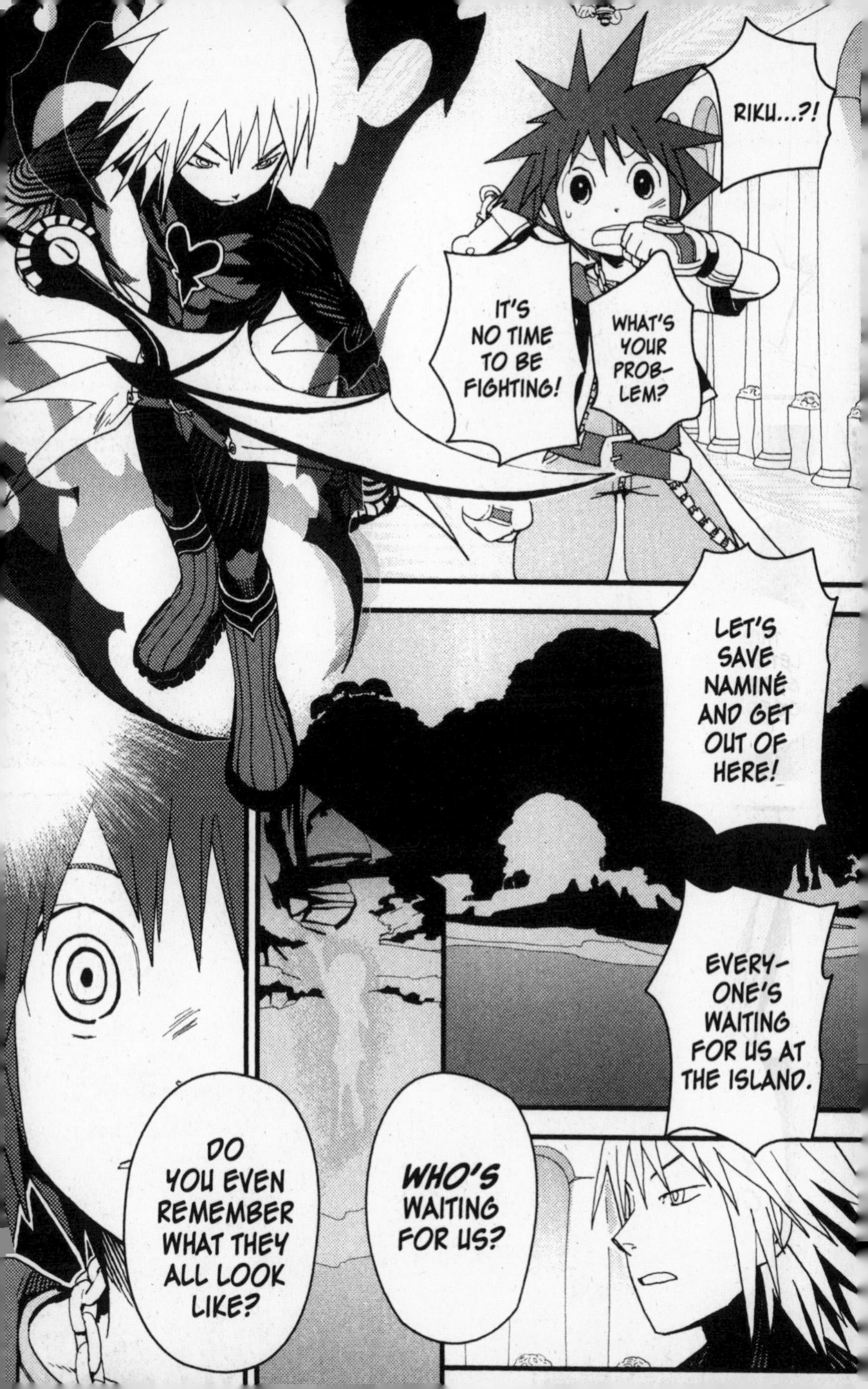

RIKU...?!
WHAT'S YOUR PROB-LEM?
IT'S NO TIME TO BE FIGHTING!
LET'S SAVE NAMINÉ AND GET OUT OF HERE!
EVERY-ONE'S WAITING FOR US AT THE ISLAND.
WHO'S WAITING FOR US?
DO YOU EVEN REMEMBER WHAT THEY ALL LOOK LIKE?

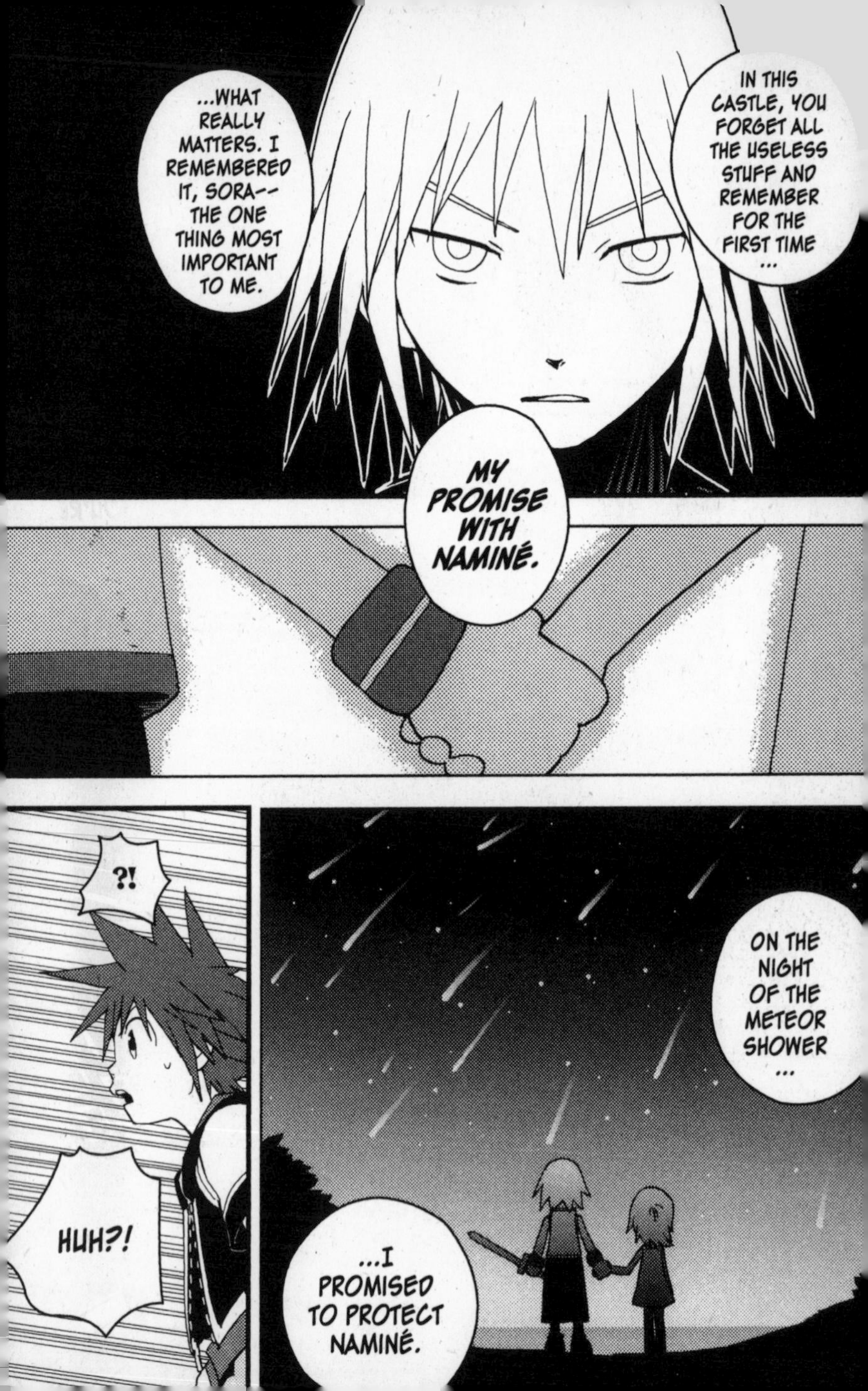
IN THIS CASTLE, YOU FORGET ALL THE USELESS STUFF AND REMEMBER FOR THE FIRST TIME ...
...WHAT REALLY MATTERS. I REMEMBERED IT, SORA-- THE ONE THING MOST IMPORTANT TO ME.
MY PROMISE WITH NAMINÉ.
ON THE NIGHT OF THE METEOR SHOWER ...
...I PROMISED TO PROTECT NAMINÉ.
?!
HUH?!

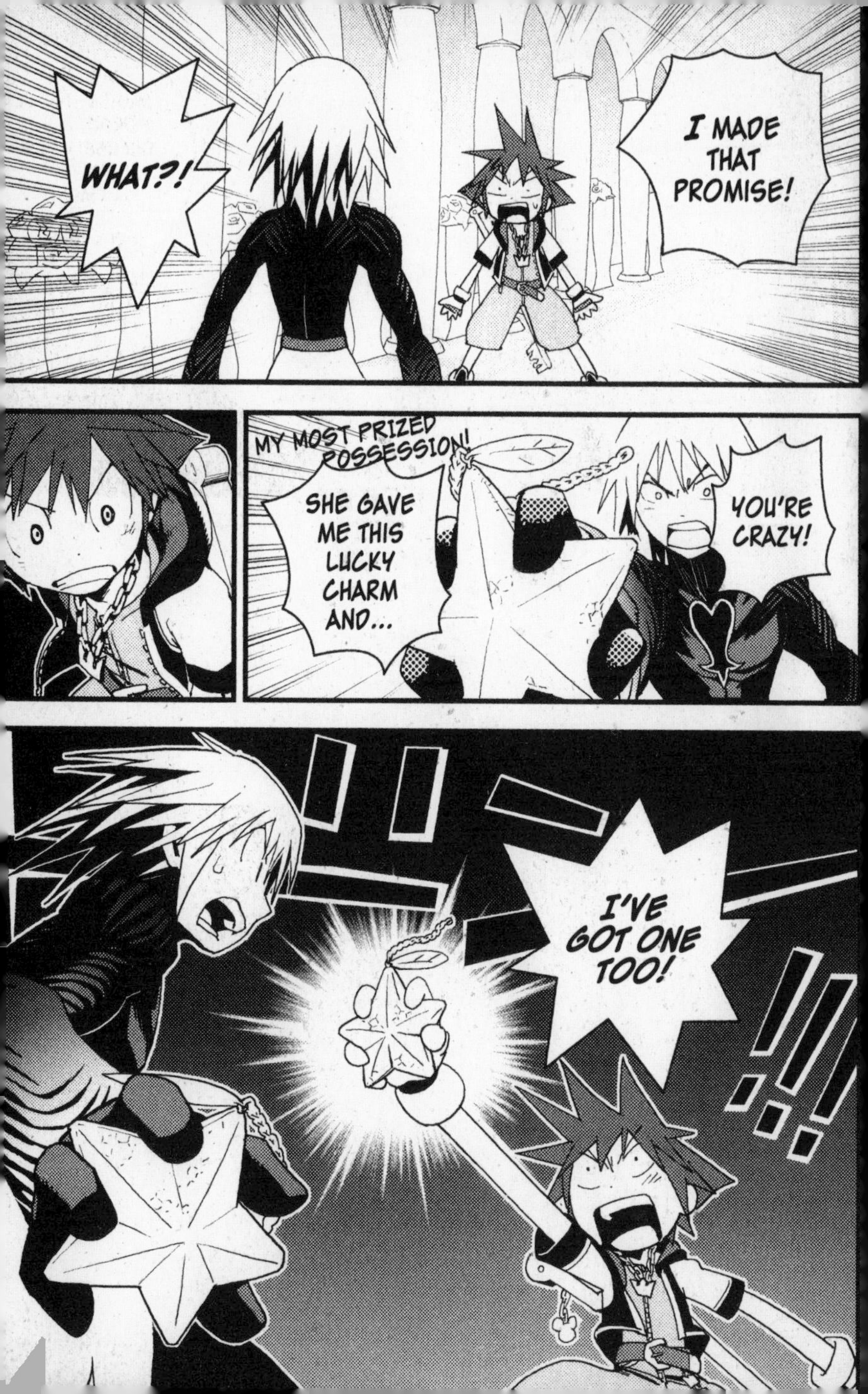
I MADE THAT PROMISE!
WHAT?!
YOU'RE CRAZY!
SHE GAVE ME THIS LUCKY CHARM AND...
MY MOST PRIZED POSSESSION!
I'VE GOT ONE TOO!

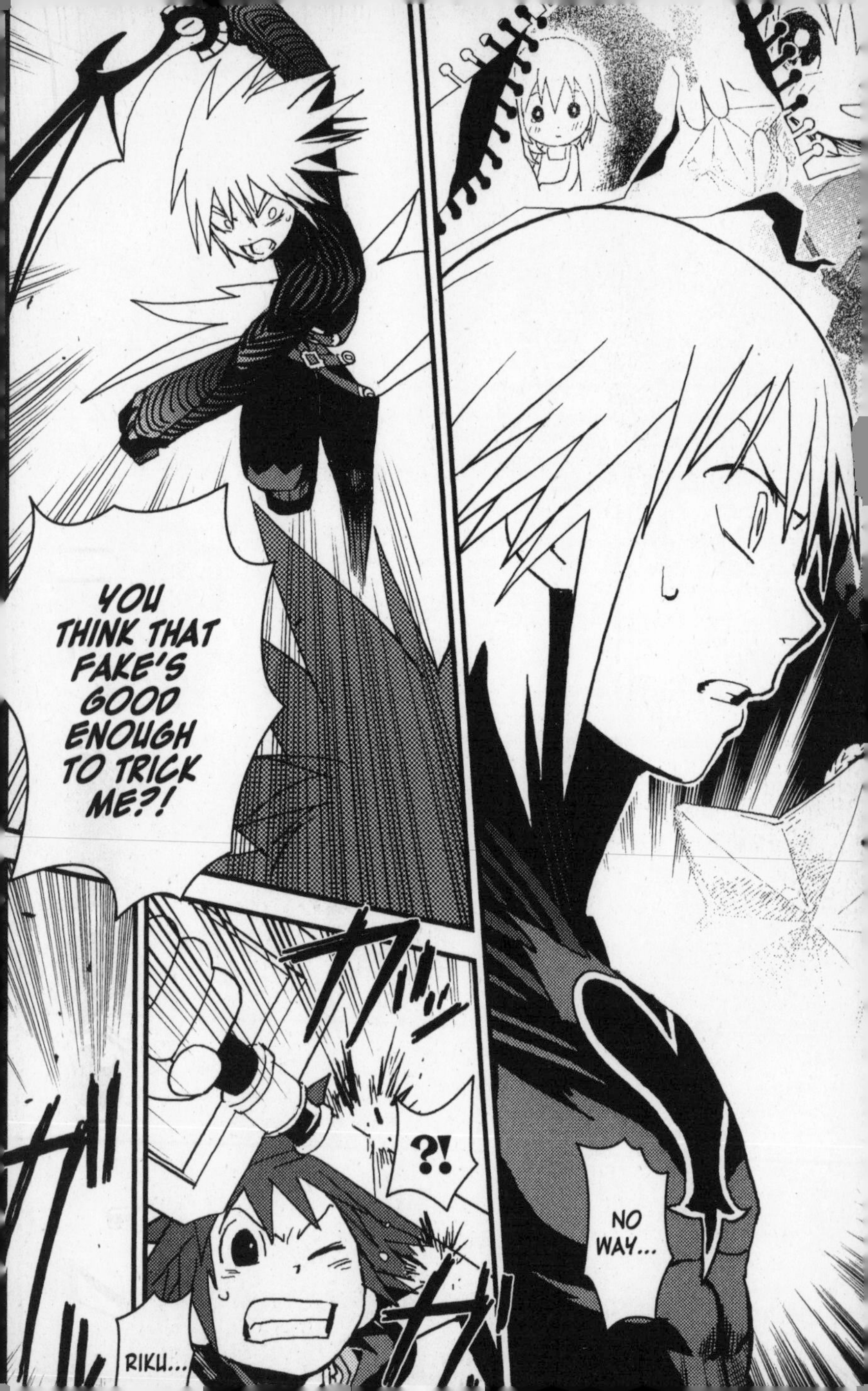
NO WAY...
YOU THINK THAT FAKE'S GOOD ENOUGH TO TRICK ME?!
?!
RIKU...

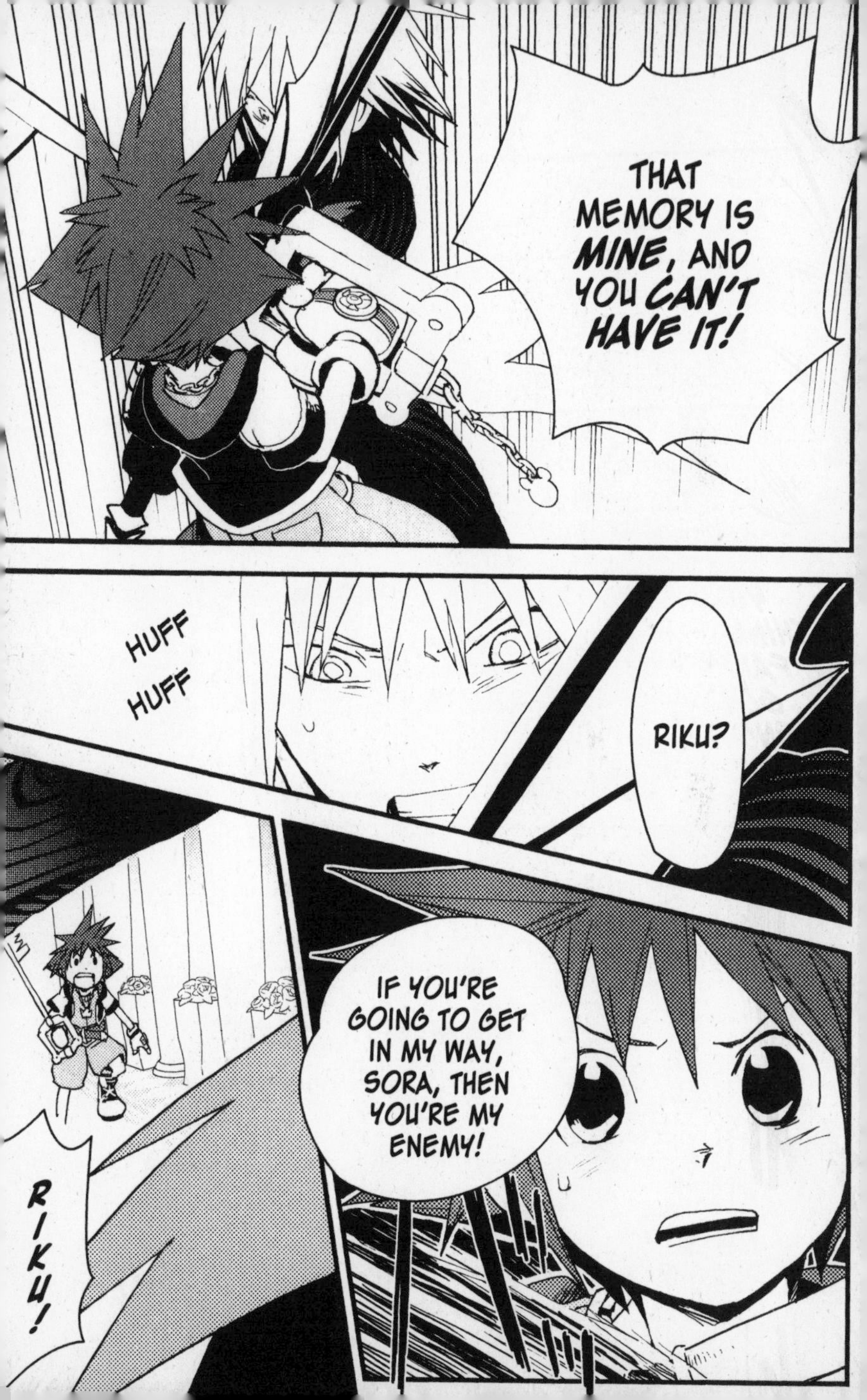
THAT MEMORY IS MINE, AND YOU CAN'T HAVE IT!
RIKU?
HUFF HUFF
IF YOU'RE GOING TO GET IN MY WAY, SORA, THEN YOU'RE MY ENEMY!
RIKU!

WE BOTH WANT THE SAME THING. WE BOTH WANT TO HELP NAMINÉ. SO WHY ARE WE FIGHTING?

WHY...? I DON'T GET IT.

ギリギリギリ

I HAVE NO PLAN B!

THE PLAN WILL BE COMPLETELY RUINED...

DON'T RUN AWAY, YOU FOOL!

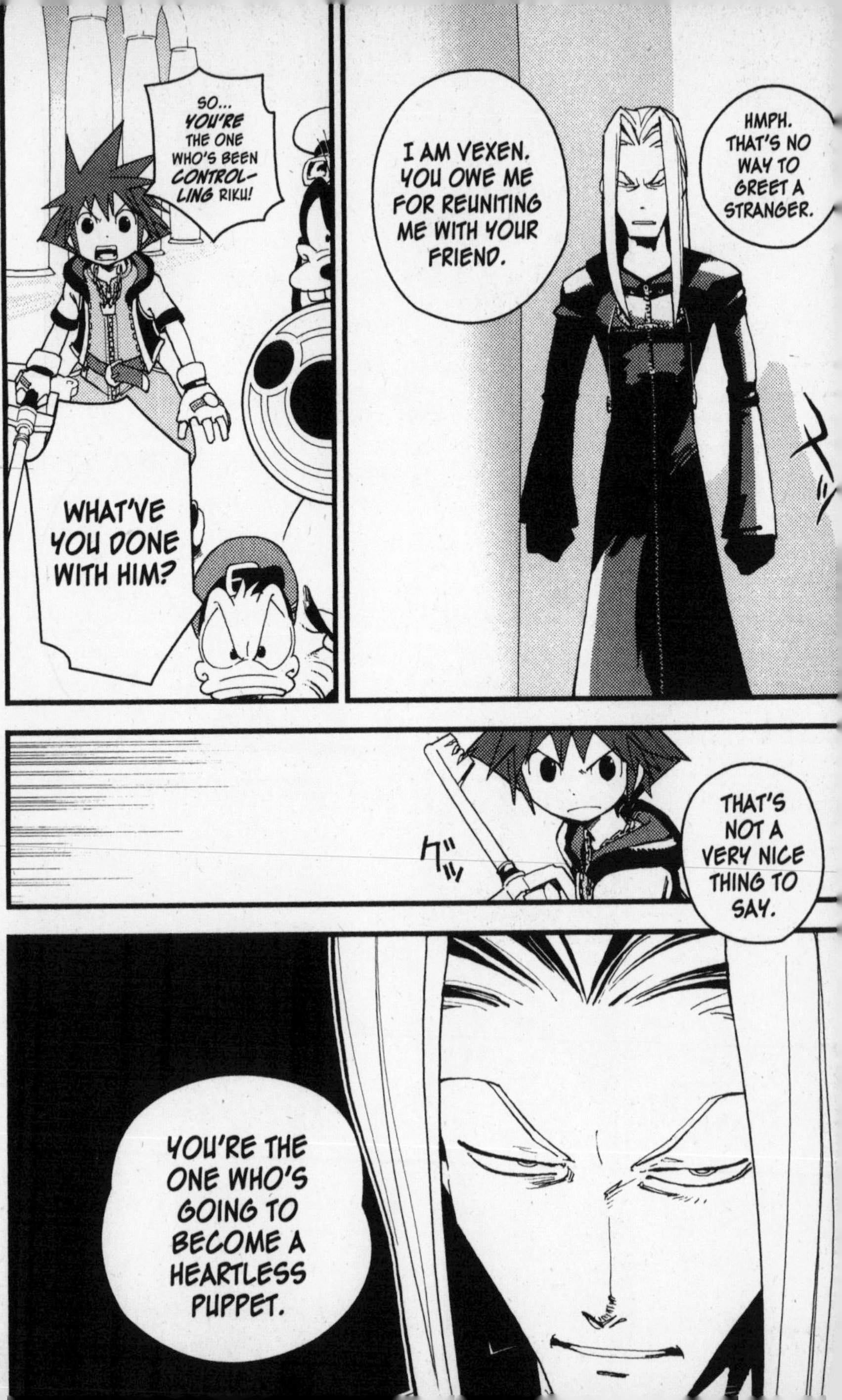
HMPH. THAT'S NO WAY TO GREET A STRANGER.
I AM VEXEN. YOU OWE ME FOR REUNITING ME WITH YOUR FRIEND.
SO... *YOU'RE* THE ONE WHO'S BEEN *CONTROLLING* RIKU!
WHAT'VE YOU DONE WITH HIM?
THAT'S NOT A VERY NICE THING TO SAY.
YOU'RE THE ONE WHO'S GOING TO BECOME A HEARTLESS PUPPET.

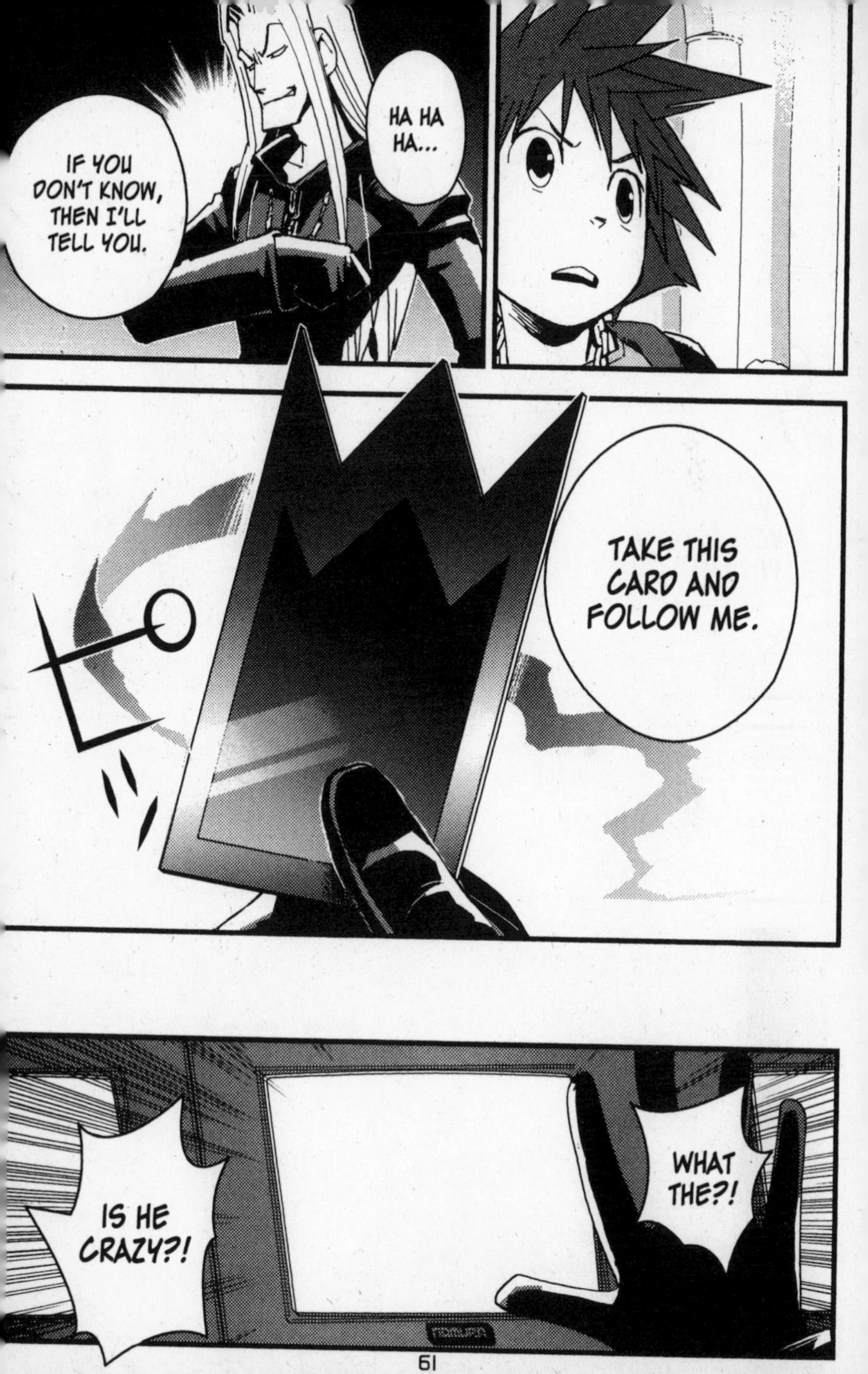
HA HA HA...
IF YOU DON'T KNOW, THEN I'LL TELL YOU.
TAKE THIS CARD AND FOLLOW ME.
WHAT THE?!
IS HE CRAZY?!

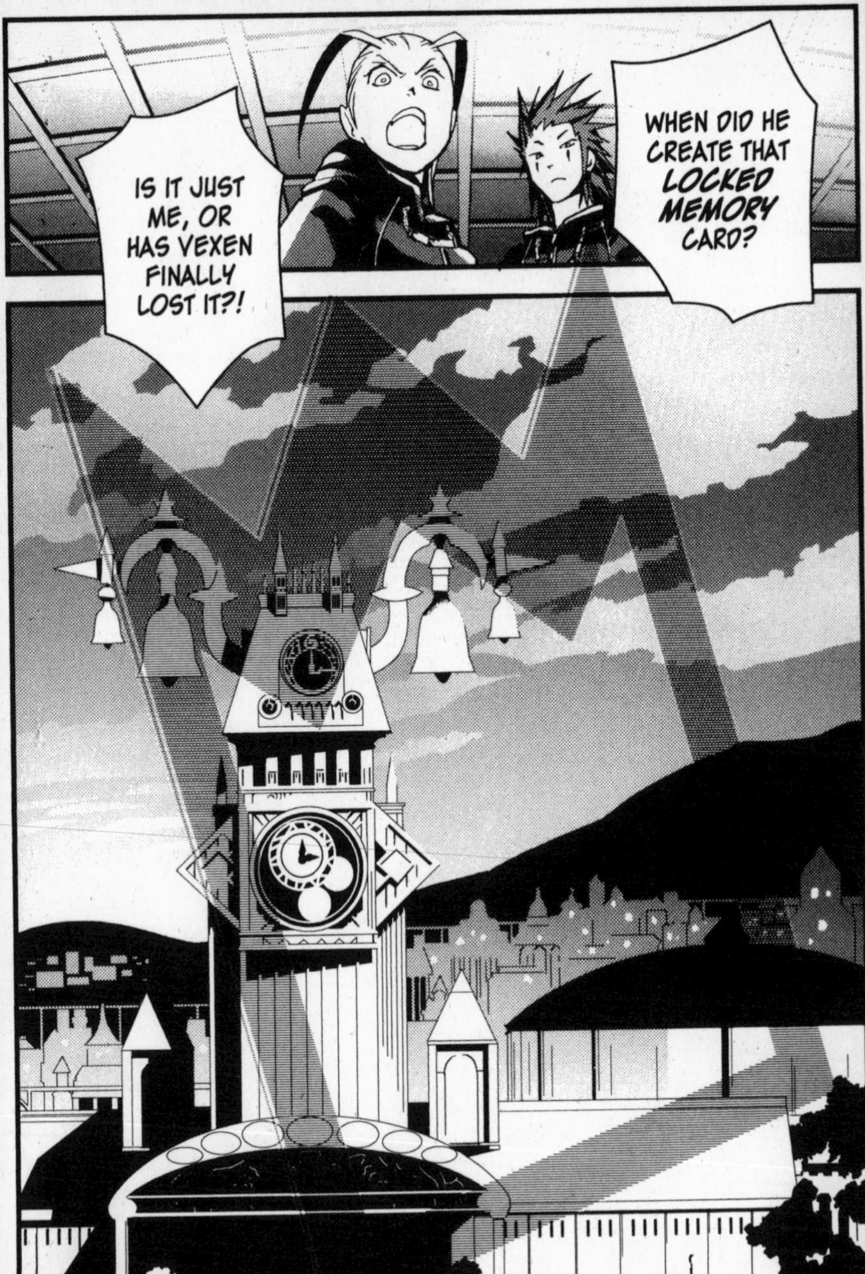
WHEN DID HE CREATE THAT LOCKED MEMORY CARD?
IS IT JUST ME, OR HAS VEXEN FINALLY LOST IT?!

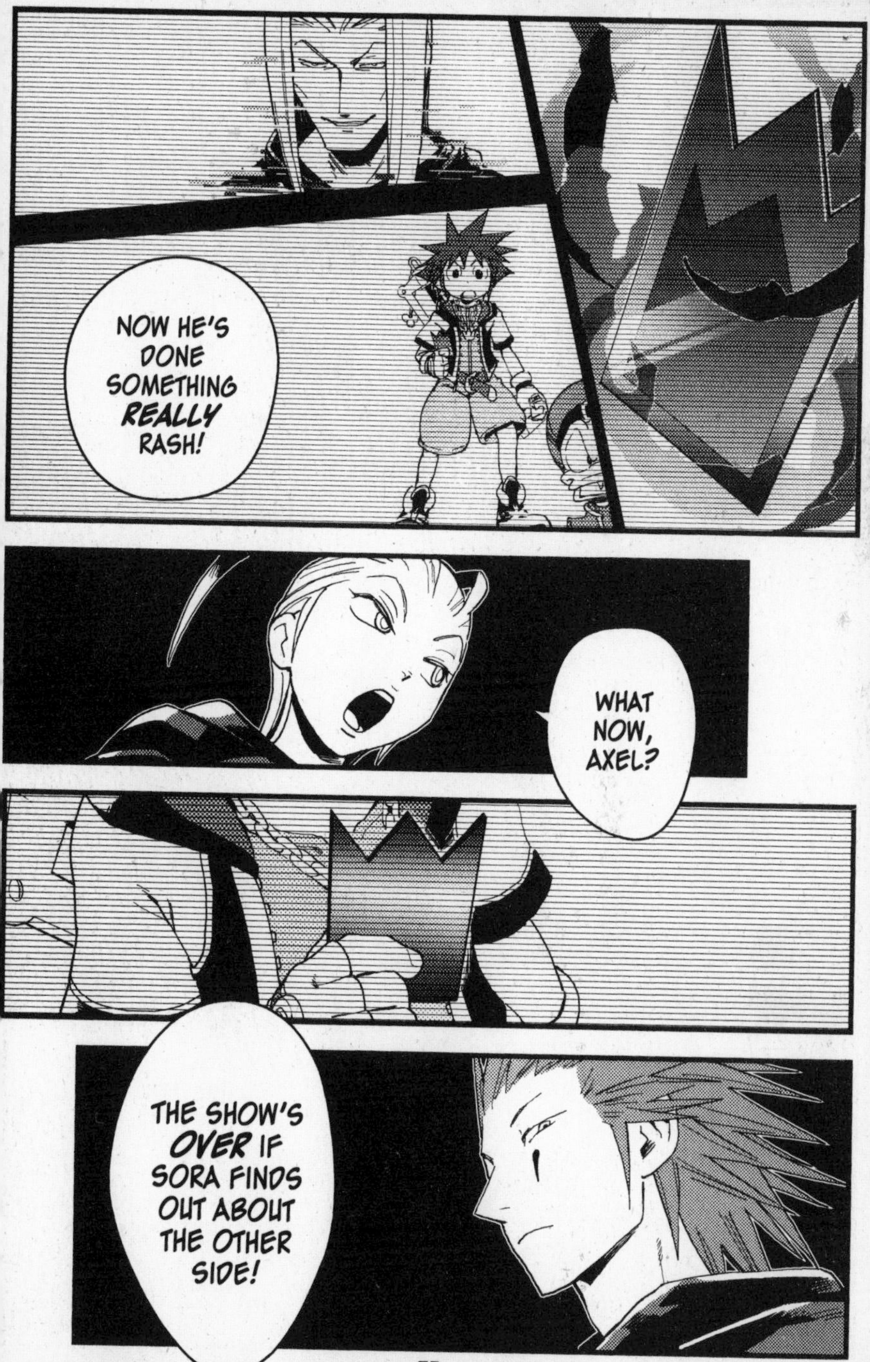
NOW HE'S DONE SOMETHING REALLY RASH!
WHAT NOW, AXEL?
THE SHOW'S OVER IF SORA FINDS OUT ABOUT THE OTHER SIDE!

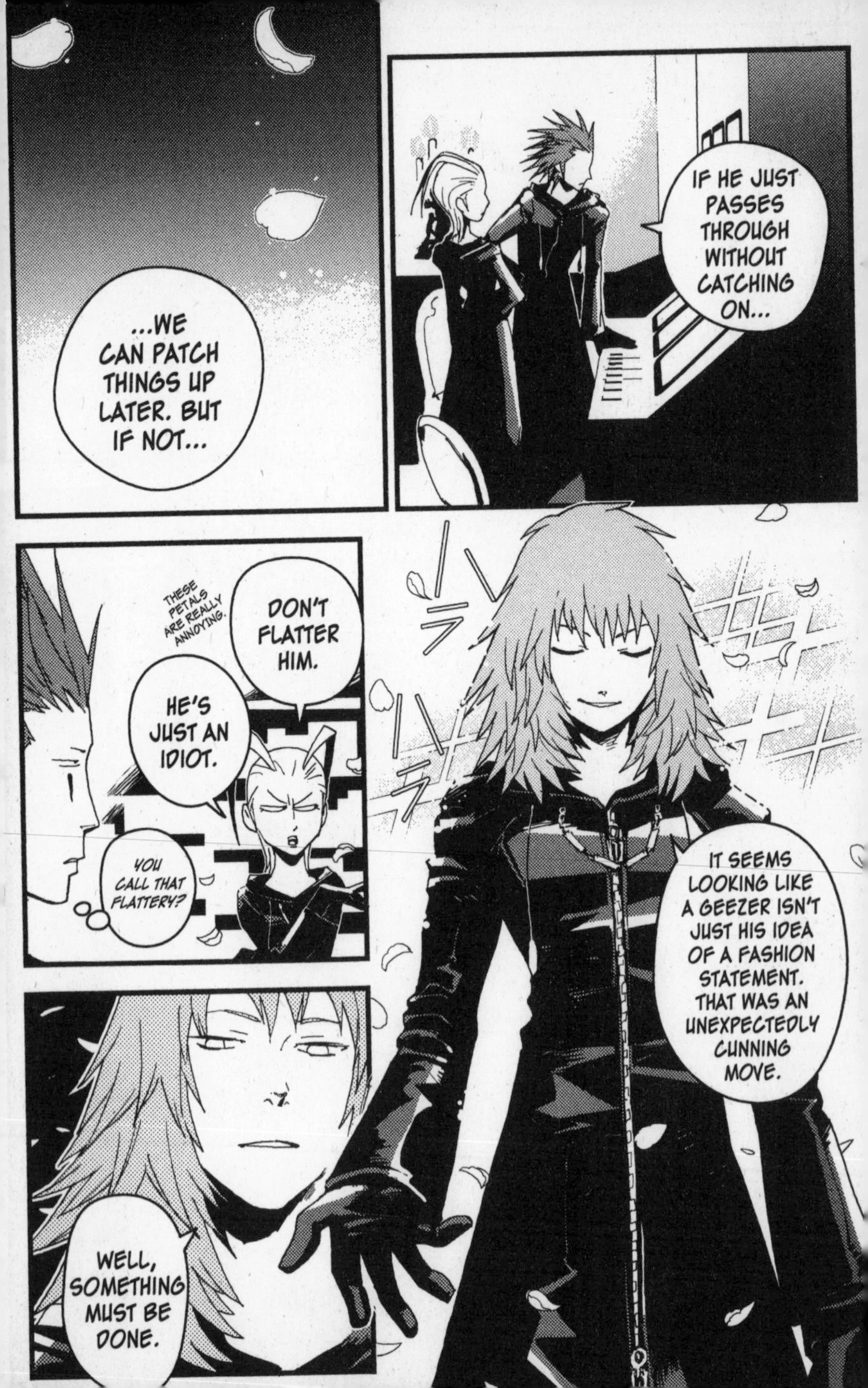
IF HE JUST PASSES THROUGH WITHOUT CATCHING ON...
...WE CAN PATCH THINGS UP LATER. BUT IF NOT...
IT SEEMS LOOKING LIKE A GEEZER ISN'T JUST HIS IDEA OF A FASHION STATEMENT. THAT WAS AN UNEXPECTEDLY CUNNING MOVE.
DON'T FLATTER HIM.
THESE PETALS ARE REALLY ANNOYING.
HE'S JUST AN IDIOT.
YOU CALL THAT FLATTERY?
WELL, SOMETHING MUST BE DONE.

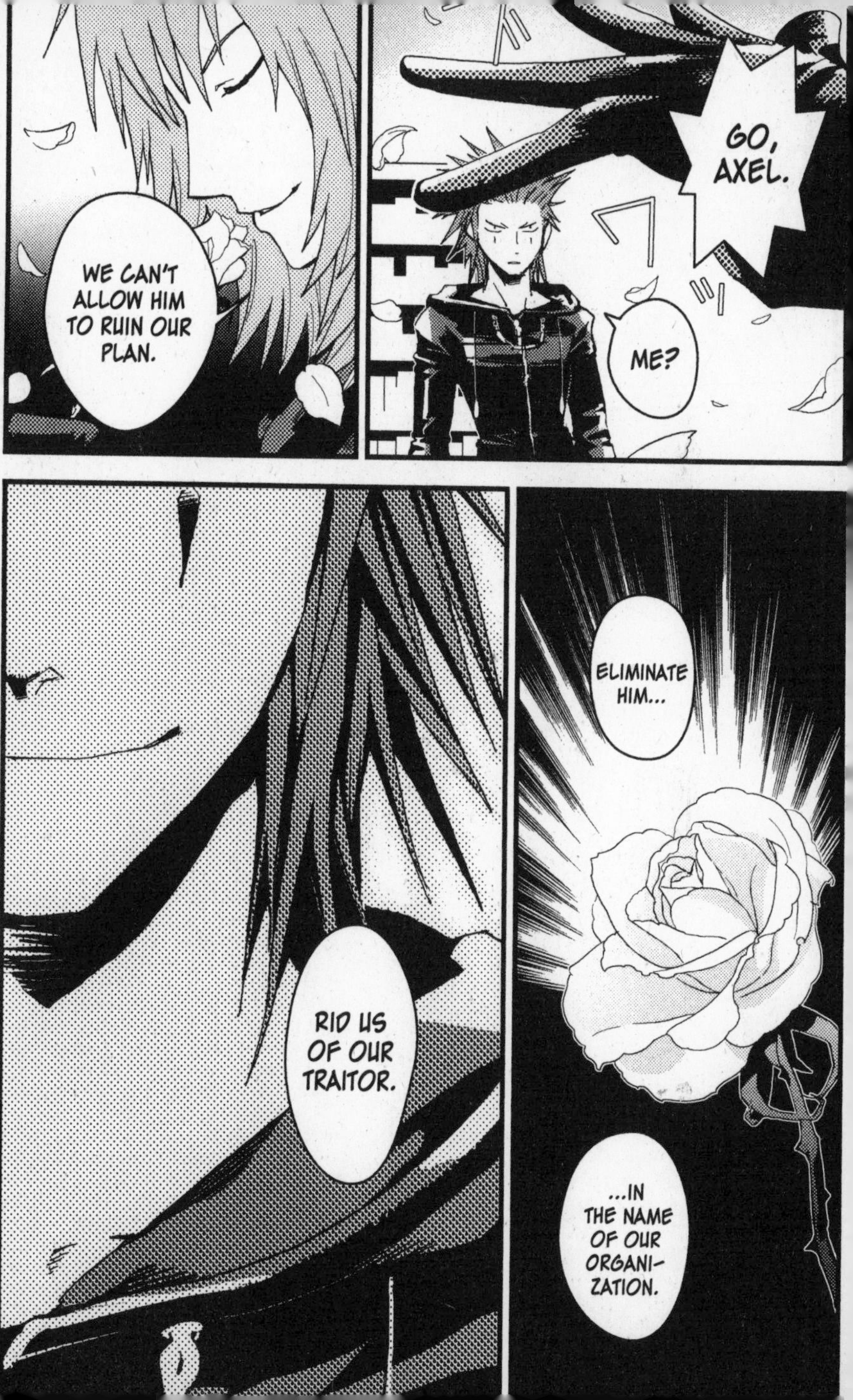
GO, AXEL.
ME?
WE CAN'T ALLOW HIM TO RUIN OUR PLAN.
ELIMINATE HIM...
...IN THE NAME OF OUR ORGANIZATION.
RID US OF OUR TRAITOR.

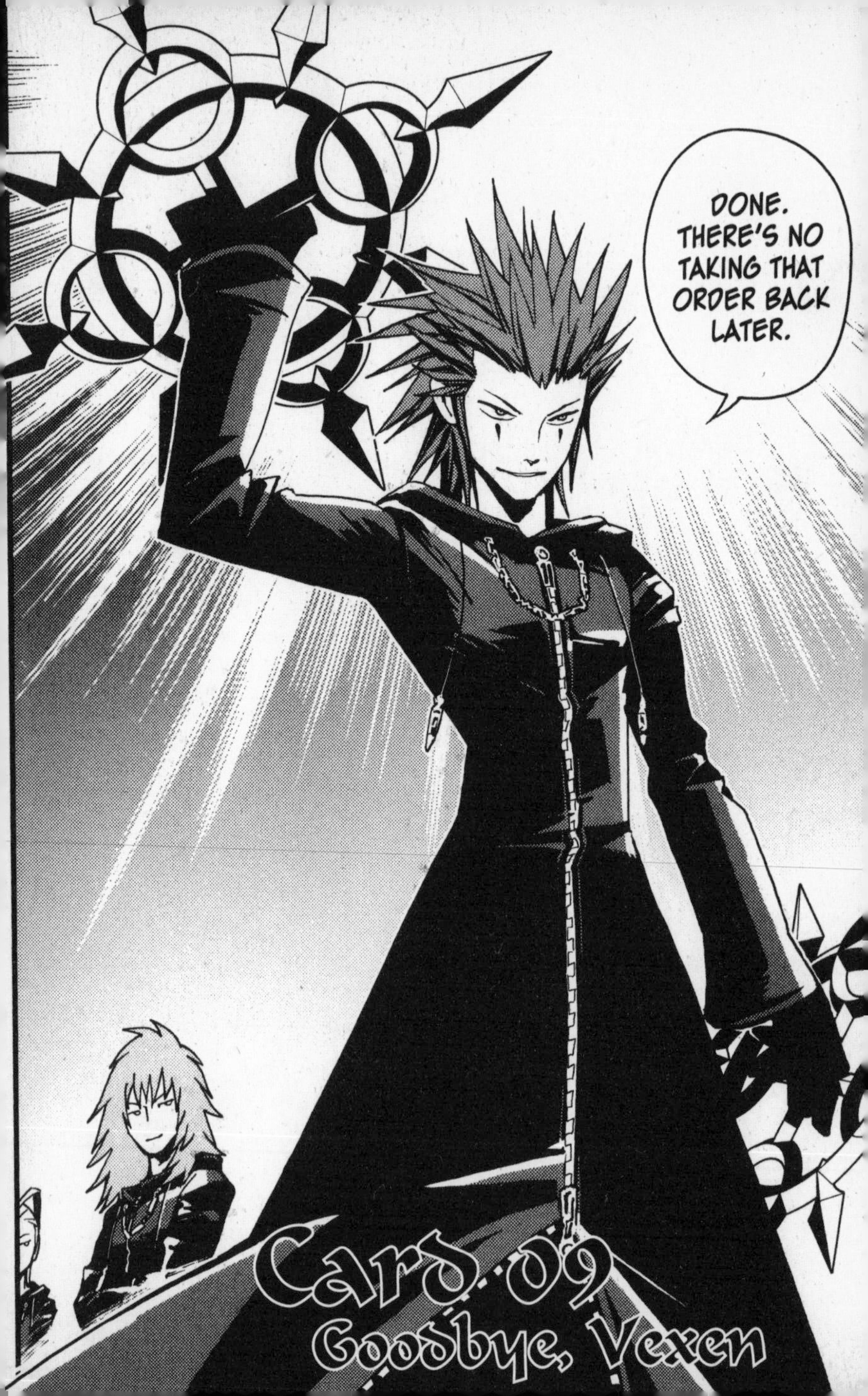

DONE. THERE'S NO TAKING THAT ORDER BACK LATER.
Card 09
Goodbye, Vexen

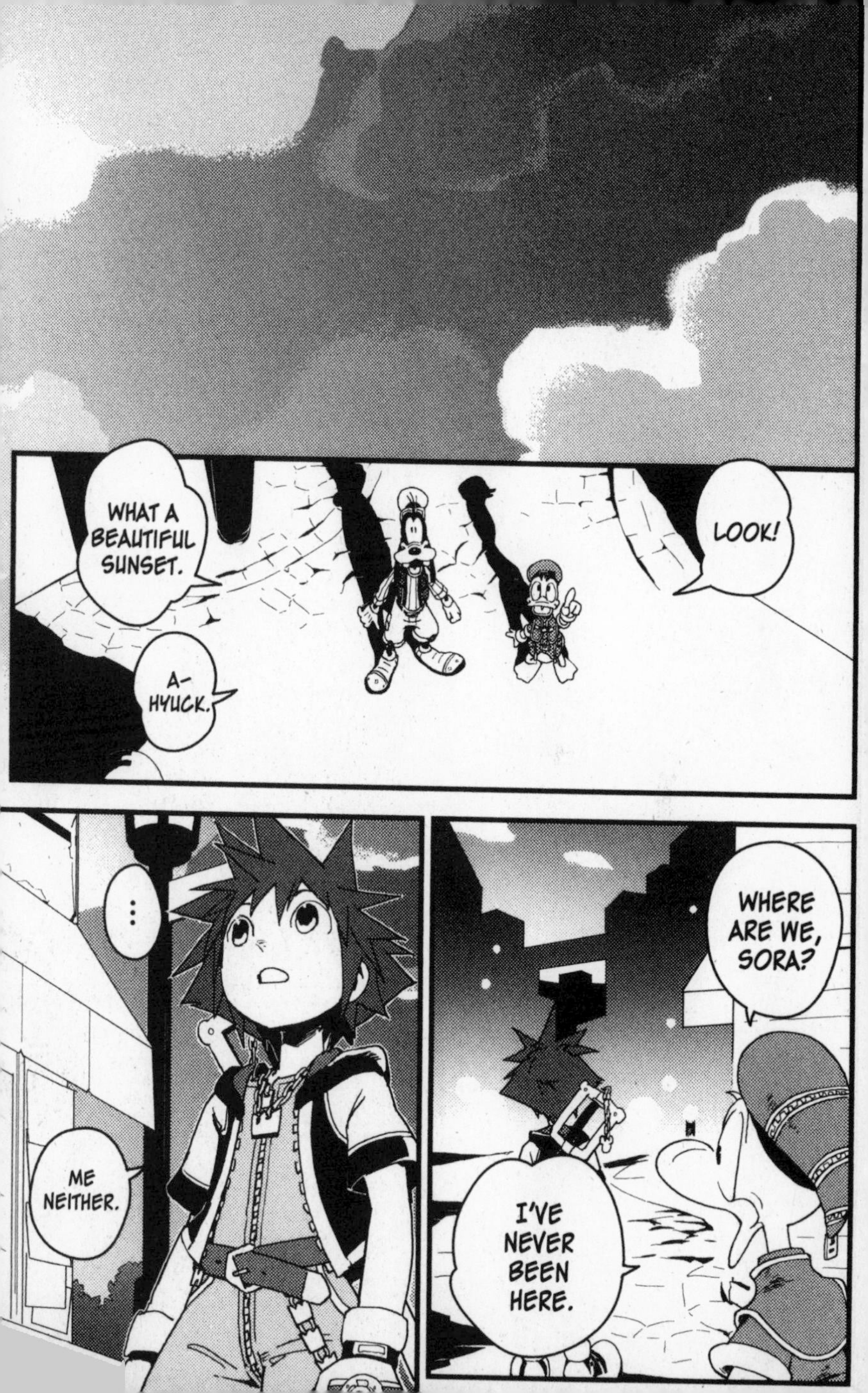
LOOK!
WHAT A BEAUTIFUL SUNSET.
A-HYUCK.
WHERE ARE WE, SORA?
I'VE NEVER BEEN HERE.
...
ME NEITHER.

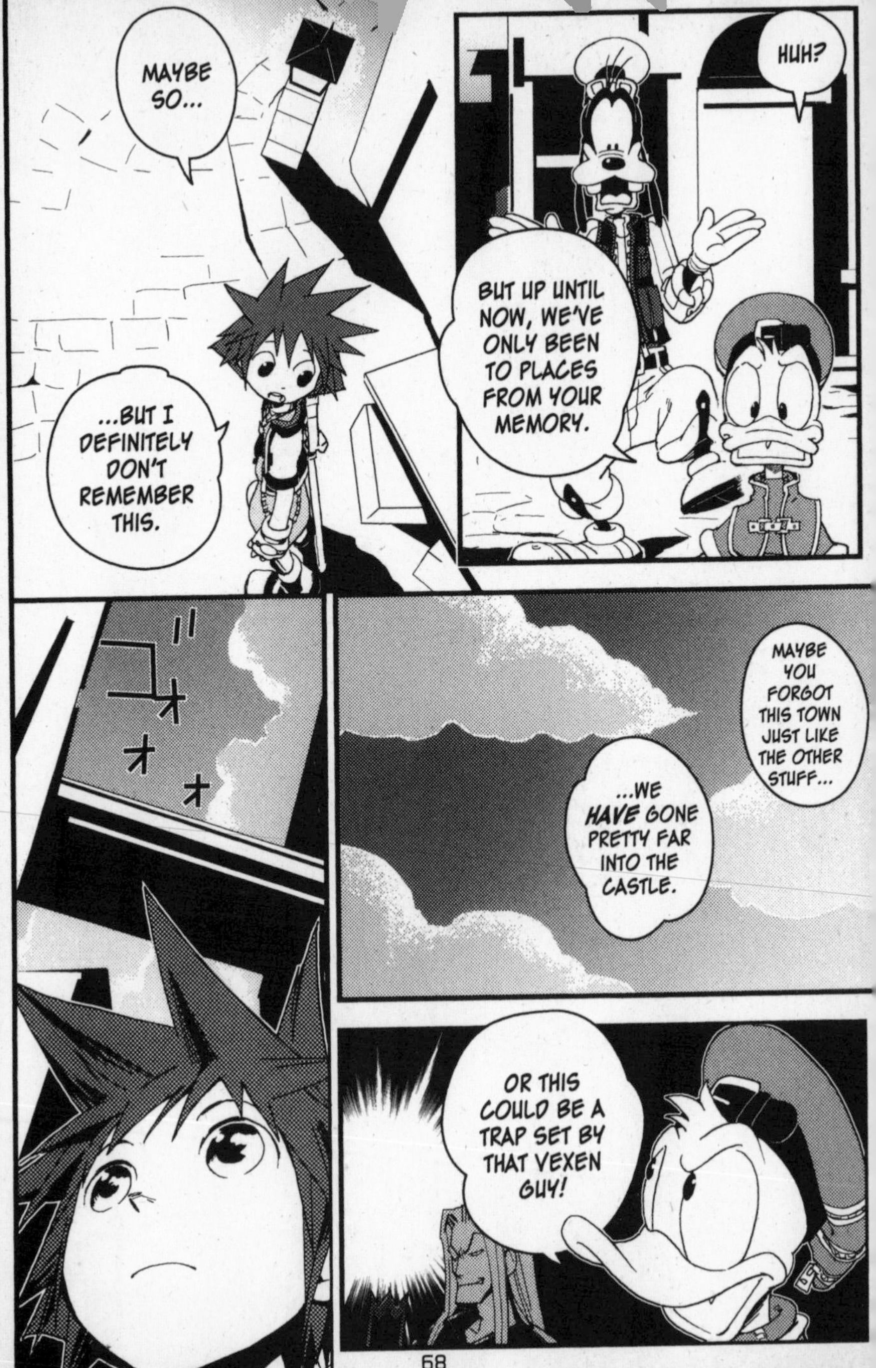
HUH?
BUT UP UNTIL NOW, WE'VE ONLY BEEN TO PLACES FROM YOUR MEMORY.
MAYBE SO...
...BUT I DEFINITELY DON'T REMEMBER THIS.
MAYBE YOU FORGOT THIS TOWN JUST LIKE THE OTHER STUFF...
...WE *HAVE* GONE PRETTY FAR INTO THE CASTLE.
OR THIS COULD BE A TRAP SET BY THAT VEXEN GUY!
ゴオォォ

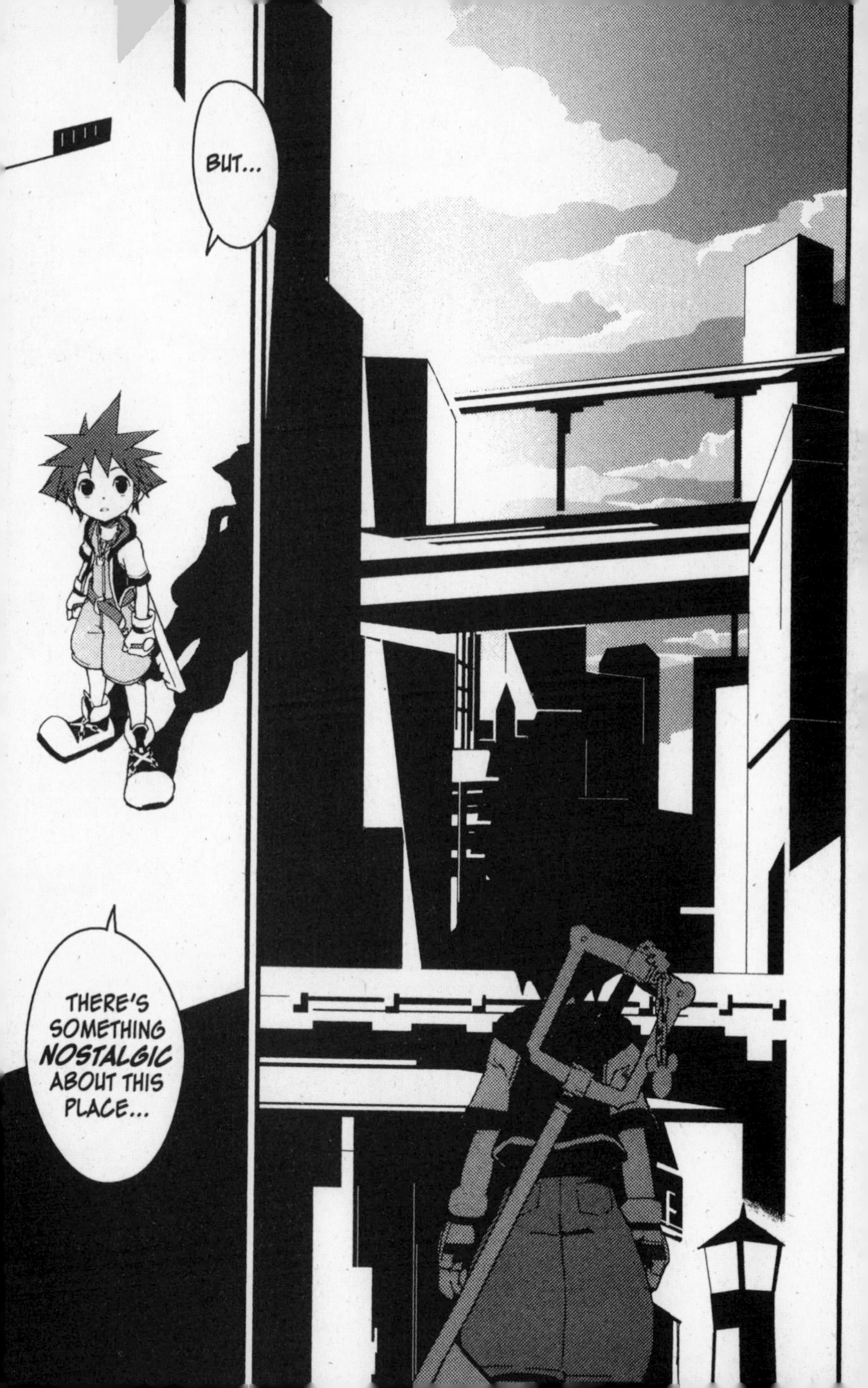
BUT...
THERE'S SOMETHING NOSTALGIC ABOUT THIS PLACE...

I FEEL KIND OF FUNNY. I'M SURE I DON'T KNOW THIS PLACE...

...BUT IT'S STARTING TO FEEL REAL FAMILIAR.

SORA?

UM...

YOU FORGOT OTHER STUFF, SO NOW YOU REMEMBER THIS PLACE.

MAYBE IT'S LIKE WITH NAMINÉ.

YOUR HEART IS A SLAVE TO YOUR MEMORY.

HA HA HA.

"LIKE WITH NAMINÉ," IS IT?

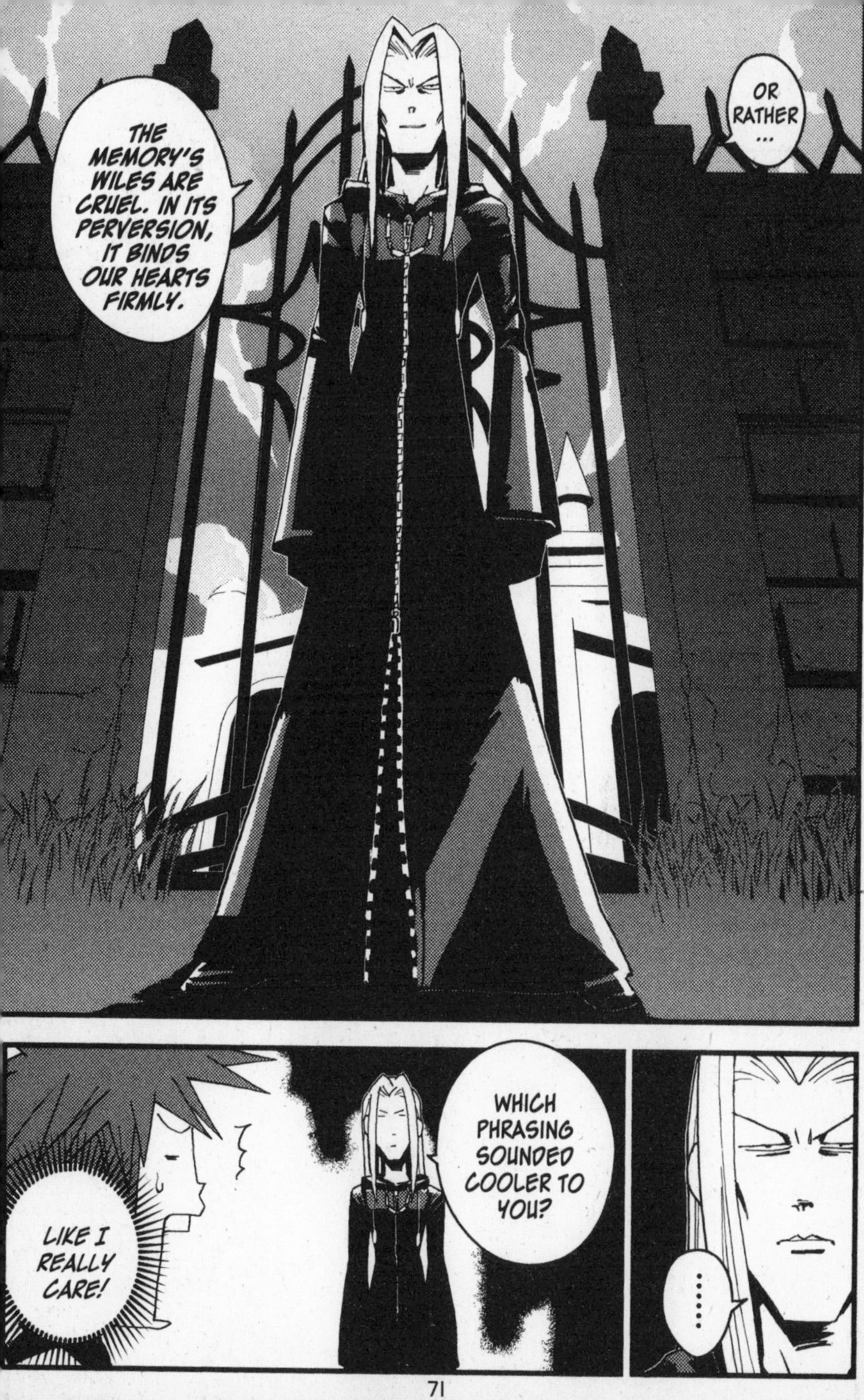
OR RATHER ...
THE MEMORY'S WILES ARE CRUEL. IN ITS PERVERSION, IT BINDS OUR HEARTS FIRMLY.
......
WHICH PHRASING SOUNDED COOLER TO YOU?
LIKE I REALLY CARE!

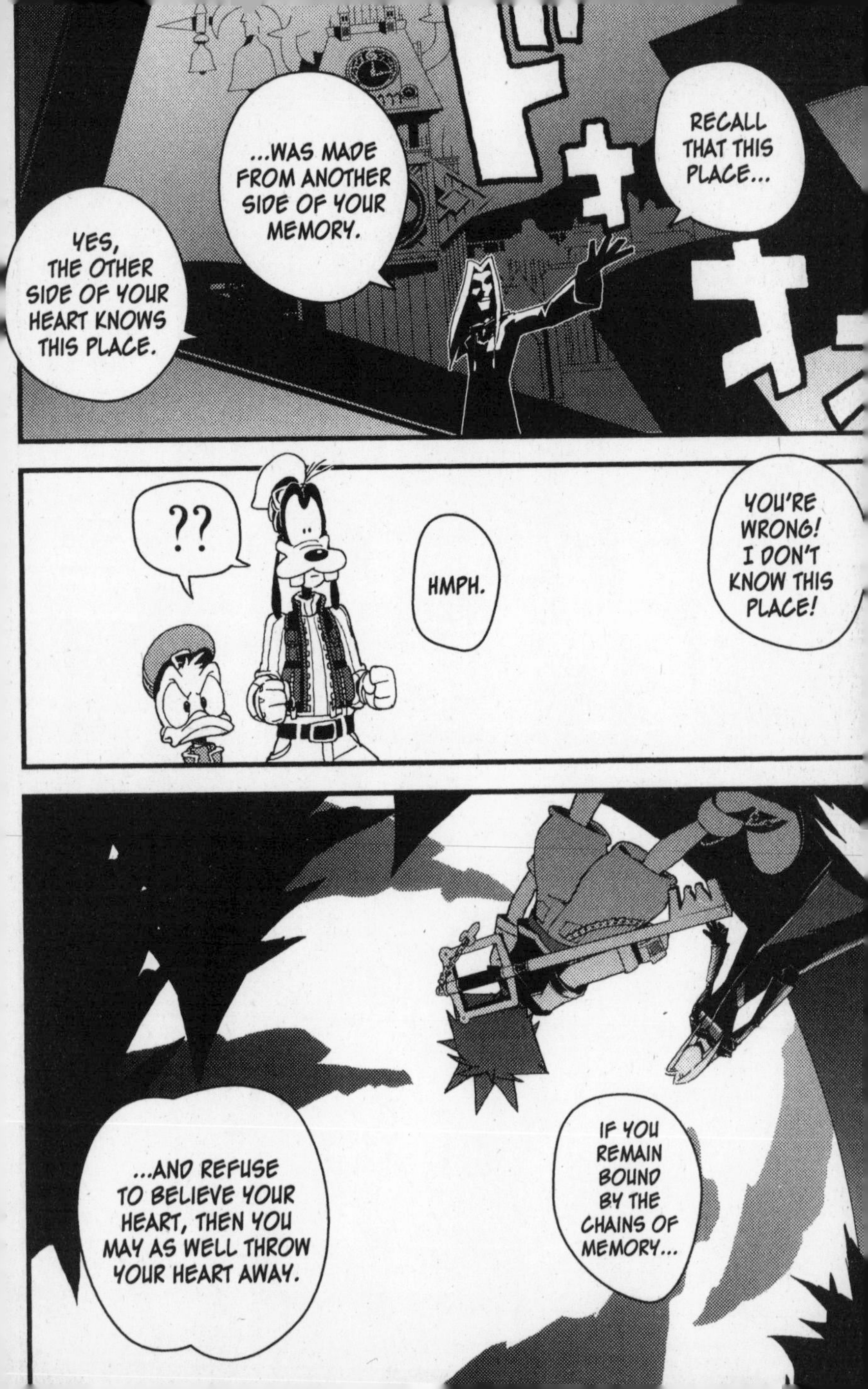
RECALL THAT THIS PLACE...
...WAS MADE FROM ANOTHER SIDE OF YOUR MEMORY.
YES, THE OTHER SIDE OF YOUR HEART KNOWS THIS PLACE.
YOU'RE WRONG! I DON'T KNOW THIS PLACE!
HMPH.
??
IF YOU REMAIN BOUND BY THE CHAINS OF MEMORY...
...AND REFUSE TO BELIEVE YOUR HEART, THEN YOU MAY AS WELL THROW YOUR HEART AWAY.

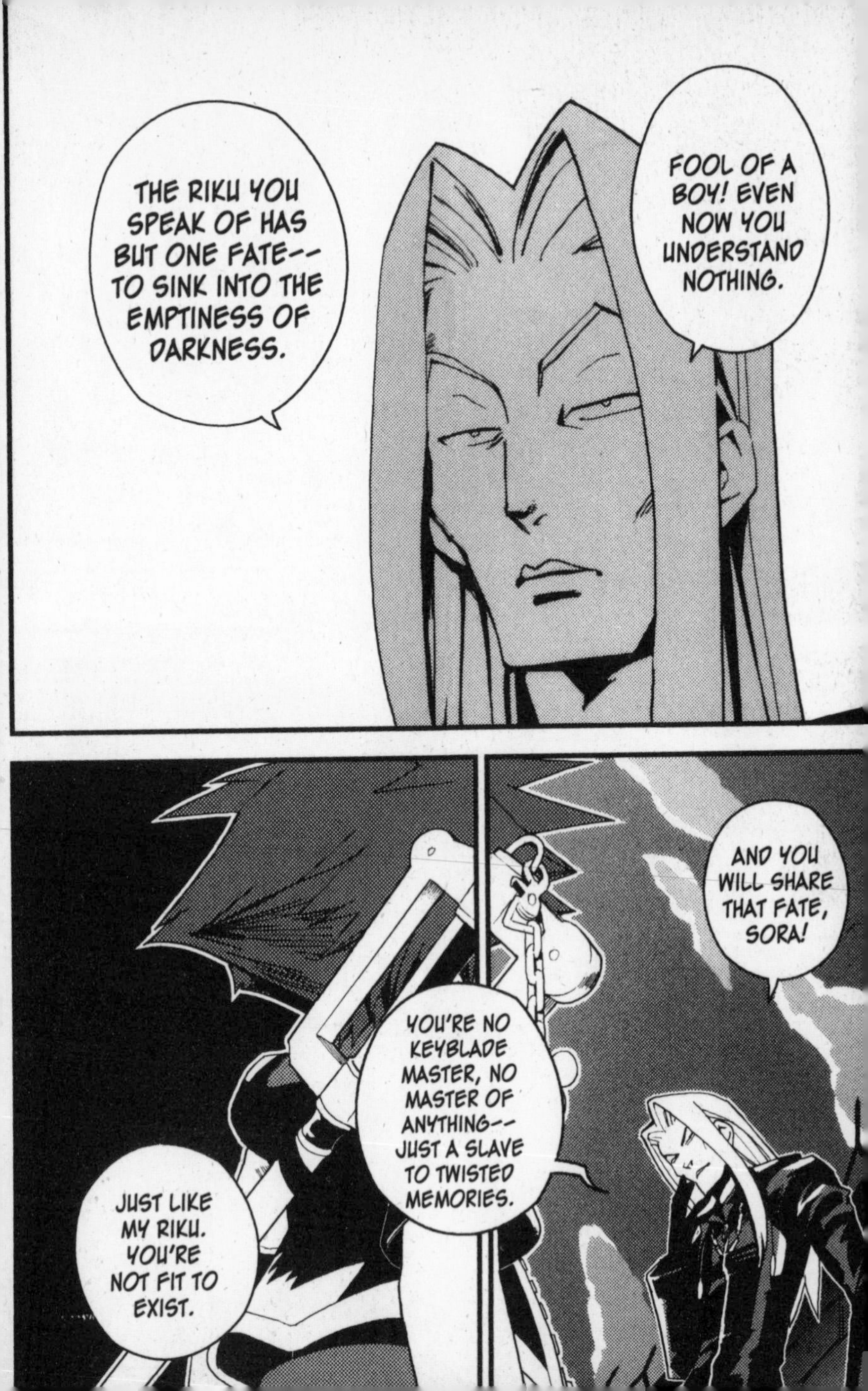
FOOL OF A BOY! EVEN NOW YOU UNDERSTAND NOTHING.
THE RIKU YOU SPEAK OF HAS BUT ONE FATE--TO SINK INTO THE EMPTINESS OF DARKNESS.
AND YOU WILL SHARE THAT FATE, SORA!
YOU'RE NO KEYBLADE MASTER, NO MASTER OF ANYTHING--JUST A SLAVE TO TWISTED MEMORIES.
JUST LIKE MY RIKU. YOU'RE NOT FIT TO EXIST.

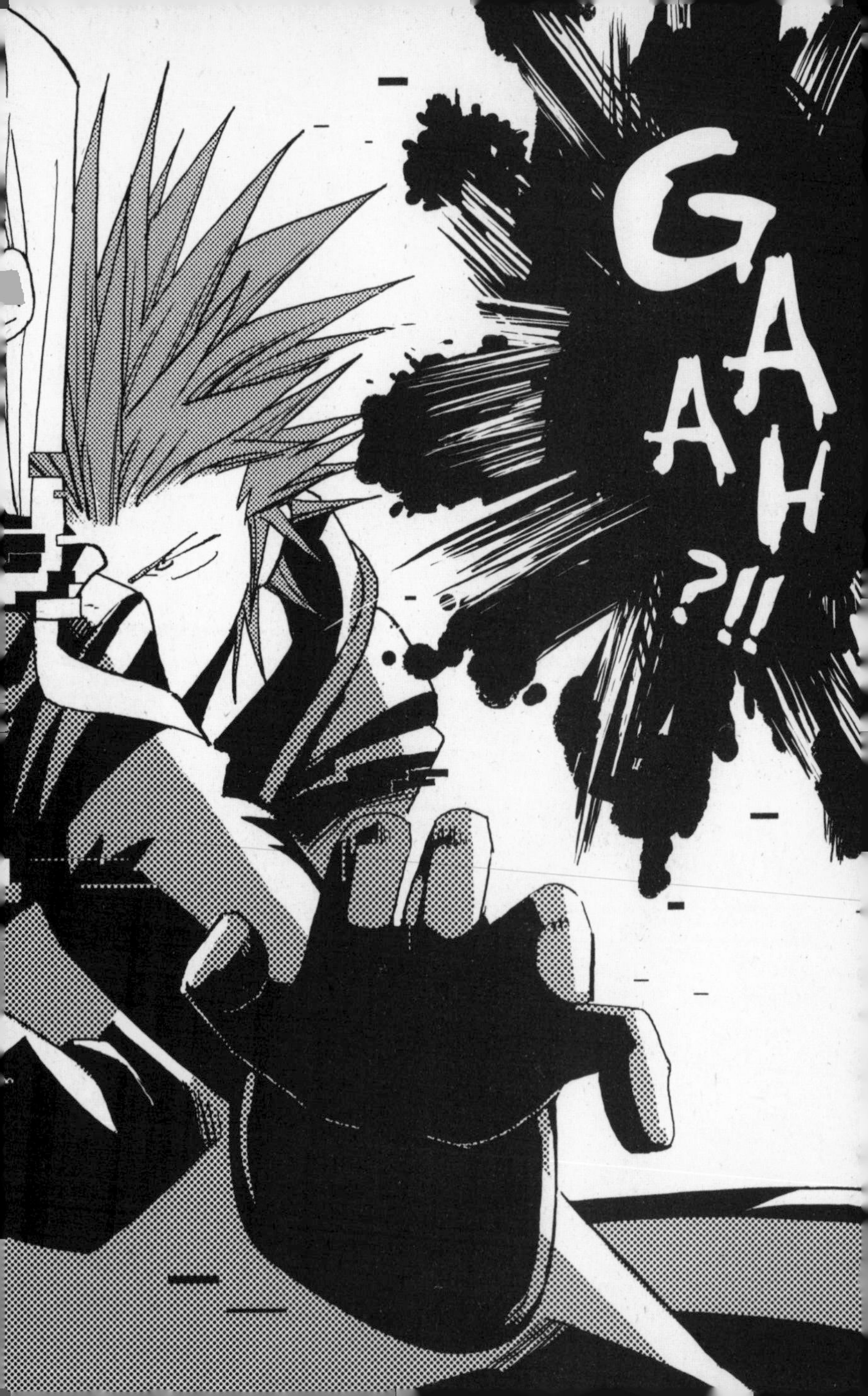
GAAAH?!!

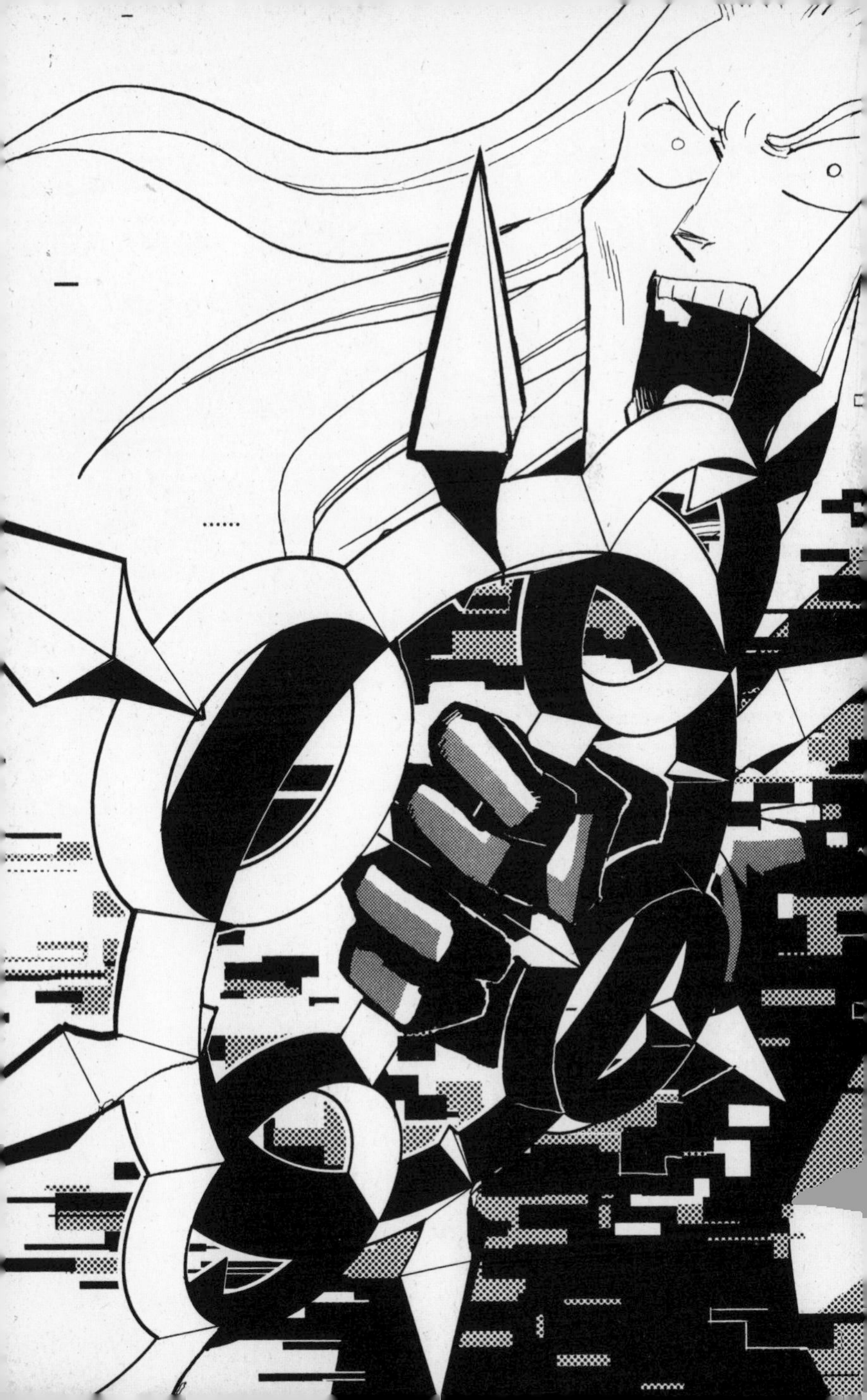

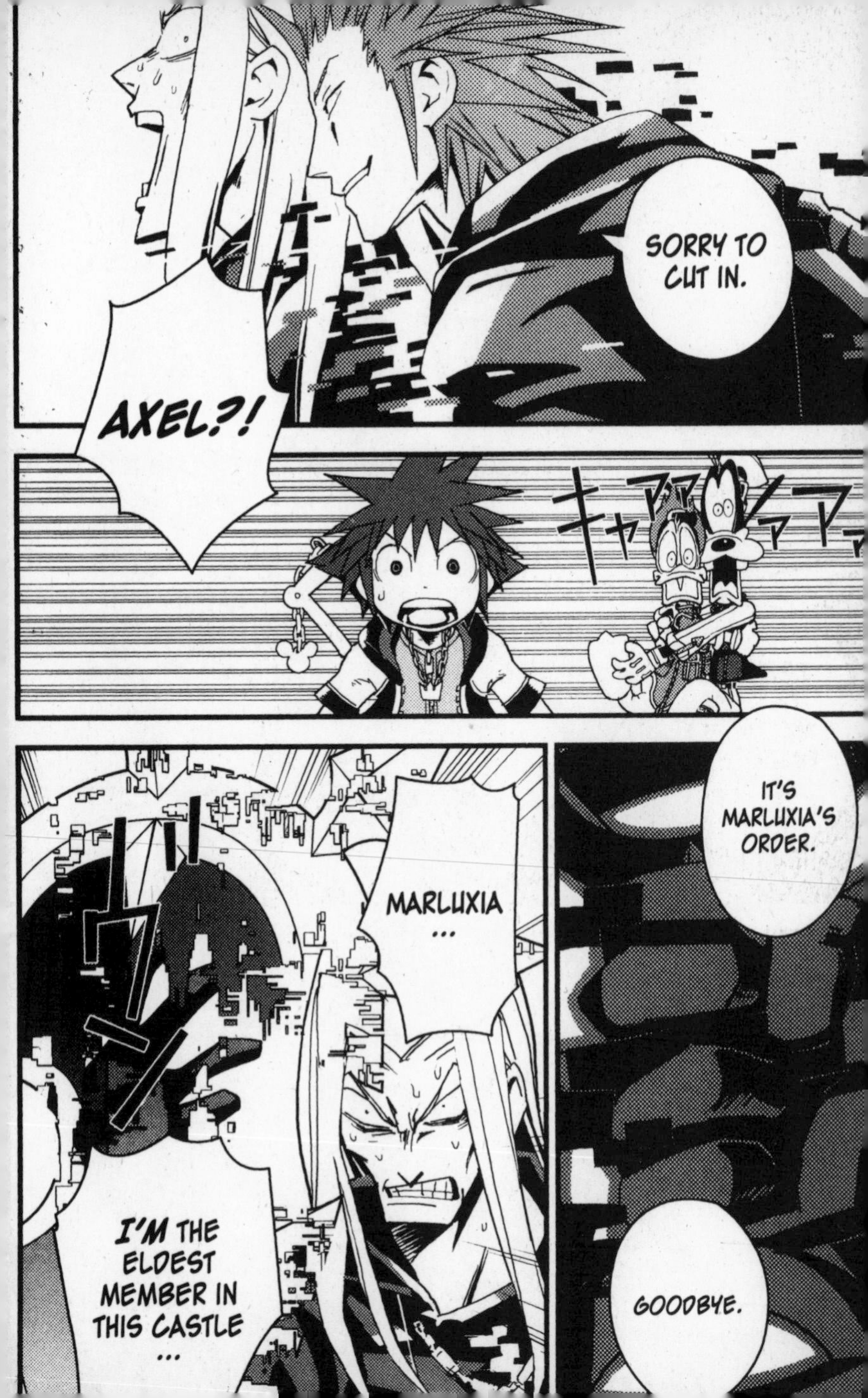
SORRY TO CUT IN.
AXEL?!
IT'S MARLUXIA'S ORDER.
GOODBYE.
MARLUXIA ...
I'M THE ELDEST MEMBER IN THIS CASTLE ...

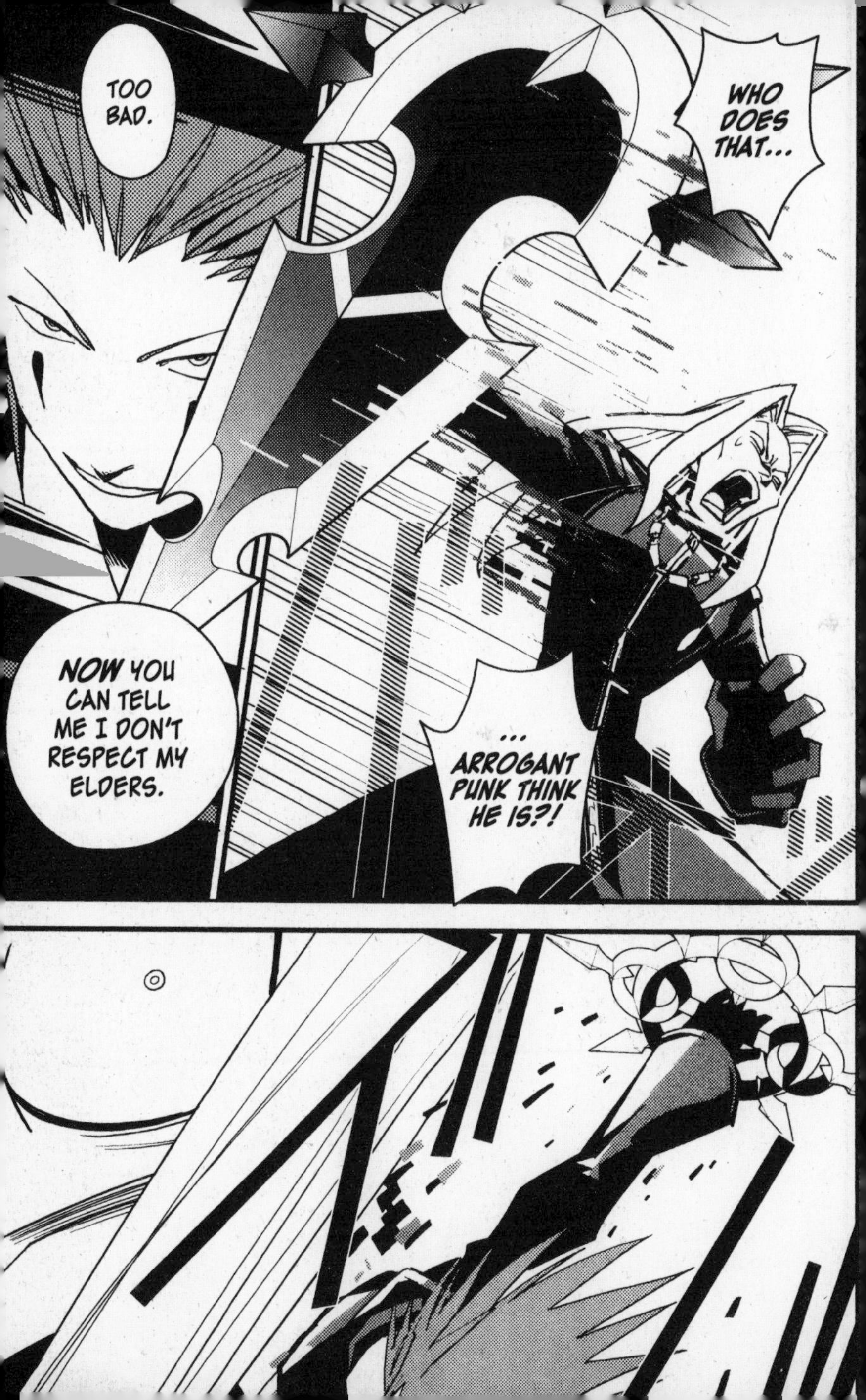
WHO DOES THAT...
...ARROGANT PUNK THINK HE IS?!
TOO BAD.
NOW YOU CAN TELL ME I DON'T RESPECT MY ELDERS.

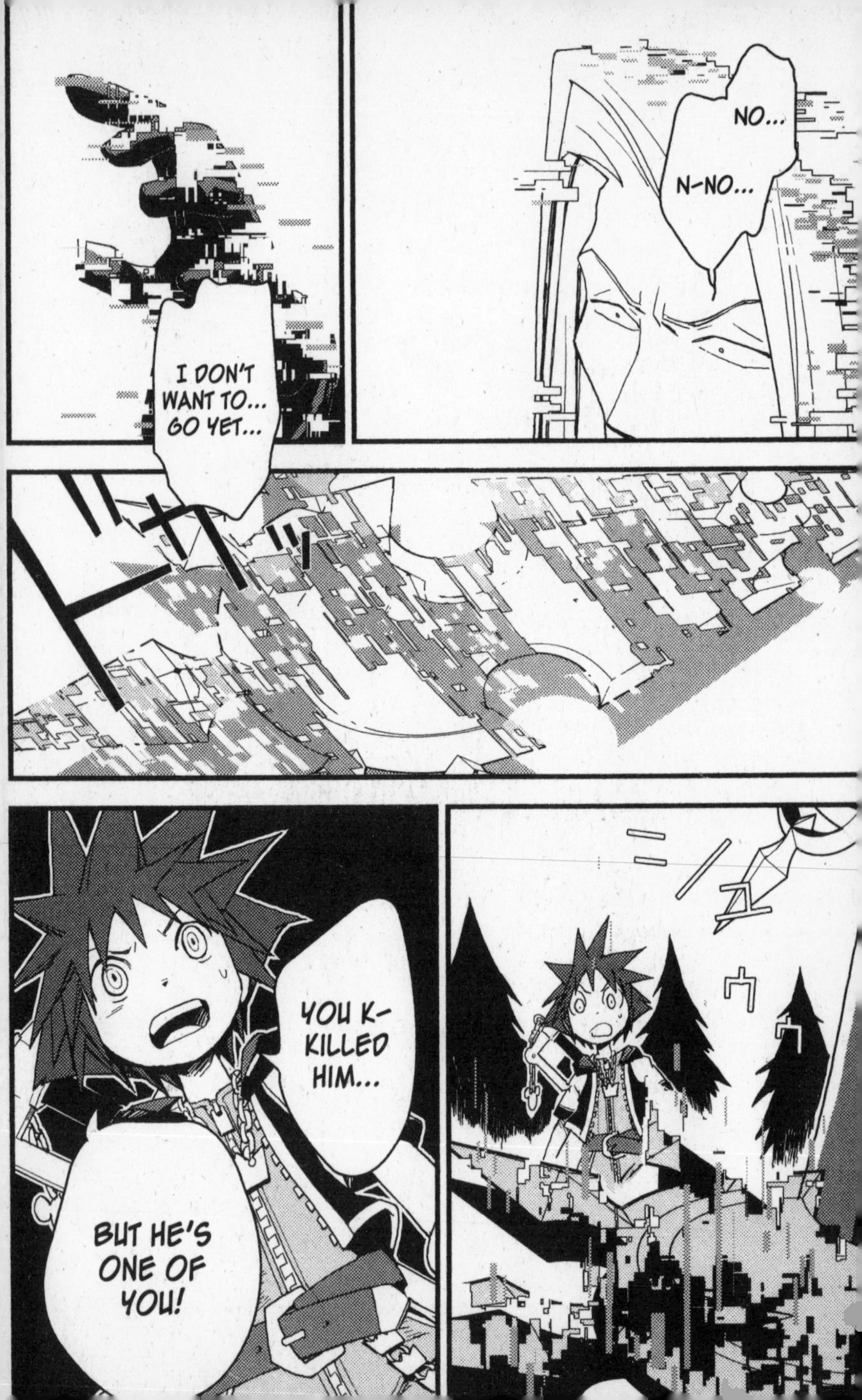
NO...
N-NO...
I DON'T WANT TO... GO YET...
YOU K-KILLED HIM...
BUT HE'S ONE OF YOU!

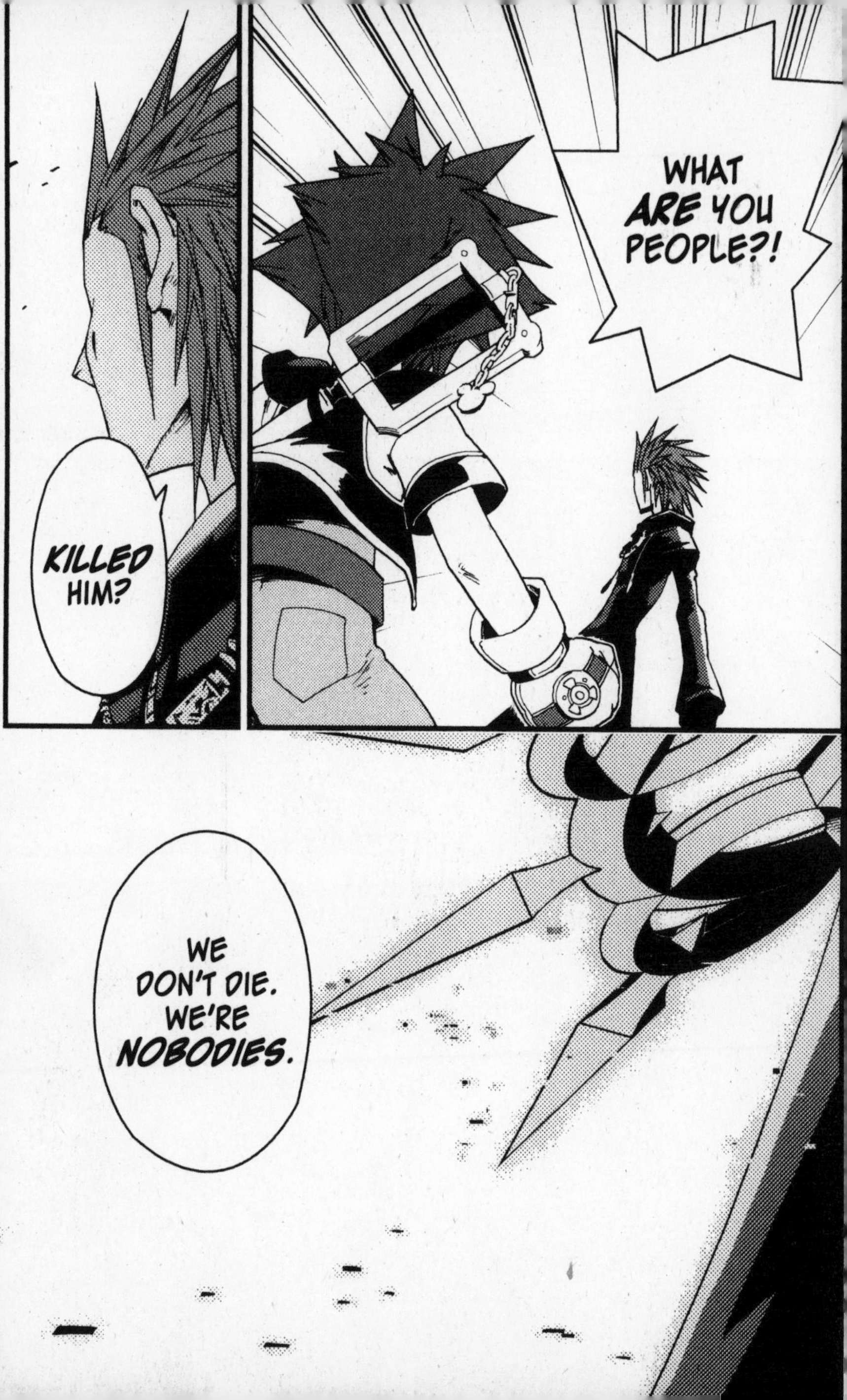
WHAT ARE YOU PEOPLE?!
KILLED HIM?
WE DON'T DIE. WE'RE NOBODIES.

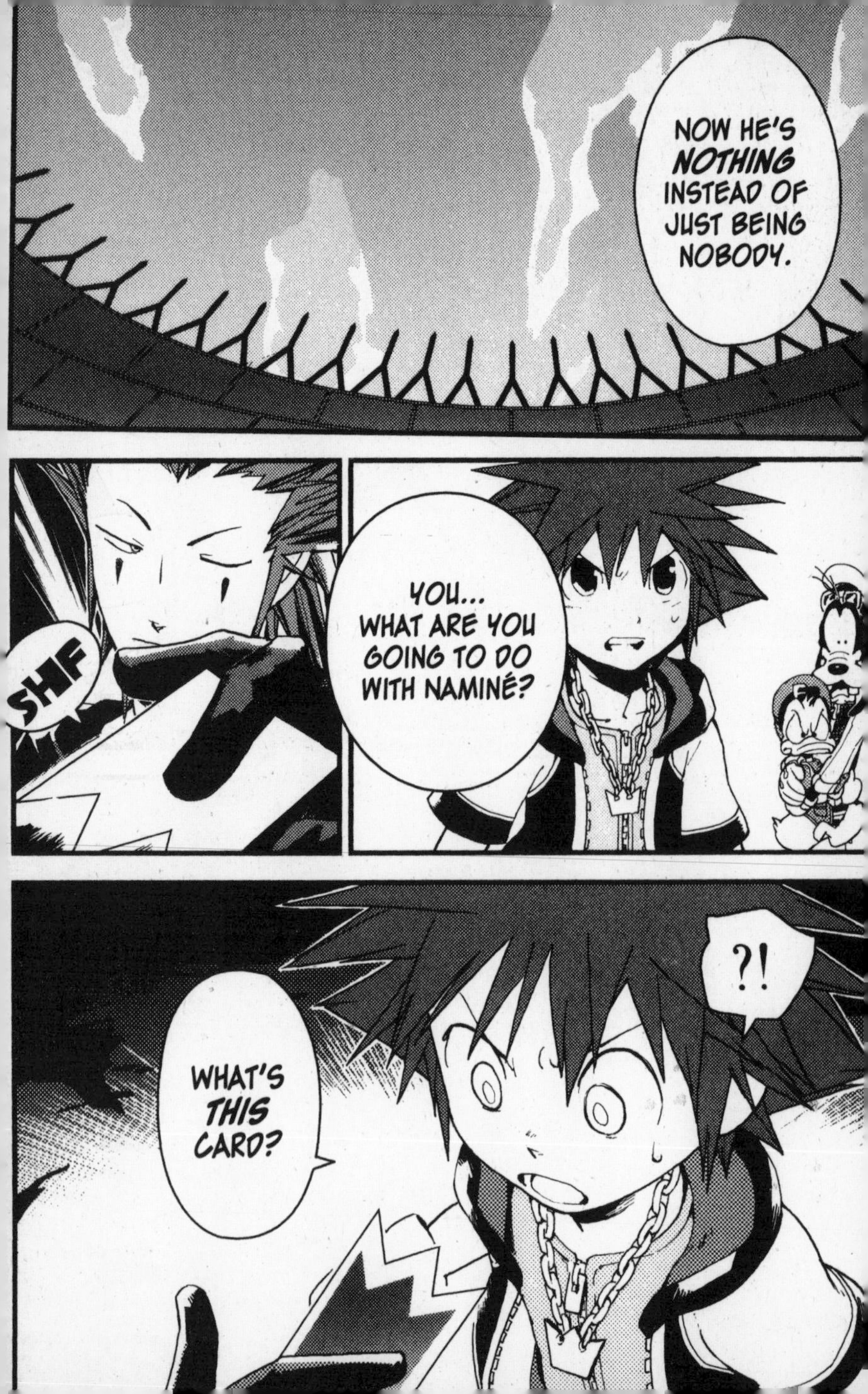
NOW HE'S *NOTHING* INSTEAD OF JUST BEING NOBODY.
YOU... WHAT ARE YOU GOING TO DO WITH NAMINÉ?
SHF
?!
WHAT'S *THIS* CARD?

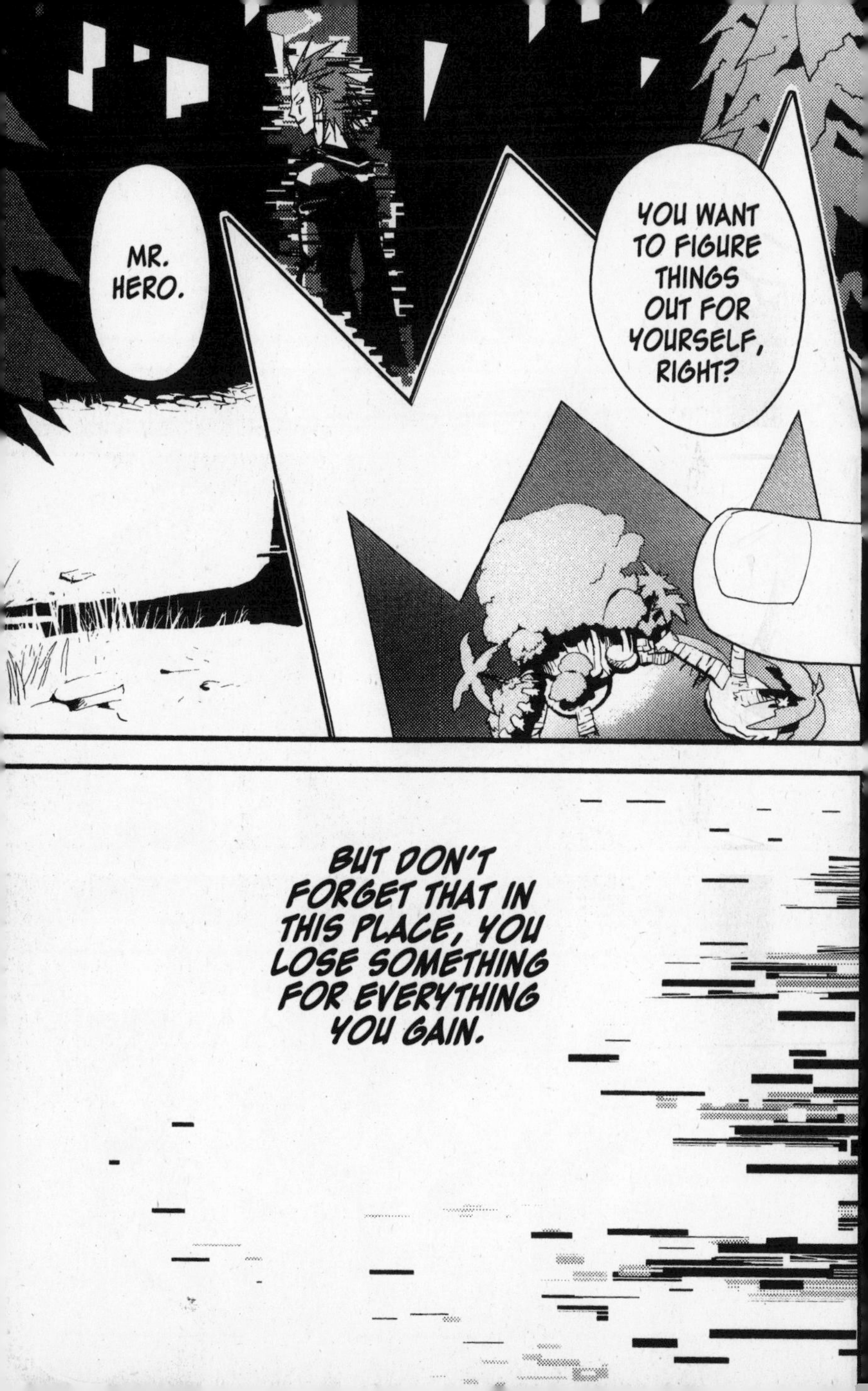
YOU WANT TO FIGURE THINGS OUT FOR YOURSELF, RIGHT?
MR. HERO.
BUT DON'T FORGET THAT IN THIS PLACE, YOU LOSE SOMETHING FOR EVERYTHING YOU GAIN.

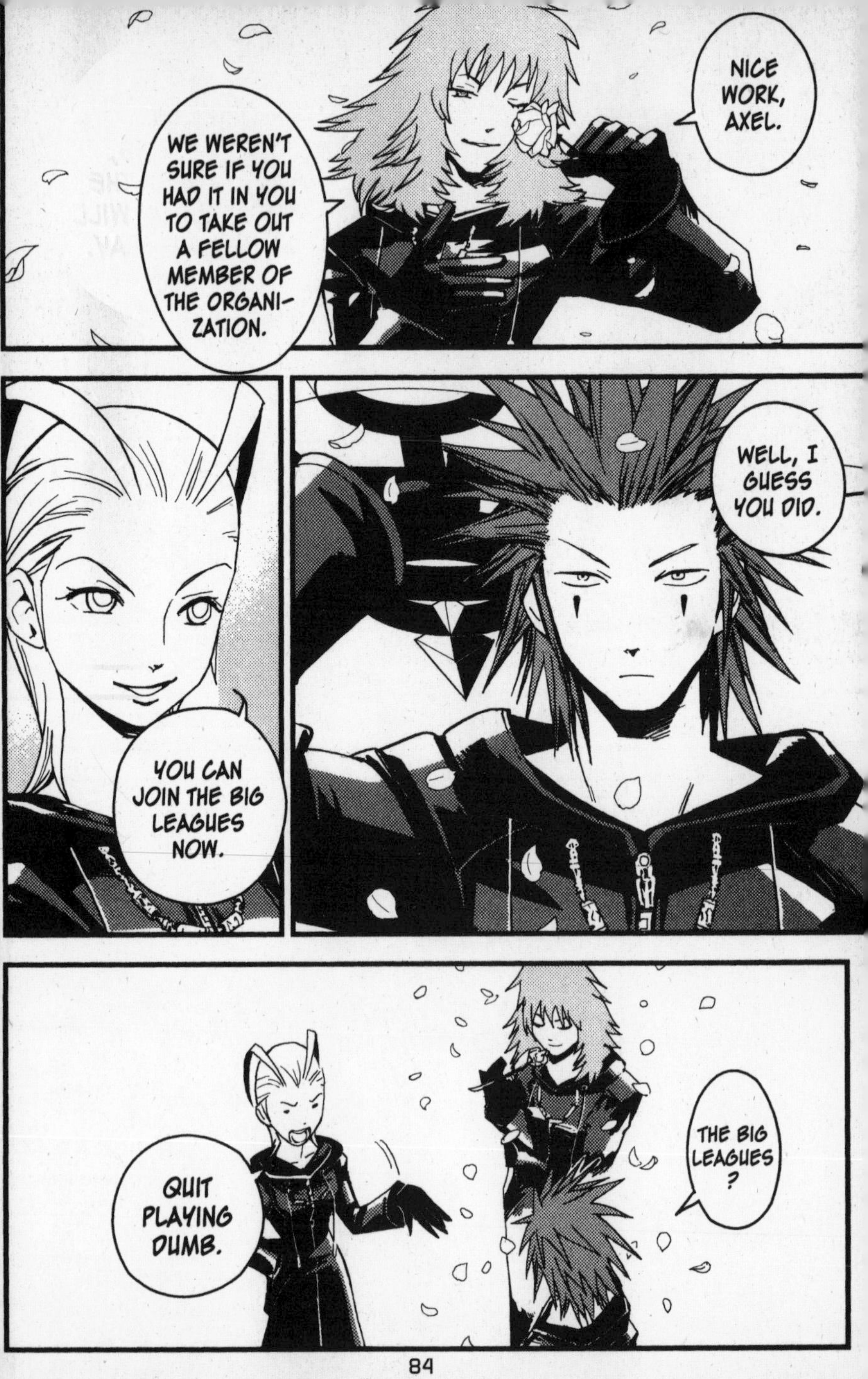
NICE WORK, AXEL.
WE WEREN'T SURE IF YOU HAD IT IN YOU TO TAKE OUT A FELLOW MEMBER OF THE ORGANI-ZATION.
WELL, I GUESS YOU DID.
YOU CAN JOIN THE BIG LEAGUES NOW.
THE BIG LEAGUES?
QUIT PLAYING DUMB.

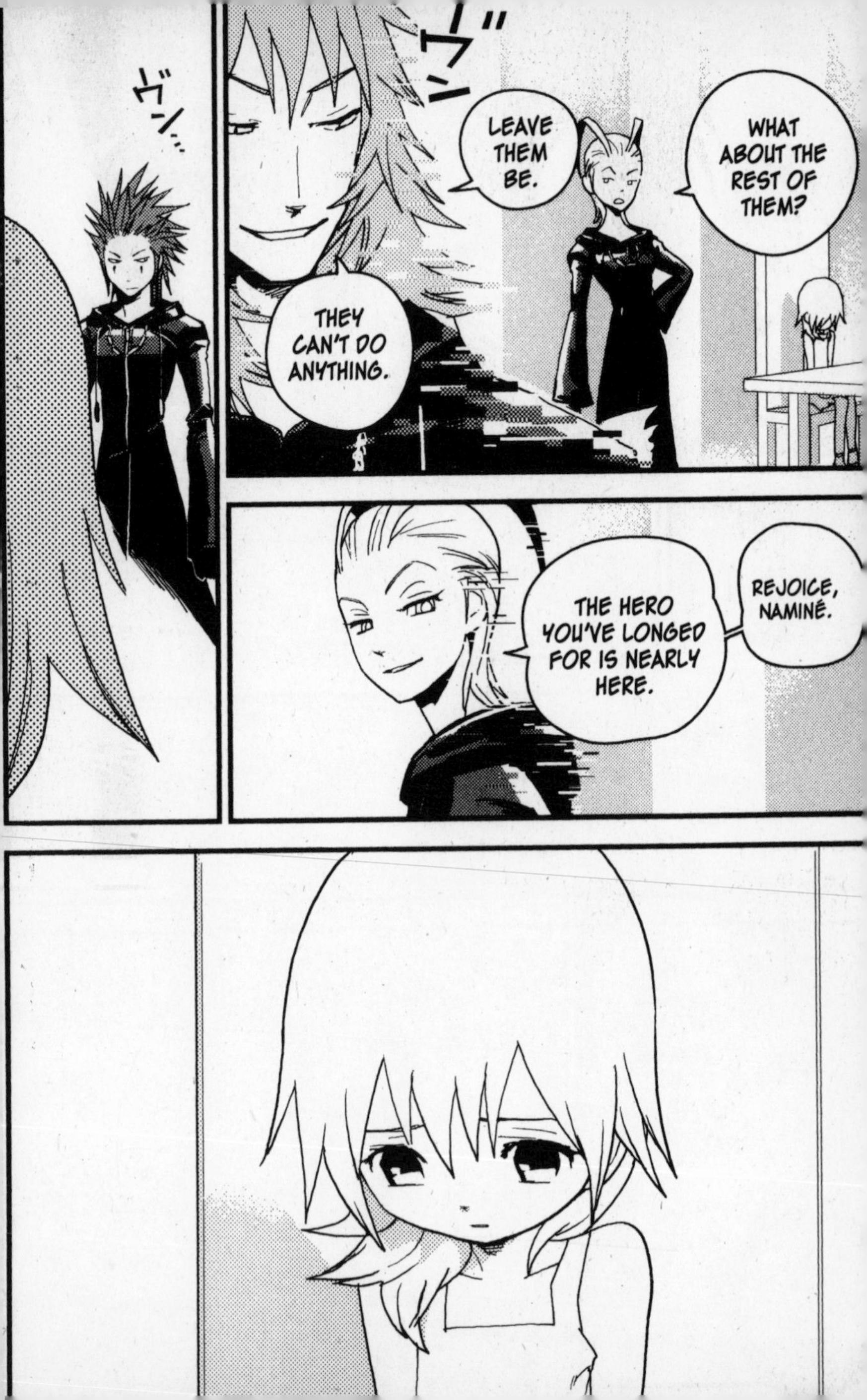
ヴン
WHAT ABOUT THE REST OF THEM?
LEAVE THEM BE.
THEY CAN'T DO ANYTHING.
REJOICE, NAMINÉ.
THE HERO YOU'VE LONGED FOR IS NEARLY HERE.
ヴン…

IT SEEMS THAT VEXEN IS NO MORE.

UH-HUH.

IT'S DEPLORABLE. AGENTS OF THE ORGANIZATION STRIKING EACH OTHER DOWN...

BUT NOW THAT HE'S GONE...

...THAT LEAVES MORE WORK FOR US.

I'VE GOT A FEELING I'LL BE DOING ALL OF VEXEN'S WORK...

Job Chart

Oblivion

Dishes

Patrol

ZEXION

VEXEN

Trash

Comms

LEXAEUS

Bathroom

Cooking

Sweeping

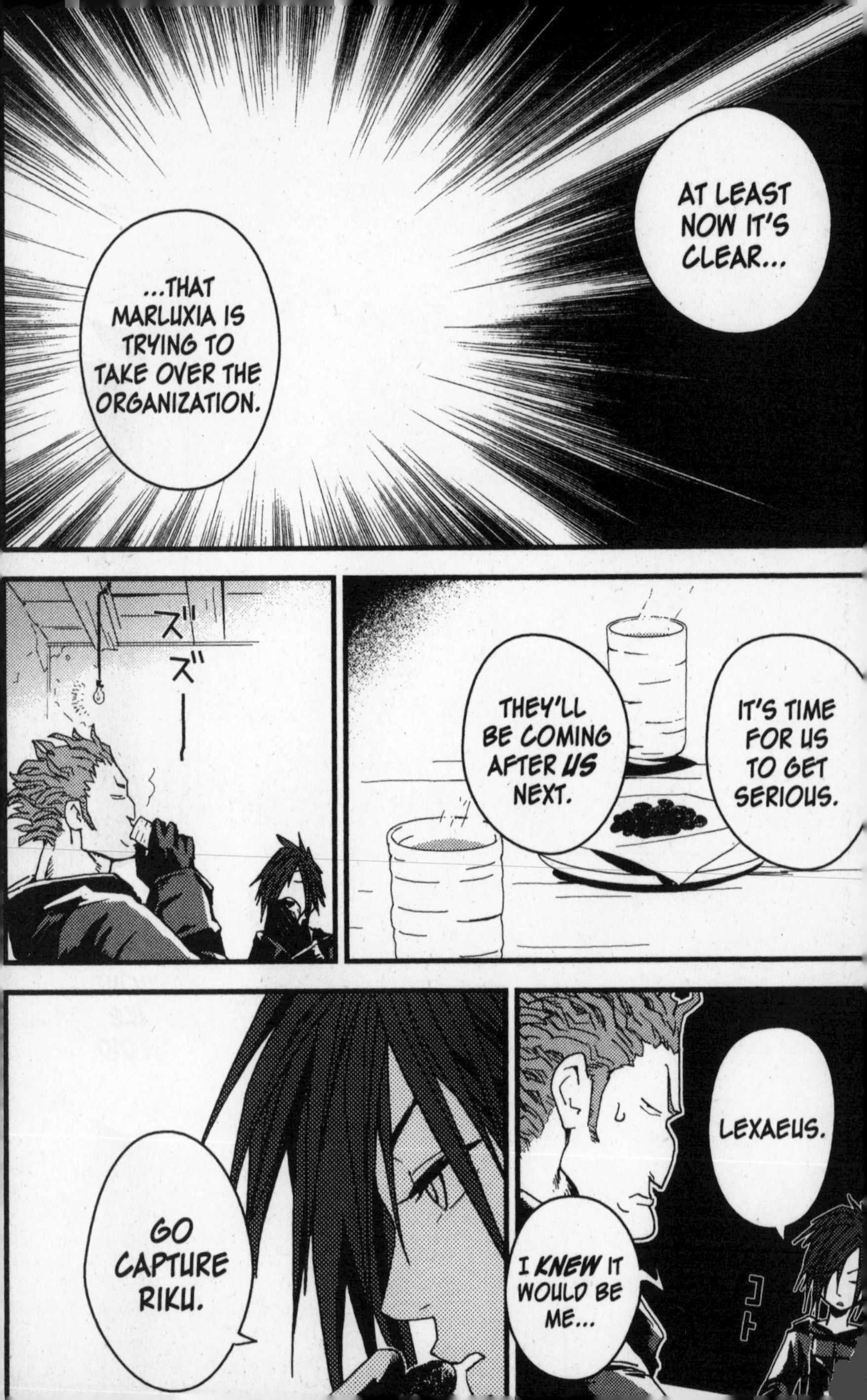
AT LEAST NOW IT'S CLEAR...
...THAT MARLUXIA IS TRYING TO TAKE OVER THE ORGANIZATION.
IT'S TIME FOR US TO GET SERIOUS.
THEY'LL BE COMING AFTER US NEXT.
ズズー
LEXAEUS.
I KNEW IT WOULD BE ME...
コト
GO CAPTURE RIKU.

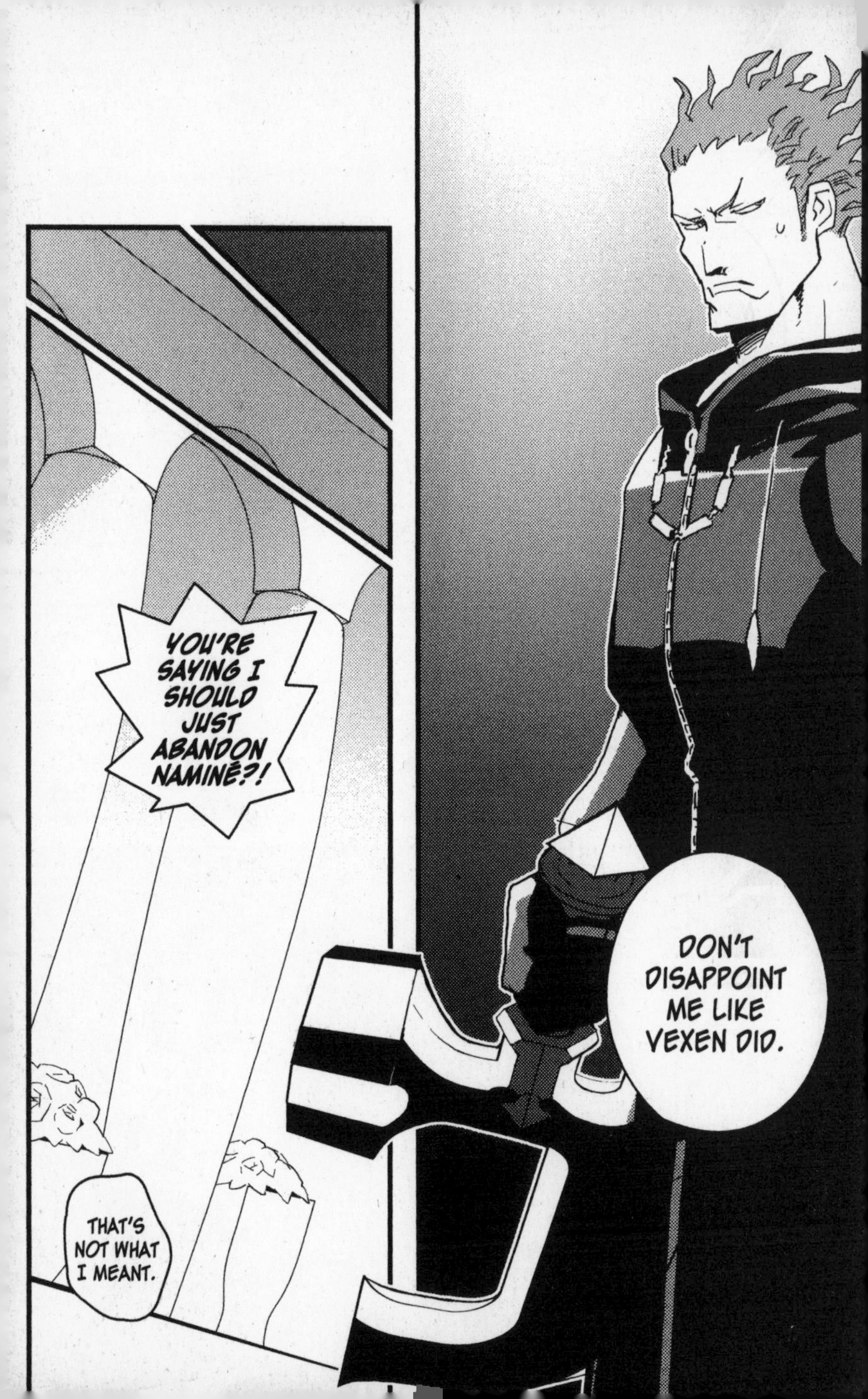
DON'T DISAPPOINT ME LIKE VEXEN DID.
YOU'RE SAYING I SHOULD JUST ABANDON NAMINÉ?!
THAT'S NOT WHAT I MEANT.

PLUS IT SEEMS LIKE ASKING FOR TROUBLE TO JUST DO WHAT THOSE GUYS SAY.

.....

THAT YOU AND RIKU HAVE THE SAME EXACT MEMORY.

YOU CAN'T BOTH BE RIGHT.

BUT DON'T YOU THINK IT'S WEIRD?

WHAT?!

AND YOU ALWAYS GET REAL TOUCHY WHEN IT COMES TO NAMINÉ. DID YOU EVER ASK YOURSELF WHY?

WHAT-EVER!

DO WHAT YOU WANT! LAY BACK, TAKE A NAP-- I DON'T CARE!

BUH-WHA?

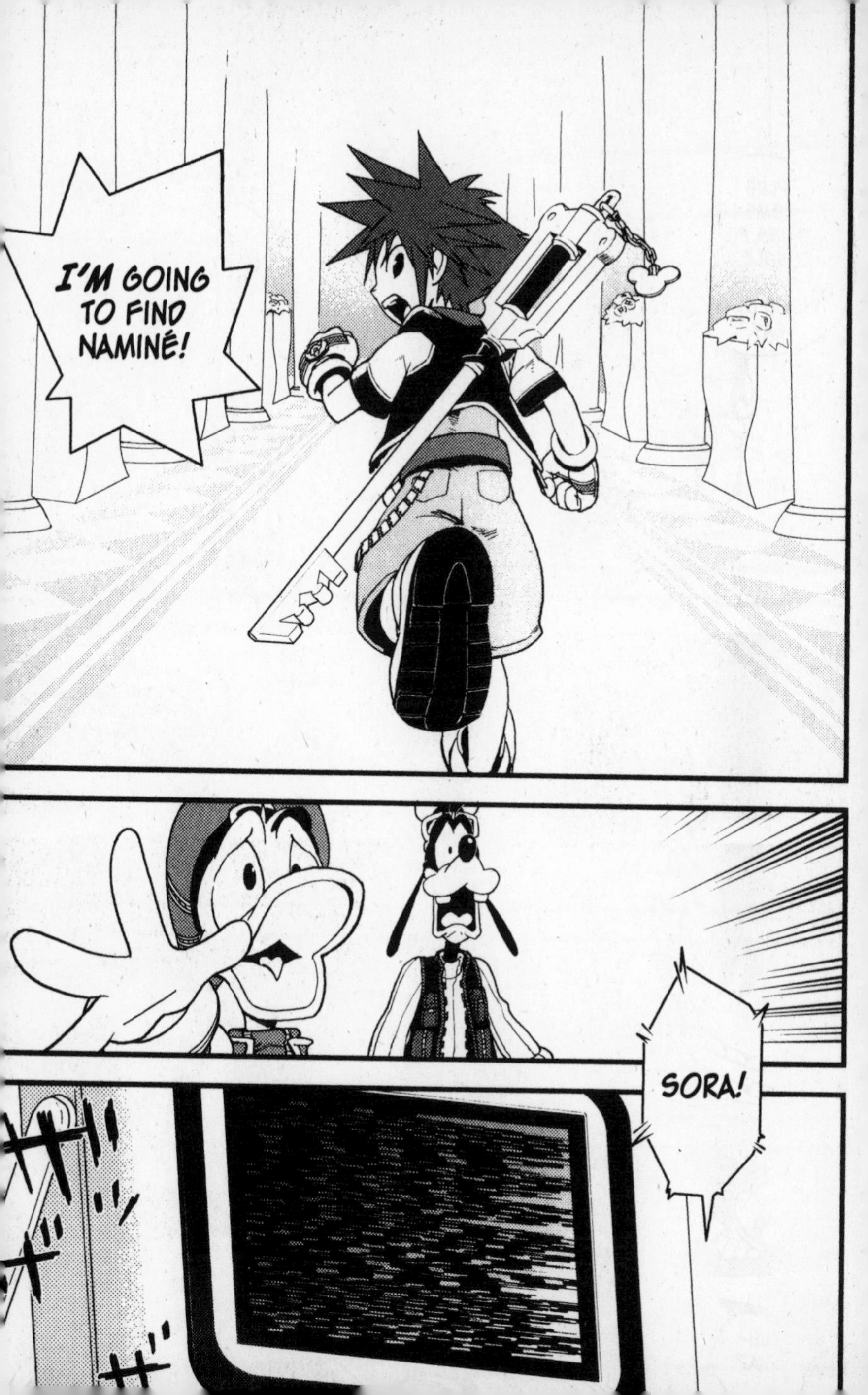
I'M GOING TO FIND NAMINÉ!
SORA!

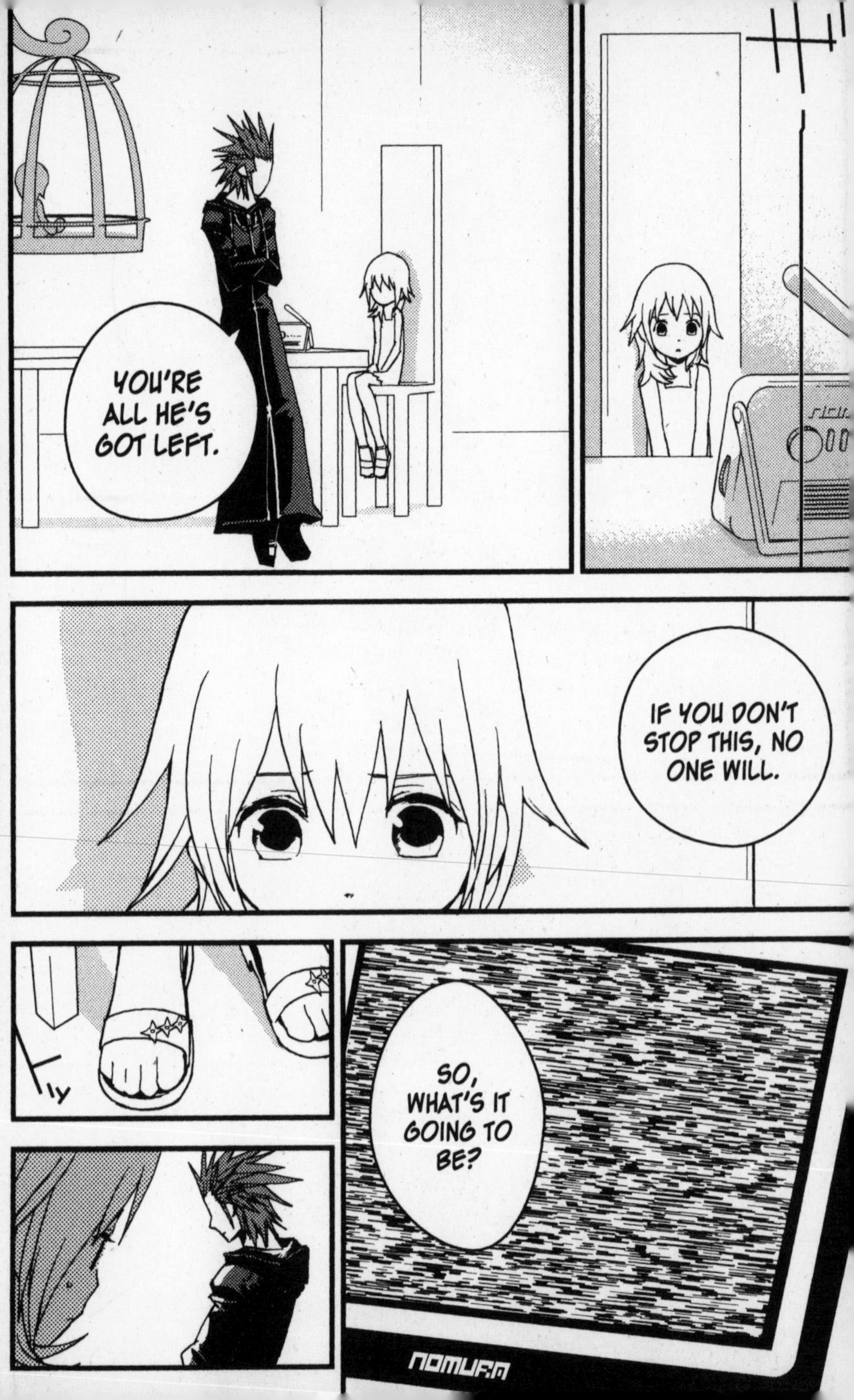
YOU'RE ALL HE'S GOT LEFT.
IF YOU DON'T STOP THIS, NO ONE WILL.
SO, WHAT'S IT GOING TO BE?

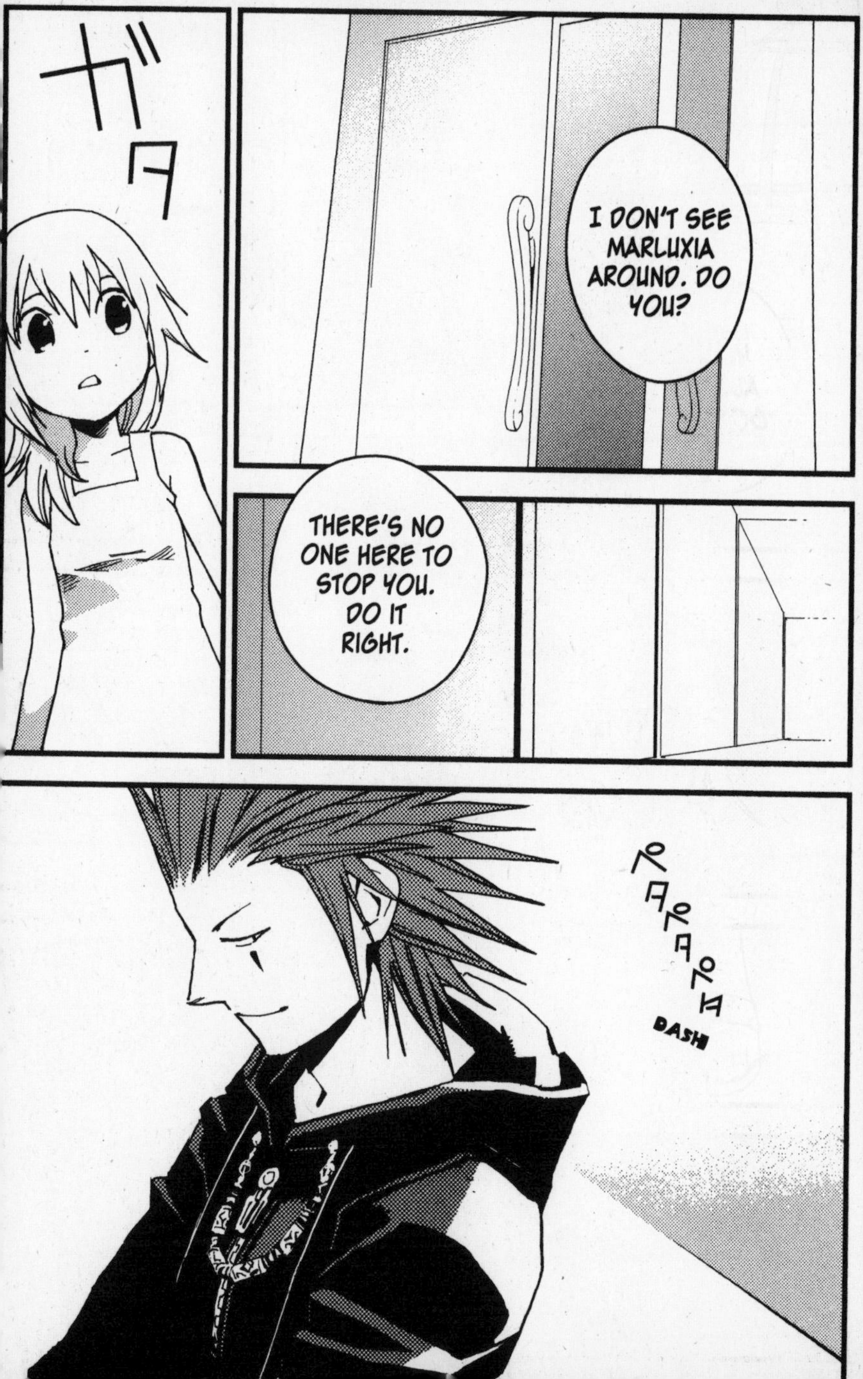
I DON'T SEE MARLUXIA AROUND. DO YOU?
THERE'S NO ONE HERE TO STOP YOU. DO IT RIGHT.
ガタ
DASH

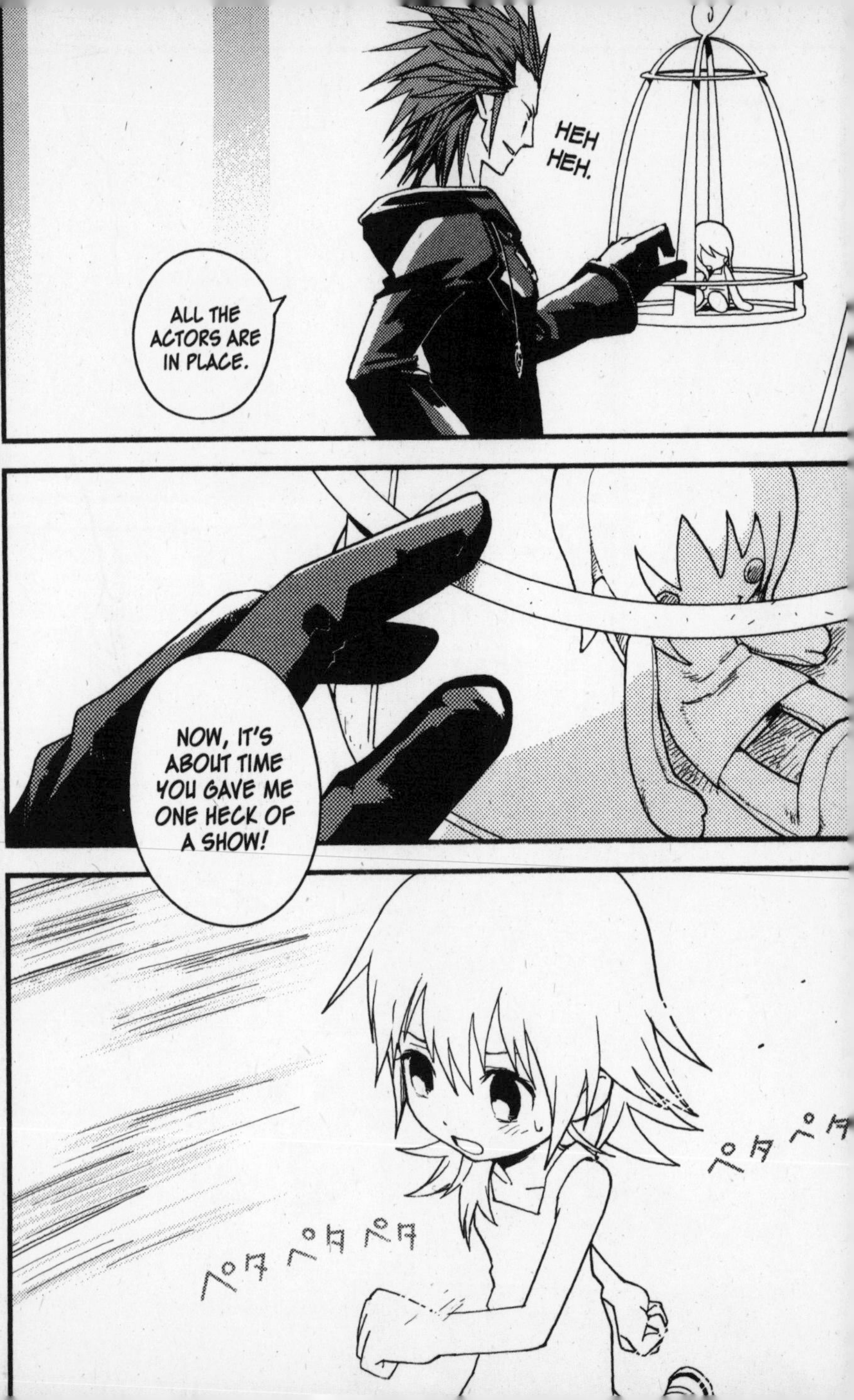
HEH HEH.
ALL THE ACTORS ARE IN PLACE.
NOW, IT'S ABOUT TIME YOU GAVE ME ONE HECK OF A SHOW!
ペタペタ
ペタペタペタ

I WAS ALWAYS ALONE...

SO LONELY...

THAT'S WHY I...

I'M SO SORRY, SORA.

Card 10
Separated Hearts

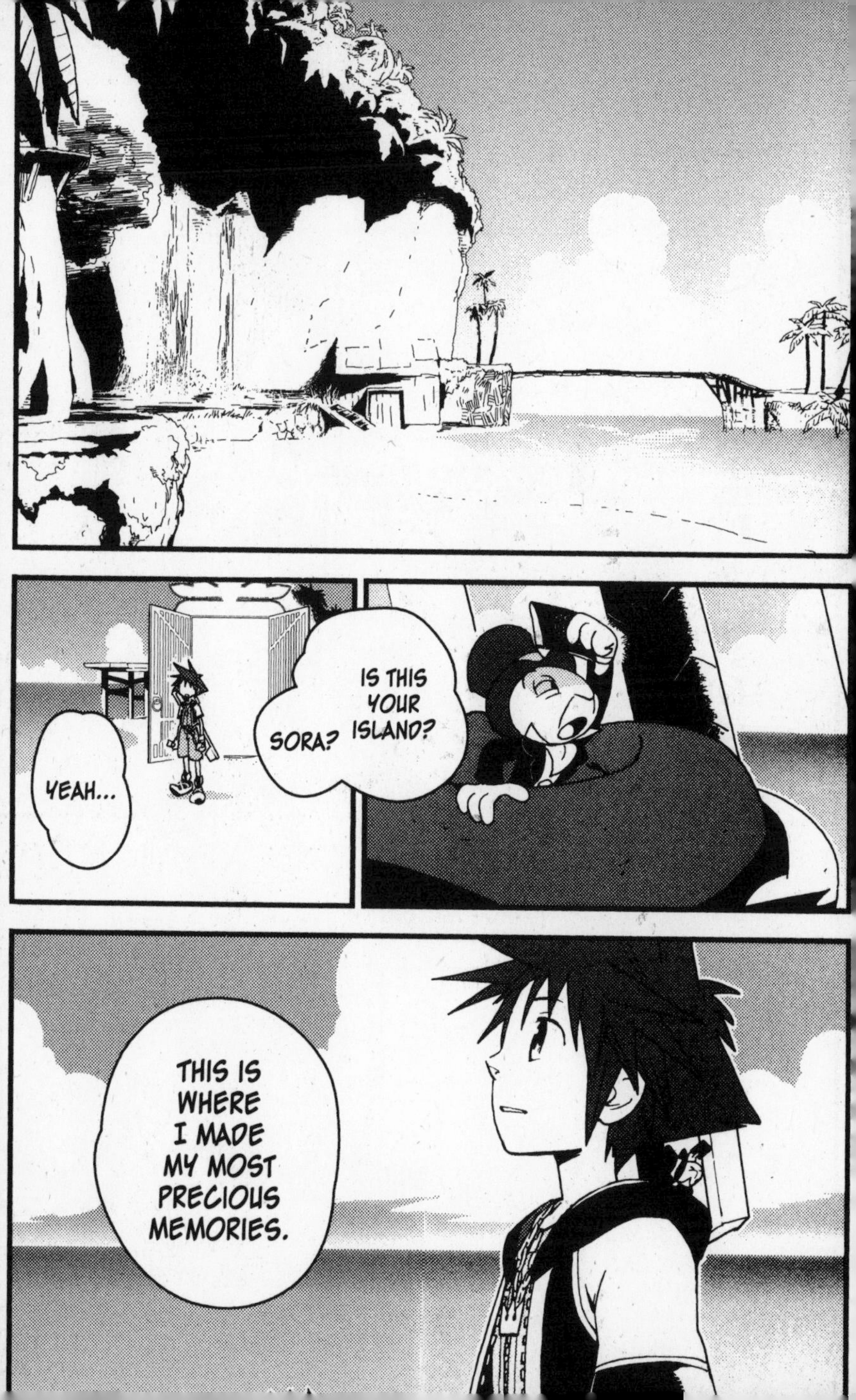
IS THIS YOUR ISLAND? SORA?
YEAH...
THIS IS WHERE I MADE MY MOST PRECIOUS MEMORIES.

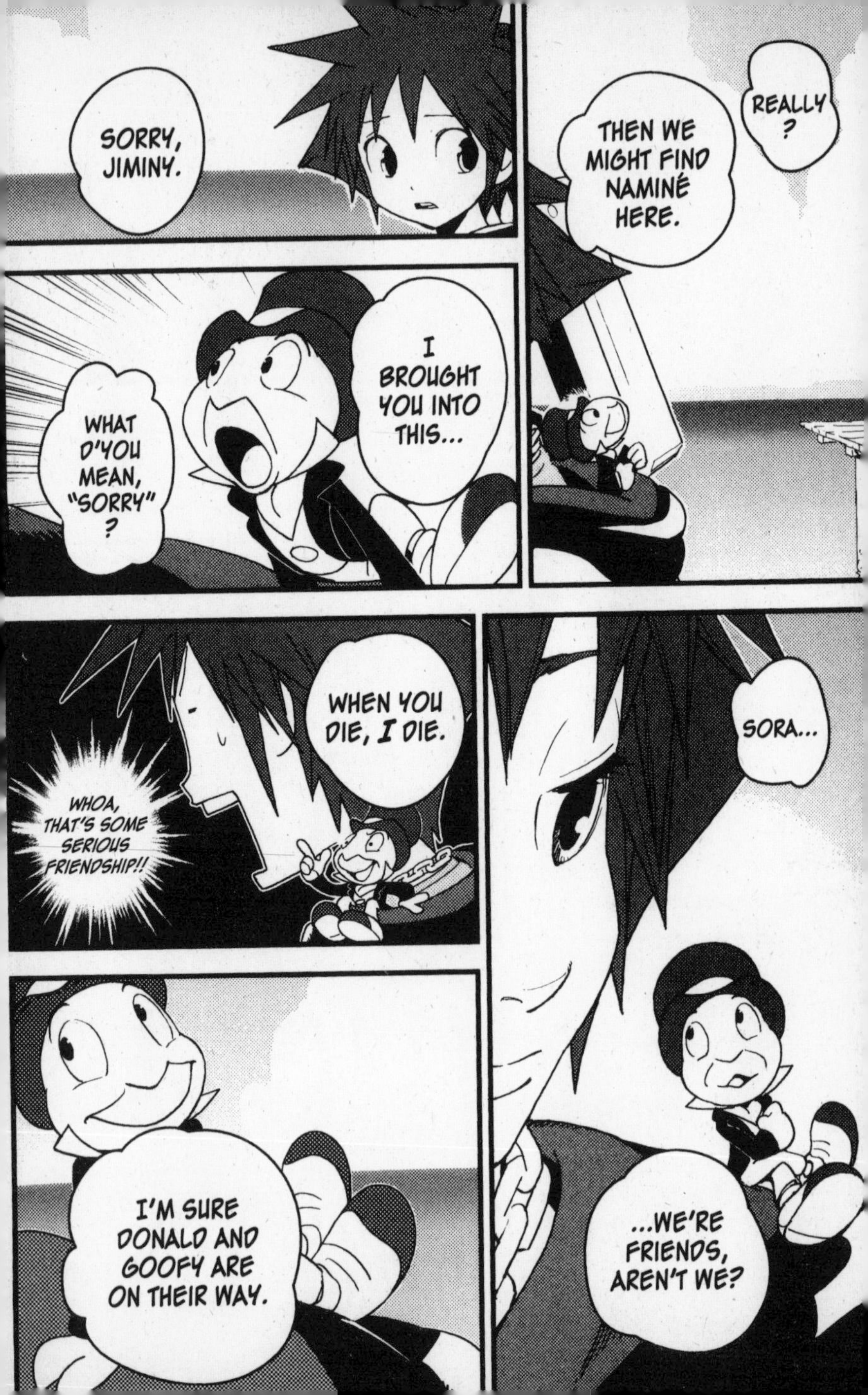
REALLY?
THEN WE MIGHT FIND NAMINÉ HERE.
SORRY, JIMINY.
I BROUGHT YOU INTO THIS...
WHAT D'YOU MEAN, "SORRY"?
SORA...
...WE'RE FRIENDS, AREN'T WE?
WHEN YOU DIE, I DIE.
WHOA, THAT'S SOME SERIOUS FRIENDSHIP!!
I'M SURE DONALD AND GOOFY ARE ON THEIR WAY.

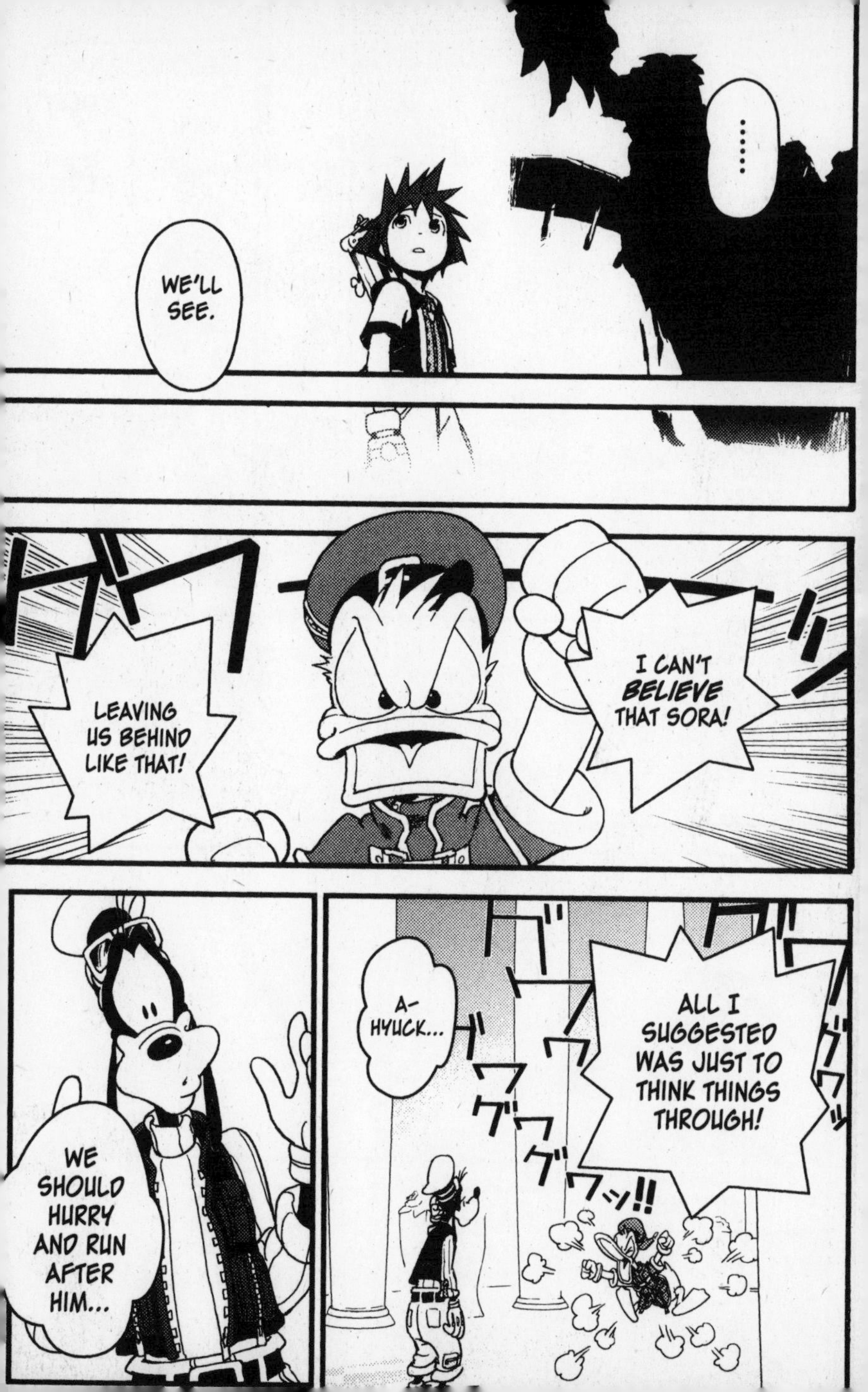
......
WE'LL SEE.
I CAN'T *BELIEVE* THAT SORA!
LEAVING US BEHIND LIKE THAT!
ALL I SUGGESTED WAS JUST TO THINK THINGS THROUGH!
A-HYUCK...
WE SHOULD HURRY AND RUN AFTER HIM...

IT TRULY IS PATHETIC.

YOU'RE PUTTING SO MUCH EFFORT INTO SEARCHING FOR NAMINÉ, WHEN SHE'S--

GAAH?!!

YOU ALWAYS GET REAL TOUCHY WHEN IT COMES TO NAMINÉ.

......

I...

I JUST WANT TO SAVE NAMINÉ.

ERK.

I DON'T THINK YOU'LL FIND HER UP HERE.

......

HEY, SORA!

WHAT WAS HE GOING TO SAY?

SORA...

SORA!

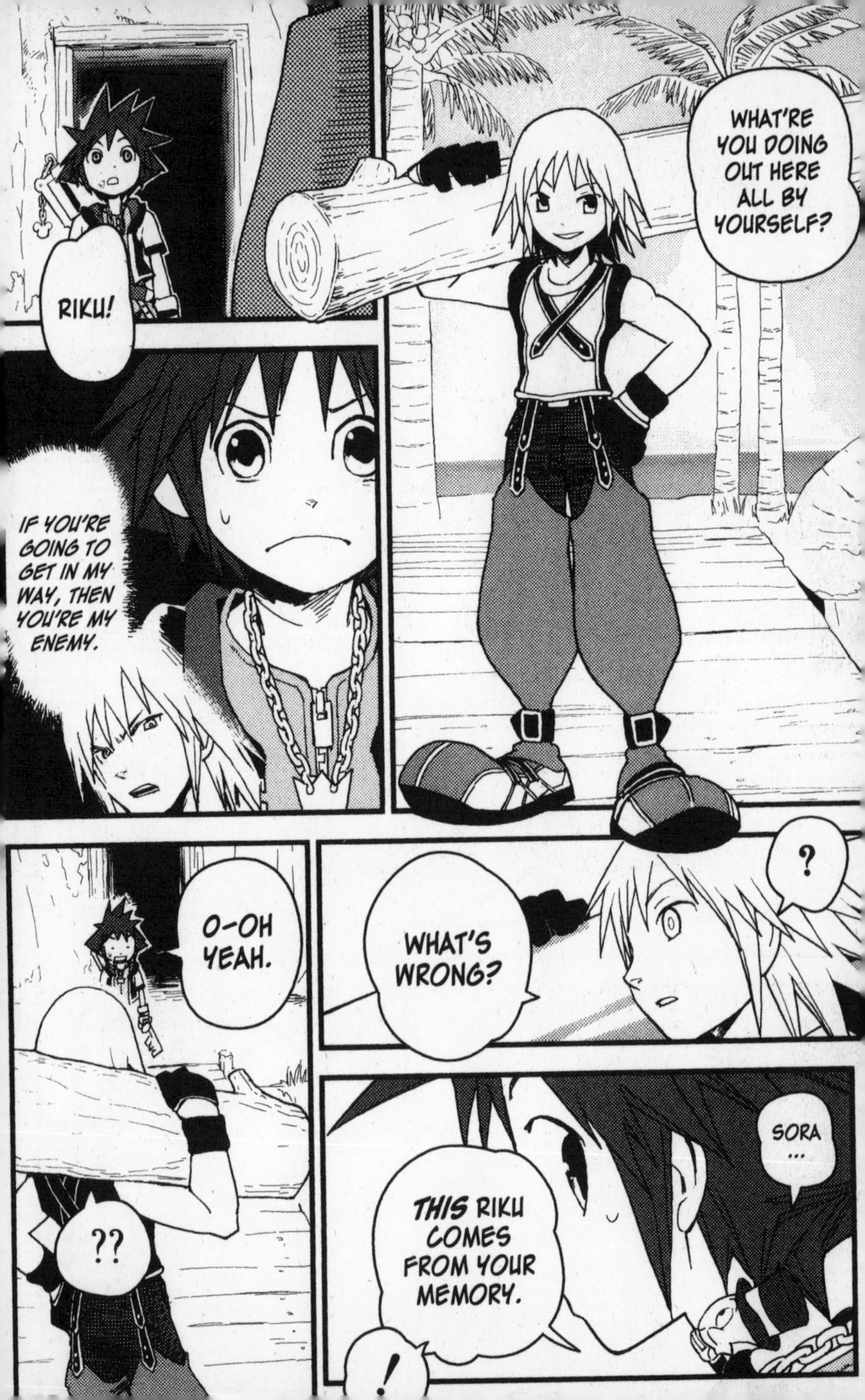
WHAT'RE YOU DOING OUT HERE ALL BY YOURSELF?
RIKU!
IF YOU'RE GOING TO GET IN MY WAY, THEN YOU'RE MY ENEMY.
?
WHAT'S WRONG?
SORA ...
THIS RIKU COMES FROM YOUR MEMORY.
!
O-OH YEAH.
??

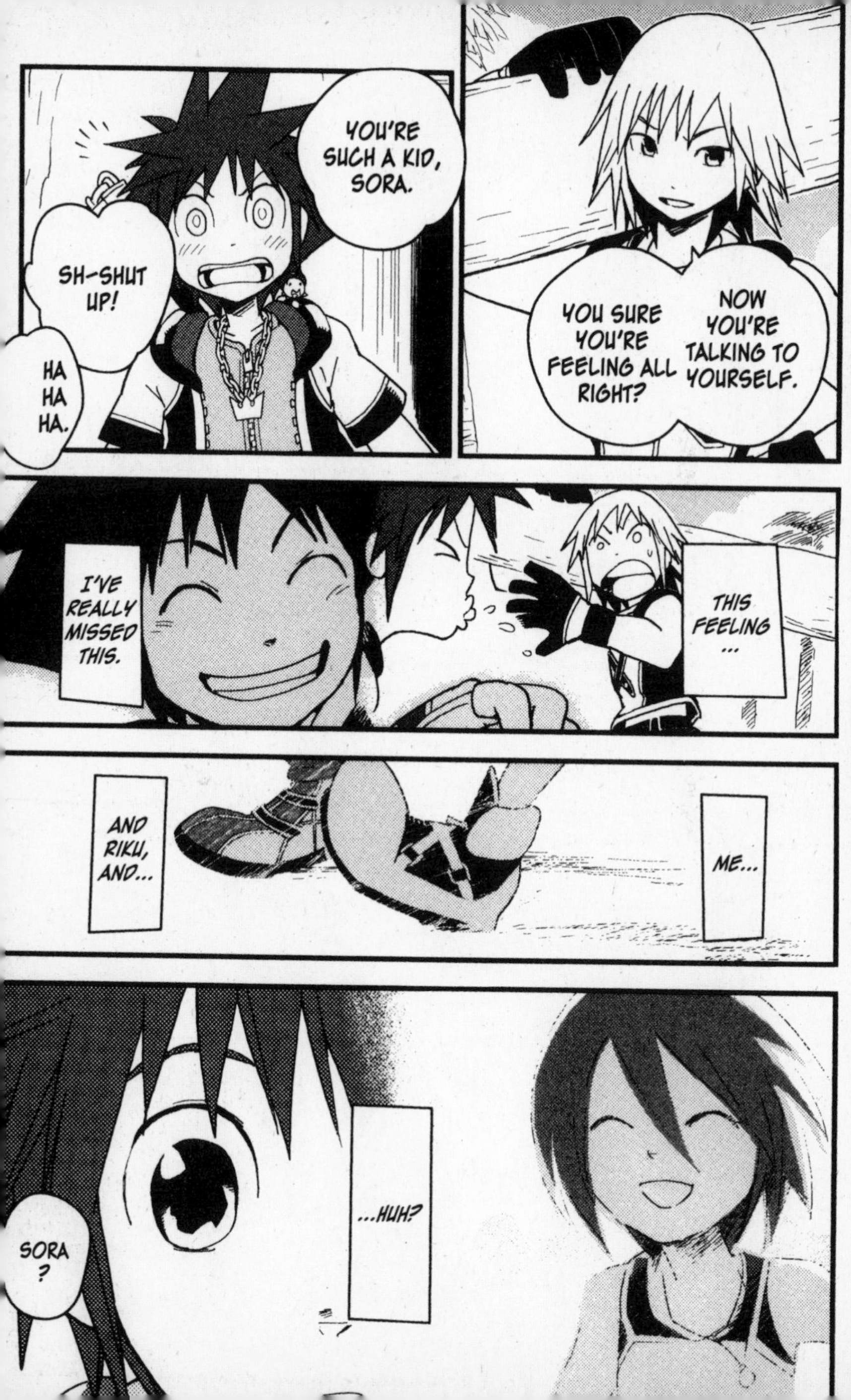
NOW YOU'RE TALKING TO YOURSELF.
YOU SURE YOU'RE FEELING ALL RIGHT?
YOU'RE SUCH A KID, SORA.
SH-SHUT UP!
HA HA HA.
THIS FEELING ...
I'VE REALLY MISSED THIS.
ME...
AND RIKU, AND...
...HUH?
SORA ?

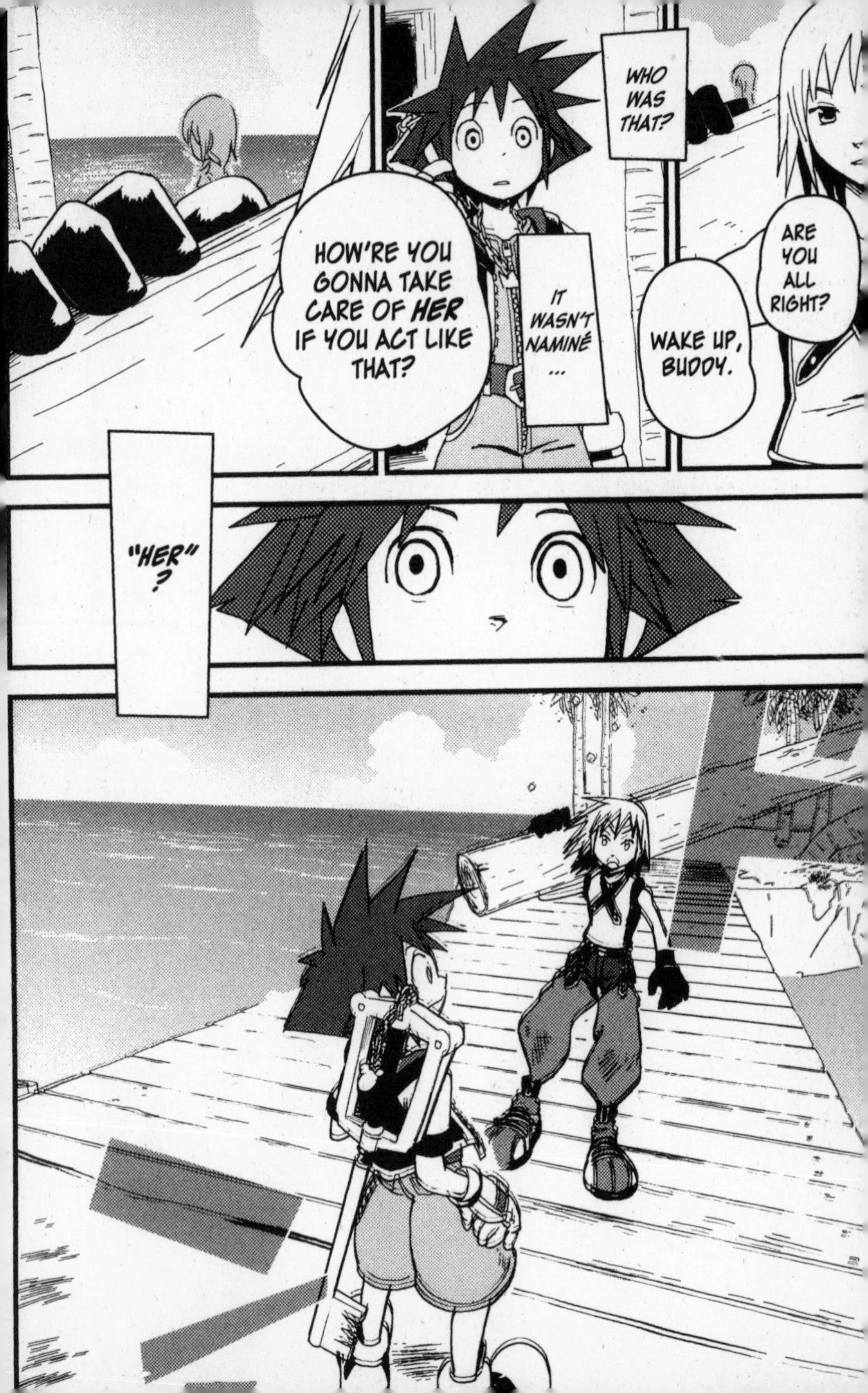
WHO WAS THAT?
ARE YOU ALL RIGHT?
WAKE UP, BUDDY.
IT WASN'T NAMINÉ...
HOW'RE YOU GONNA TAKE CARE OF HER IF YOU ACT LIKE THAT?
"HER"?

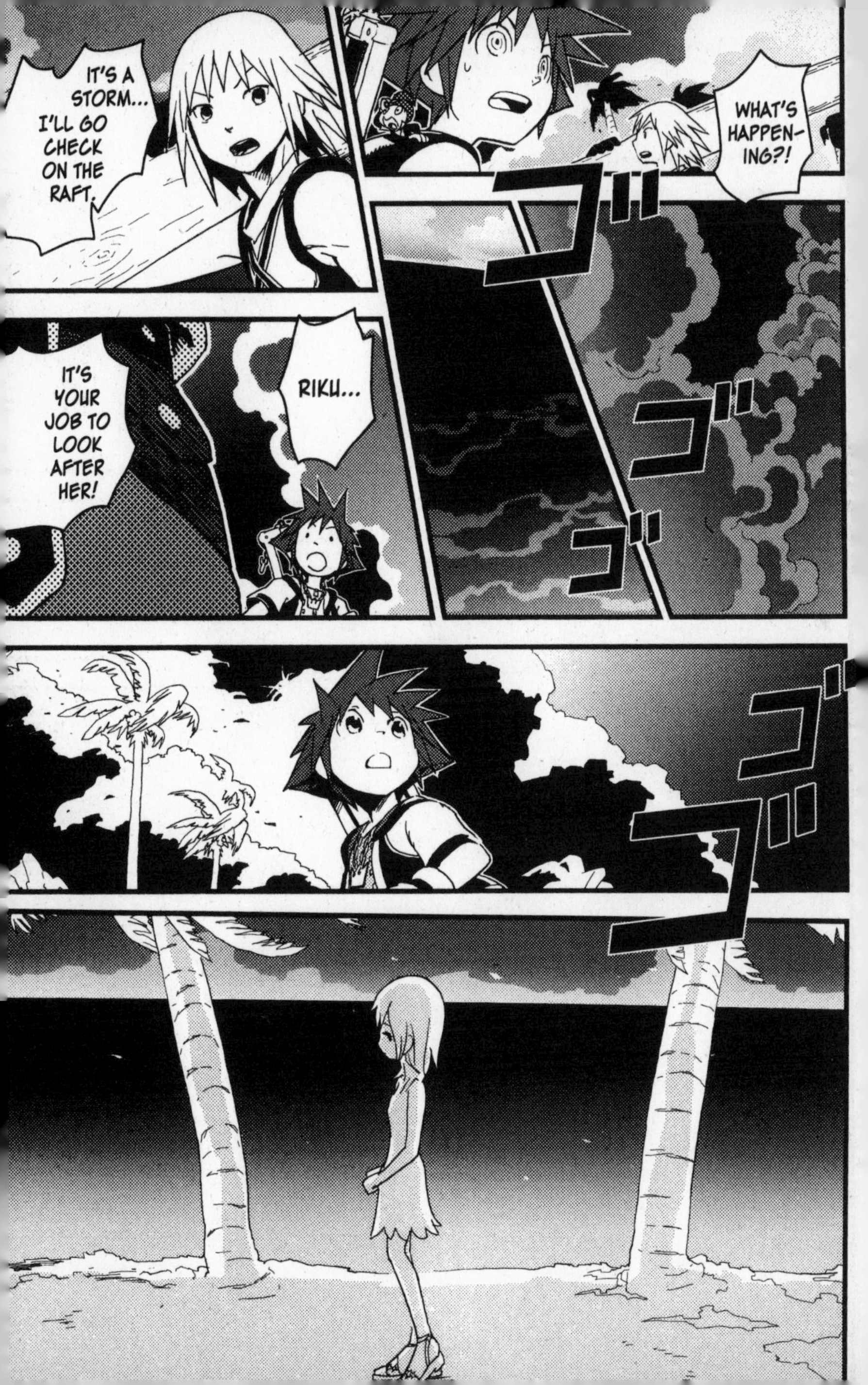
WHAT'S HAPPEN-ING?!
IT'S A STORM... I'LL GO CHECK ON THE RAFT.
ゴ
ゴ
ゴ
RIKU...
IT'S YOUR JOB TO LOOK AFTER HER!
ゴ
ゴ
ゴ

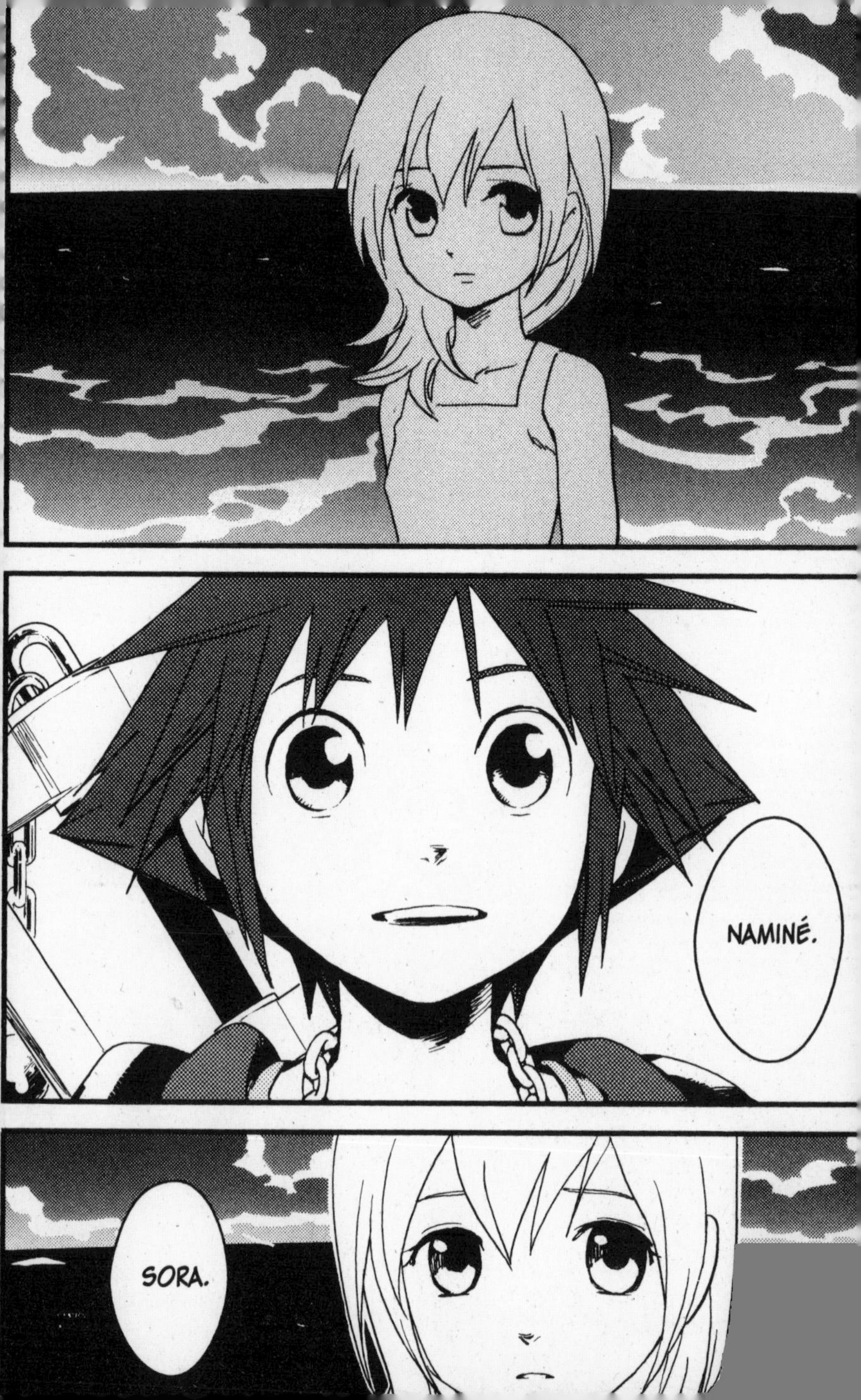
NAMINÉ.
SORA.

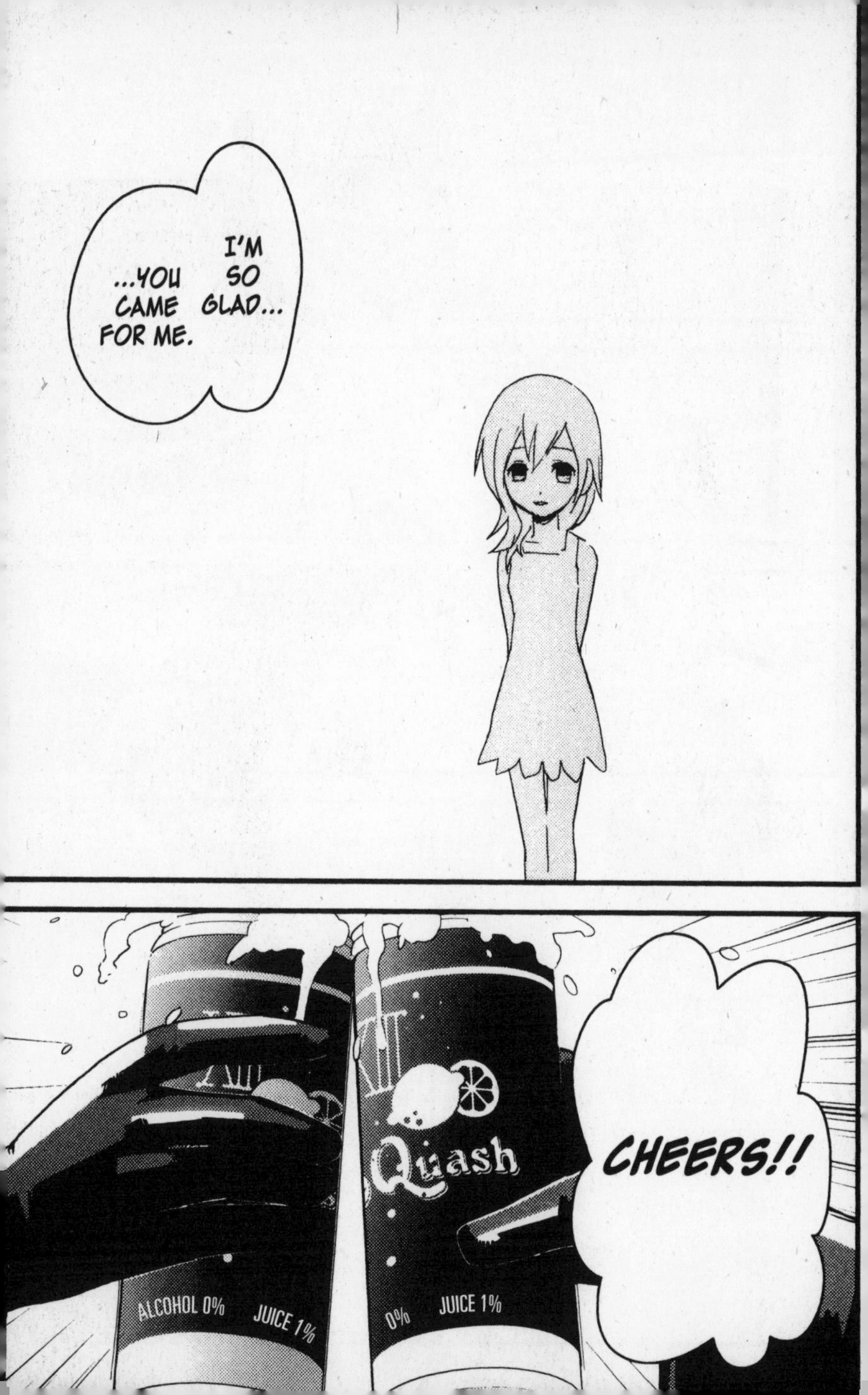
I'M SO GLAD...
...YOU CAME FOR ME.
CHEERS!!
Quash
ALCOHOL 0%
JUICE 1%
0%
JUICE 1%

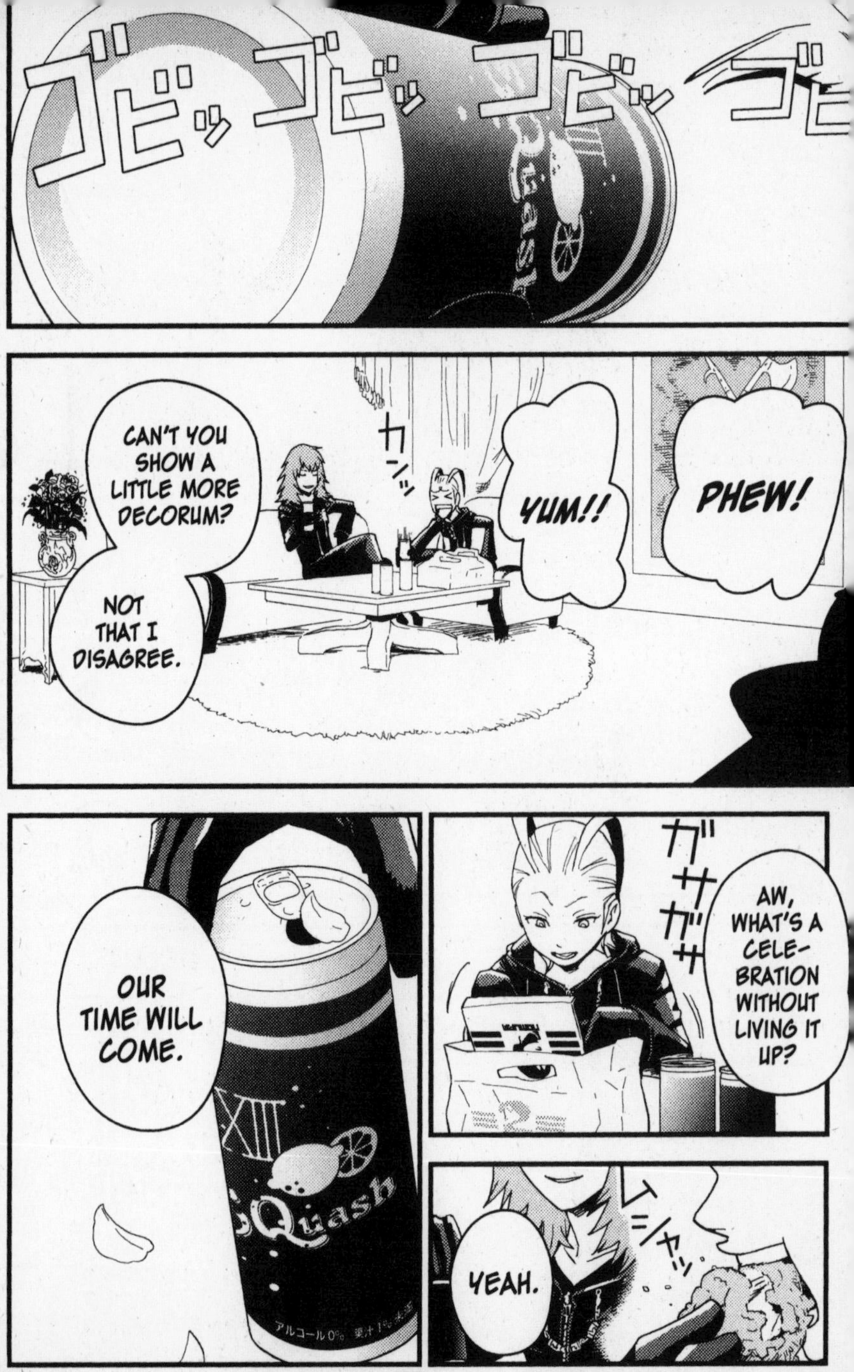
ゴビッ ゴビッ ゴビッ ゴビ
PHEW!
YUM!!
カンッ
CAN'T YOU SHOW A LITTLE MORE DECORUM?
NOT THAT I DISAGREE.
ガサガサ
AW, WHAT'S A CELE-BRATION WITHOUT LIVING IT UP?
YEAH.
ムシャッ
OUR TIME WILL COME.
XIII
SQuash
アルコール0%

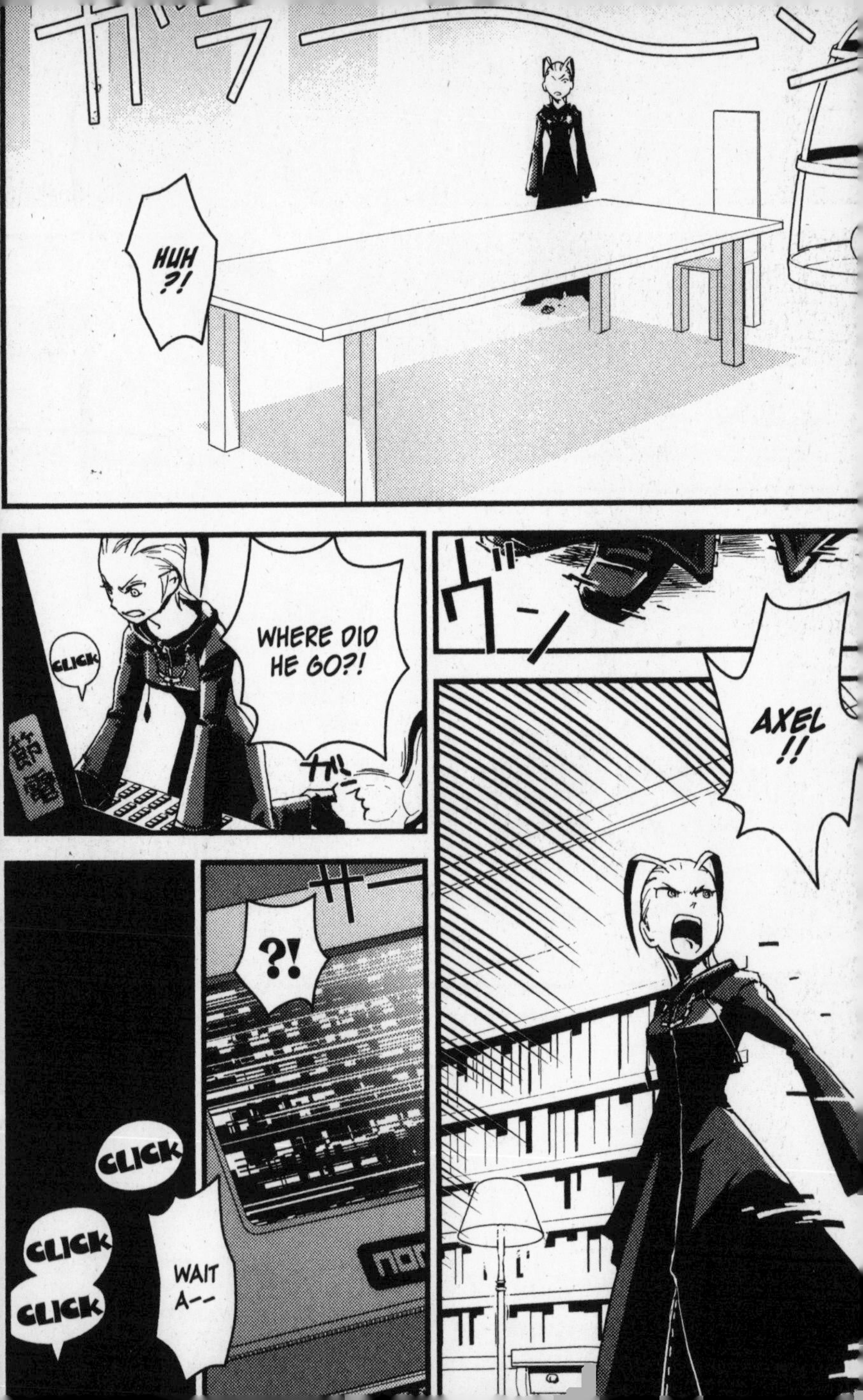

ガラーン
HUH ?!
ドゥー
AXEL !!
WHERE DID HE GO?!
CLICK
節電
ガッ
?!
サー
WAIT A--
CLICK
CLICK
CLICK

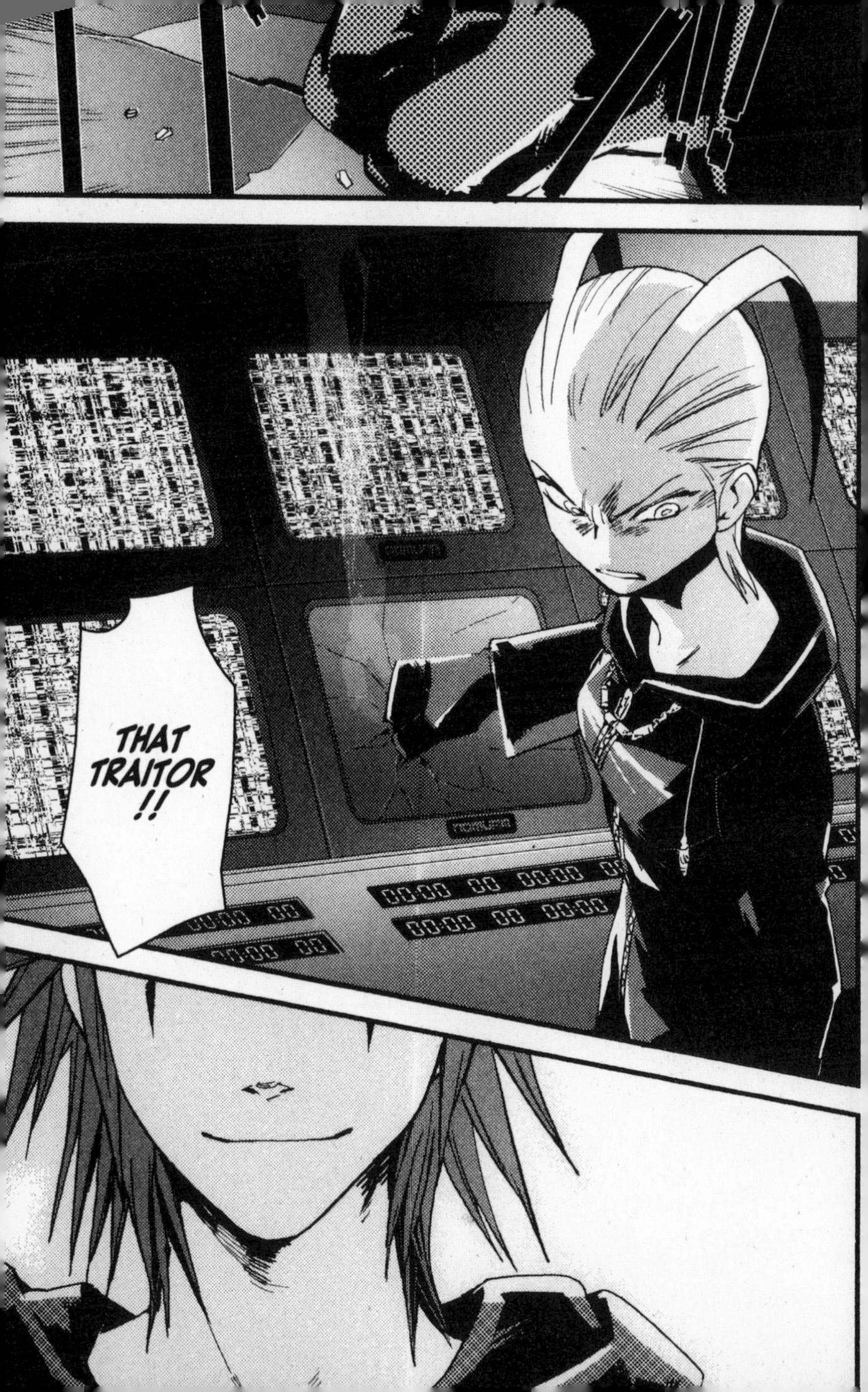
THAT TRAITOR !!

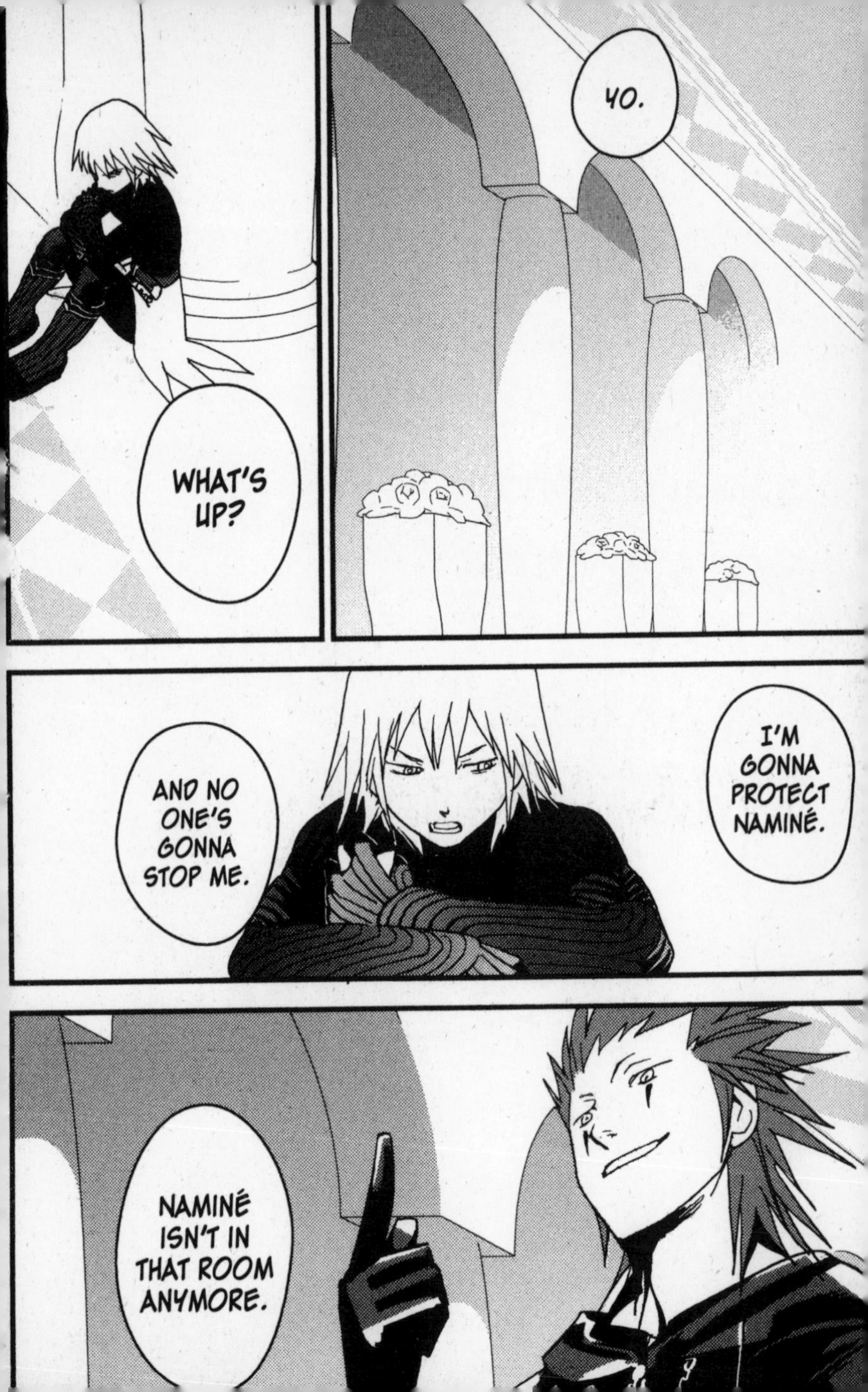
YO.
WHAT'S UP?
I'M GONNA PROTECT NAMINÉ.
AND NO ONE'S GONNA STOP ME.
NAMINÉ ISN'T IN THAT ROOM ANYMORE.

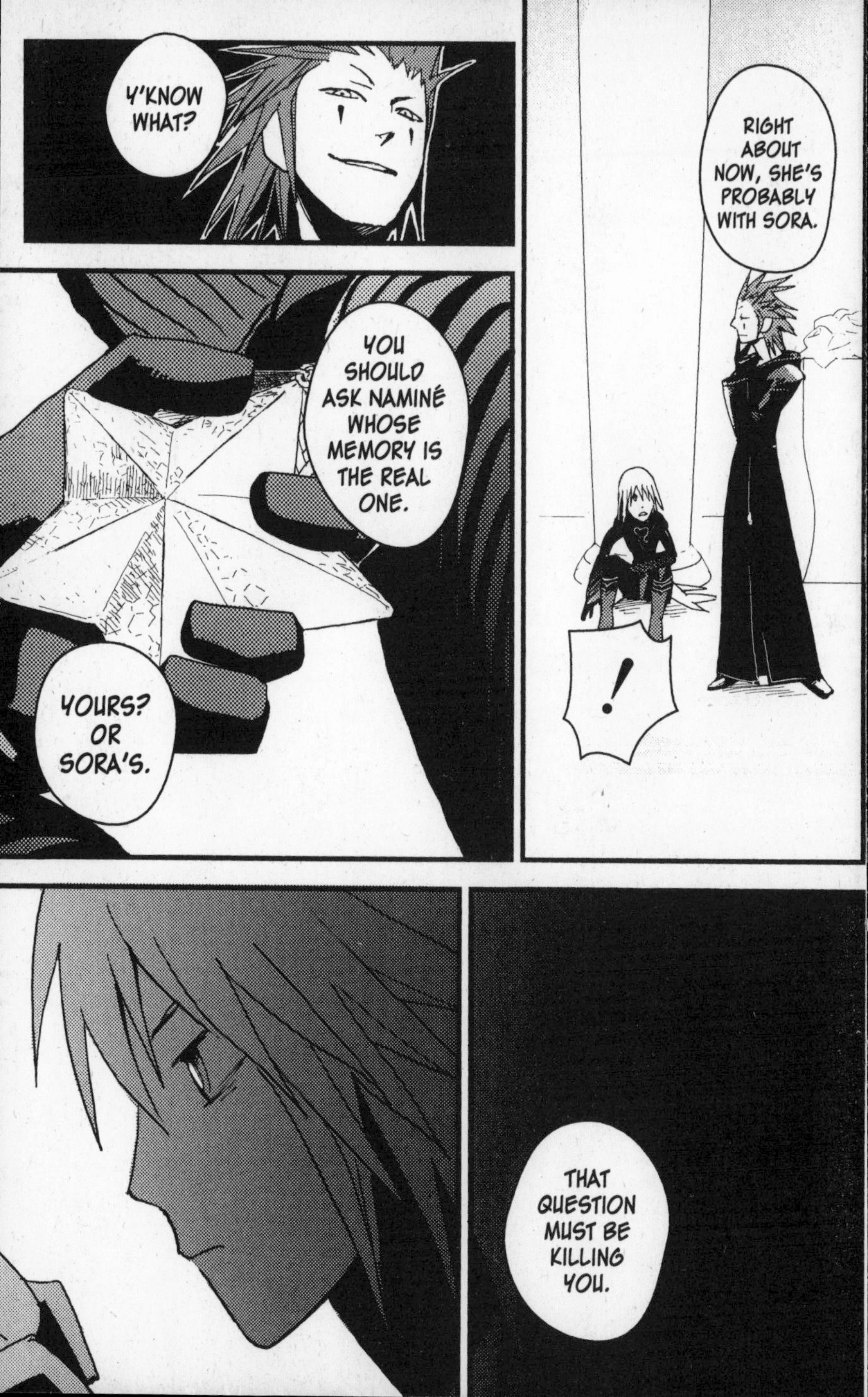

RIGHT ABOUT NOW, SHE'S PROBABLY WITH SORA.
!
Y'KNOW WHAT?
YOU SHOULD ASK NAMINÉ WHOSE MEMORY IS THE REAL ONE.
YOURS? OR SORA'S.
THAT QUESTION MUST BE KILLING YOU.

SQK

SQK

LET'S SEE...

IT'S NO EASY JOB, PULLING EVERYONE'S STRINGS.

HEH HEH...

I'M INTERESTED TO SEE HOW YOU'LL HANDLE THIS.

HMM, SORA?

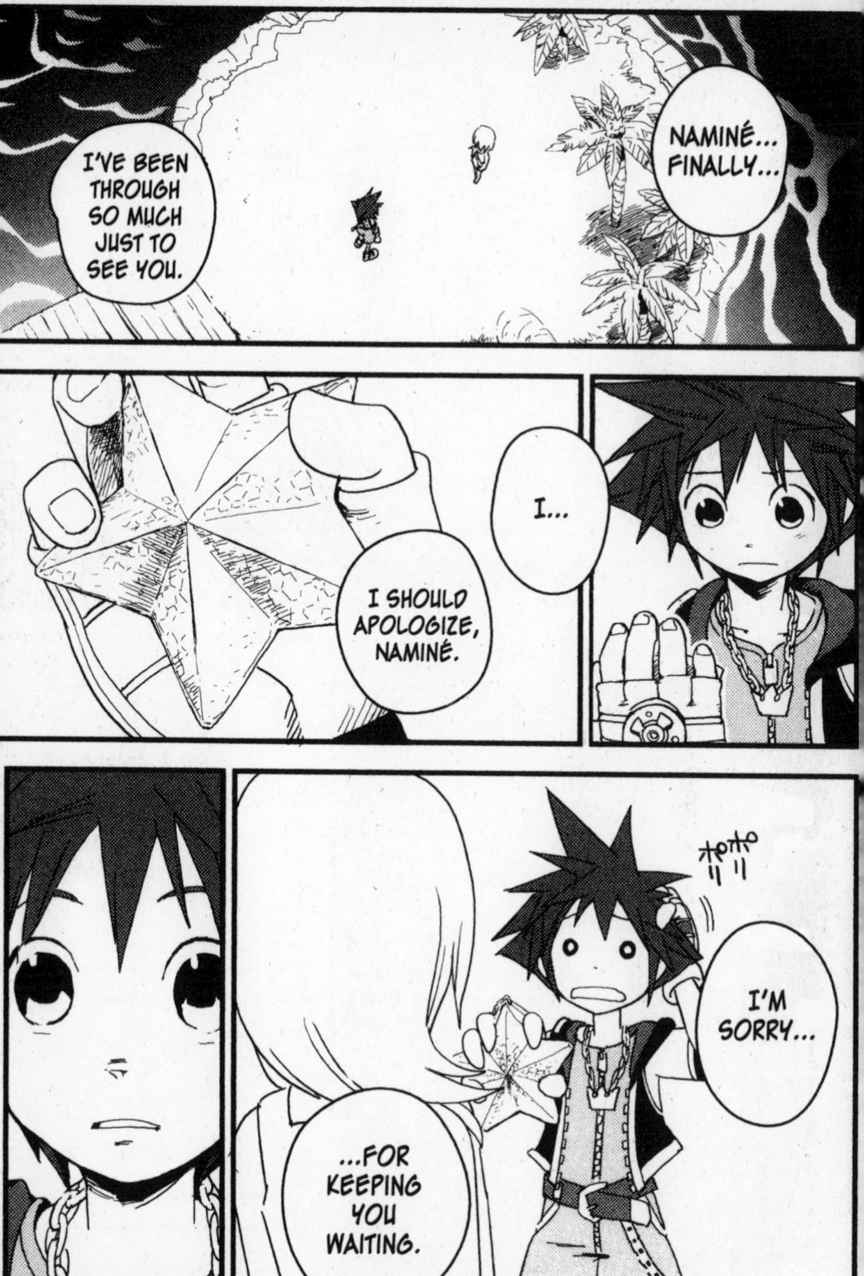
NAMINÉ... FINALLY...
I'VE BEEN THROUGH SO MUCH JUST TO SEE YOU.
I...
I SHOULD APOLOGIZE, NAMINÉ.
I'M SORRY...
...FOR KEEPING YOU WAITING.

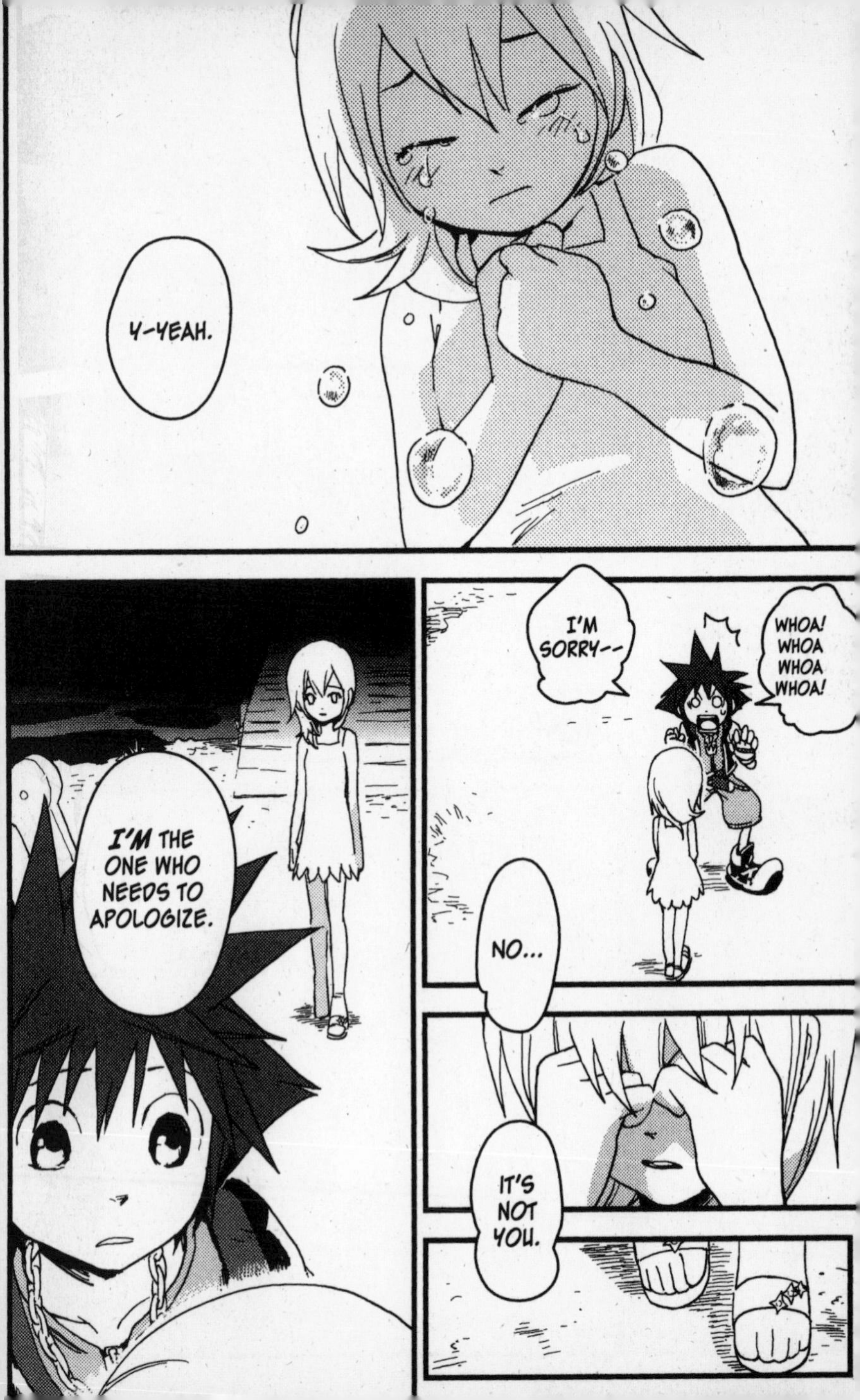
Y-YEAH.
WHOA! WHOA WHOA WHOA!
I'M SORRY--
NO...
IT'S NOT YOU.
I'M THE ONE WHO NEEDS TO APOLOGIZE.

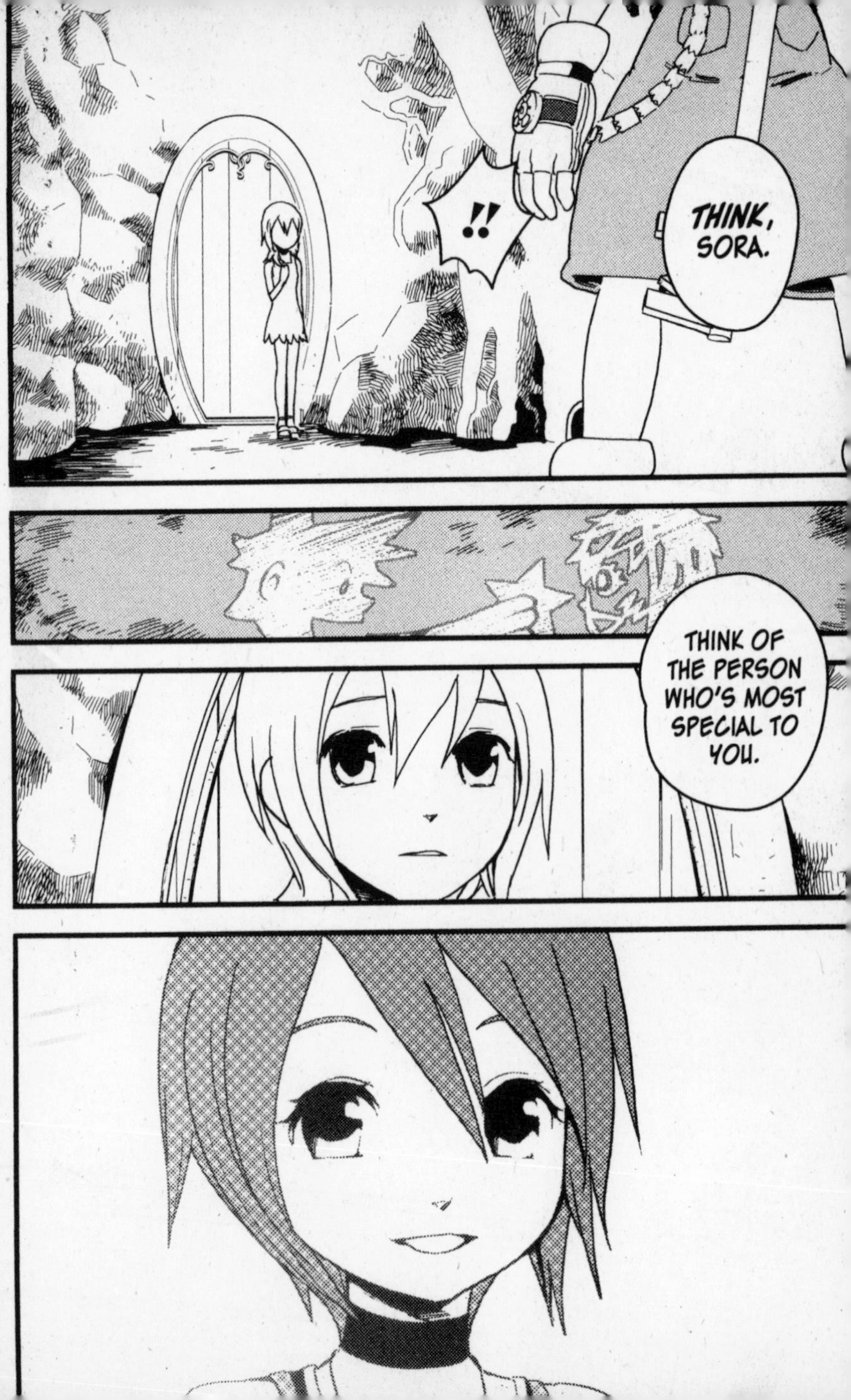
THINK, SORA.
!!
THINK OF THE PERSON WHO'S MOST SPECIAL TO YOU.

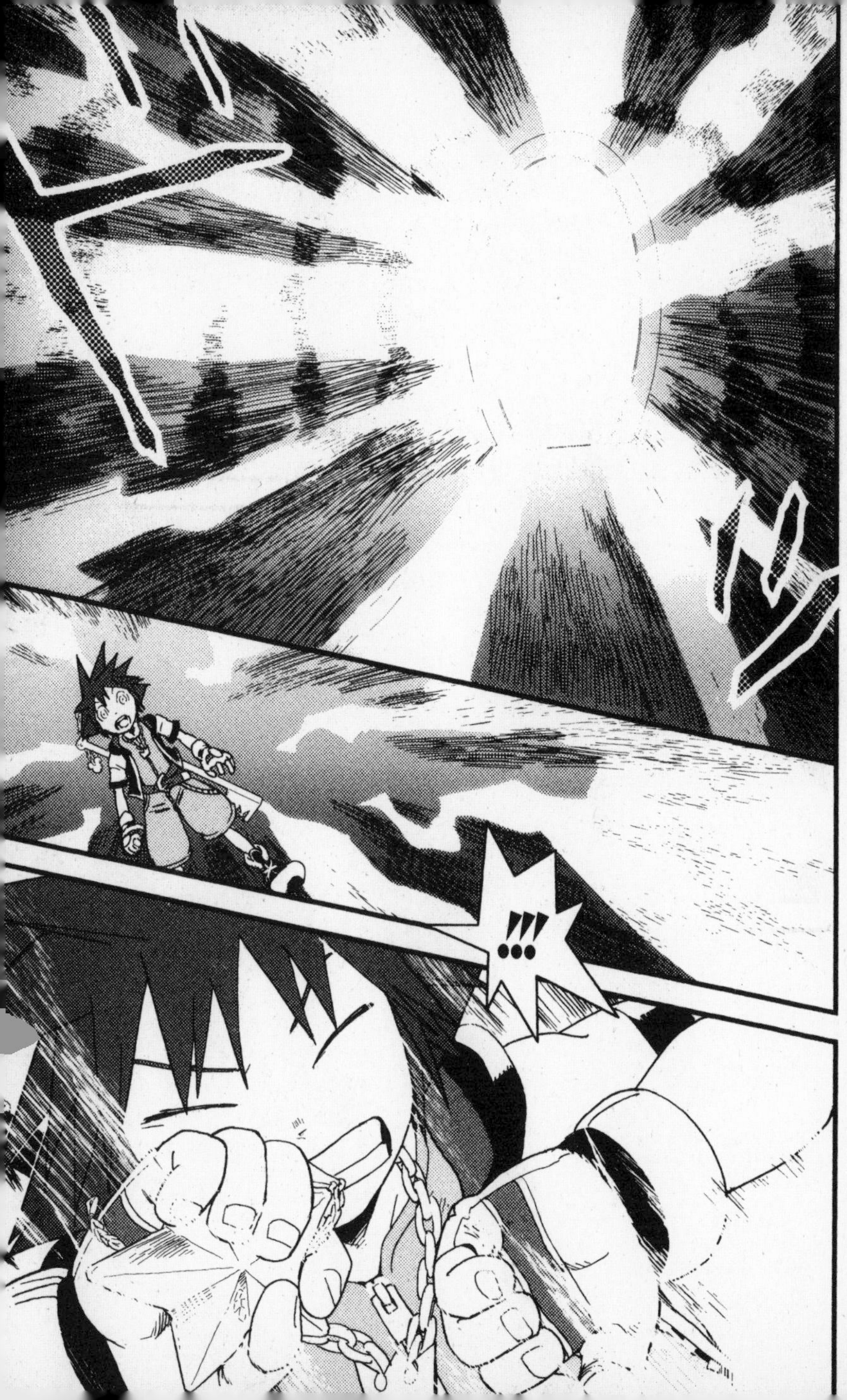
!!!

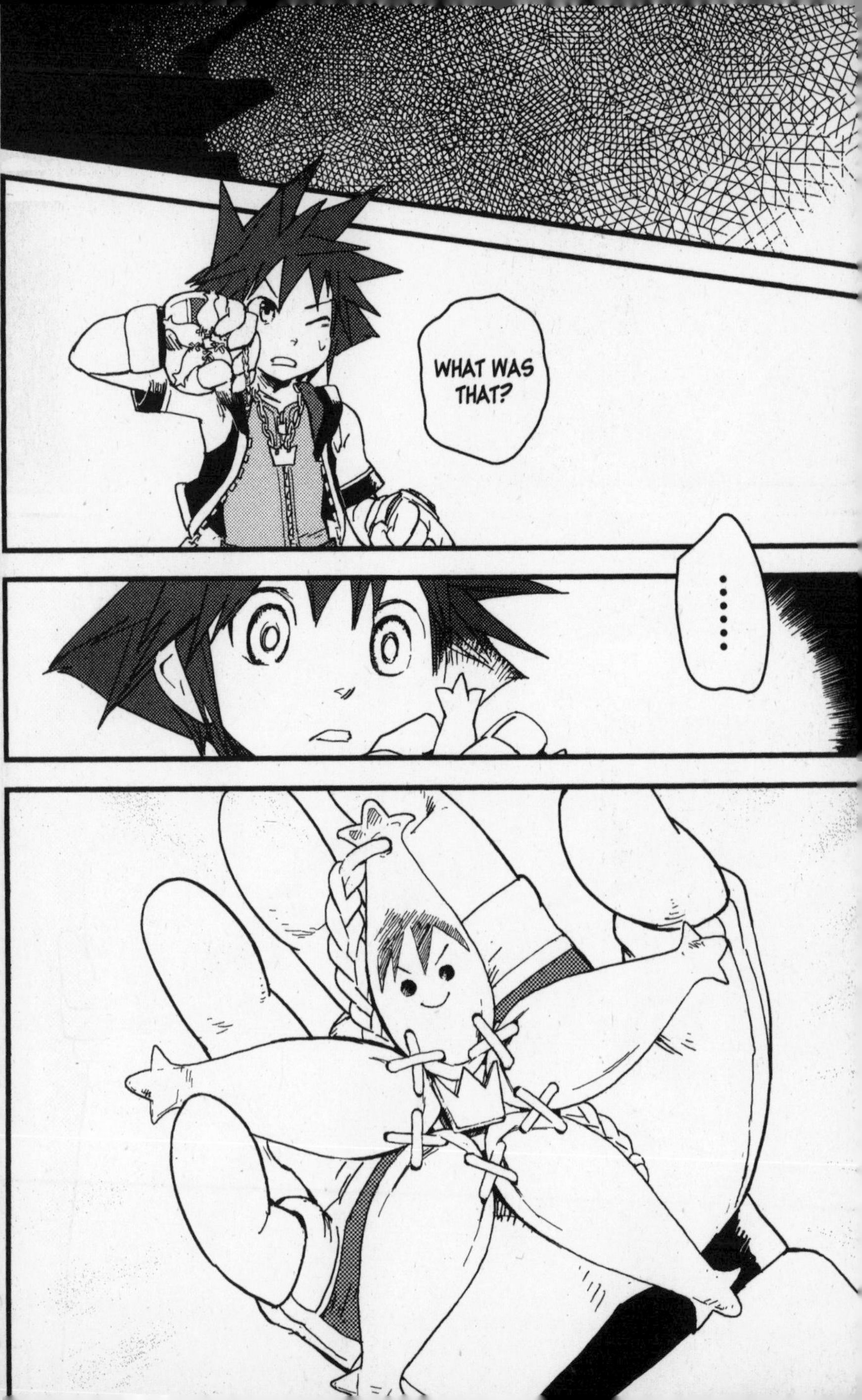
WHAT WAS THAT?
......

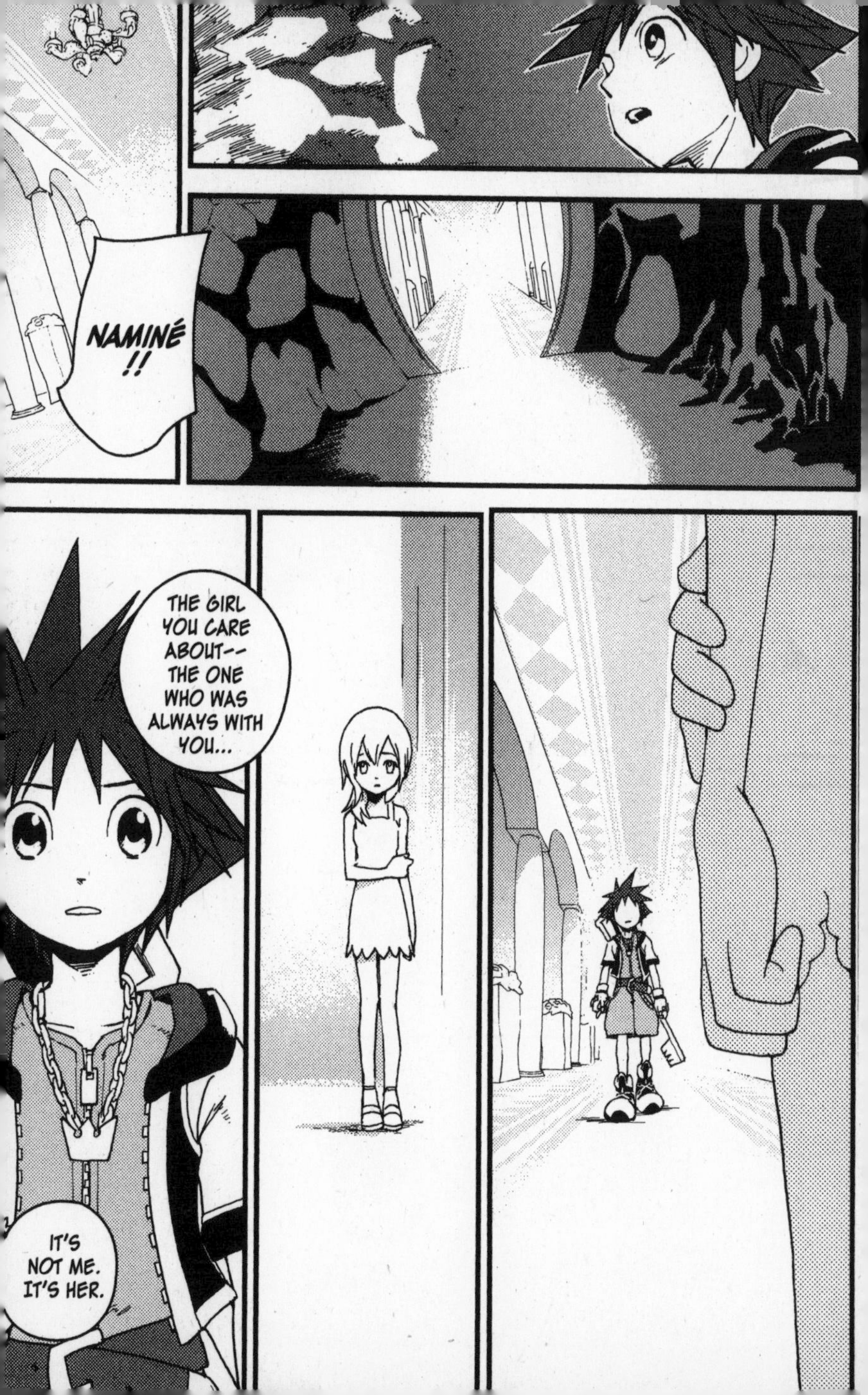
NAMINÉ !!
THE GIRL YOU CARE ABOUT-- THE ONE WHO WAS ALWAYS WITH YOU...
IT'S NOT ME. IT'S HER.

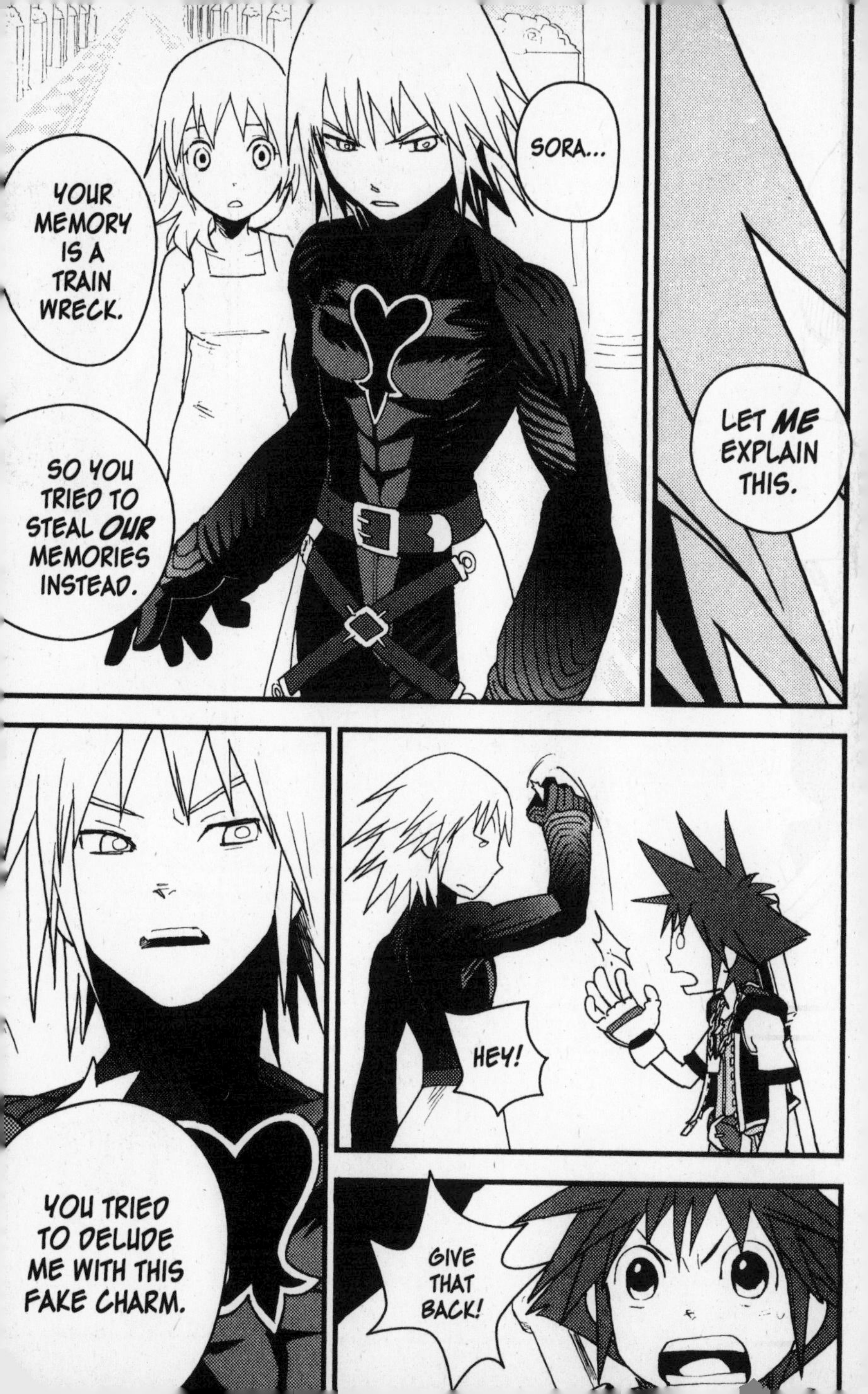
LET *ME* EXPLAIN THIS.
SORA...
YOUR MEMORY IS A TRAIN WRECK.
SO YOU TRIED TO STEAL *OUR* MEMORIES INSTEAD.
HEY!
GIVE THAT BACK!
YOU TRIED TO DELUDE ME WITH THIS FAKE CHARM.

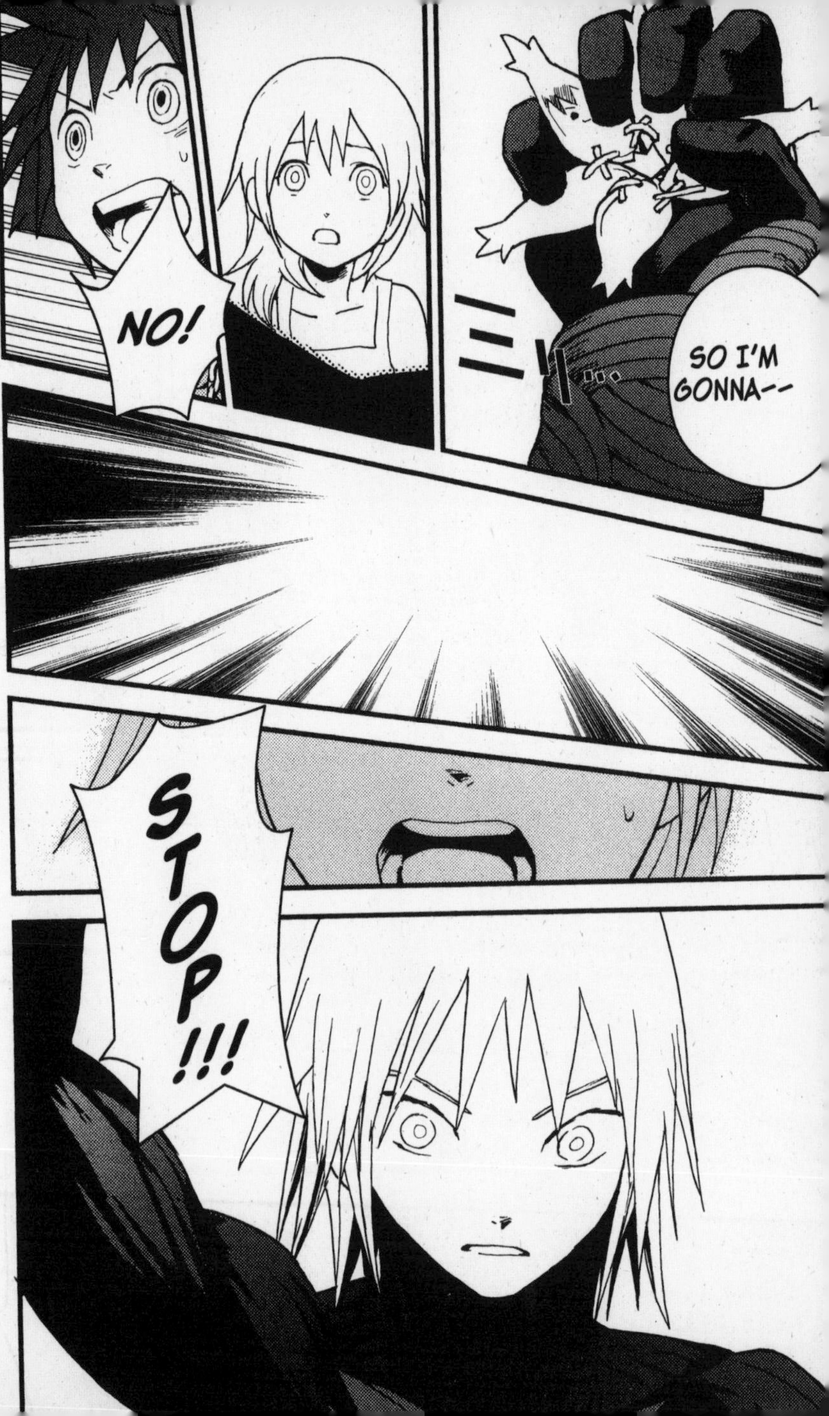
SO I'M GONNA--
NO!
STOP!!!

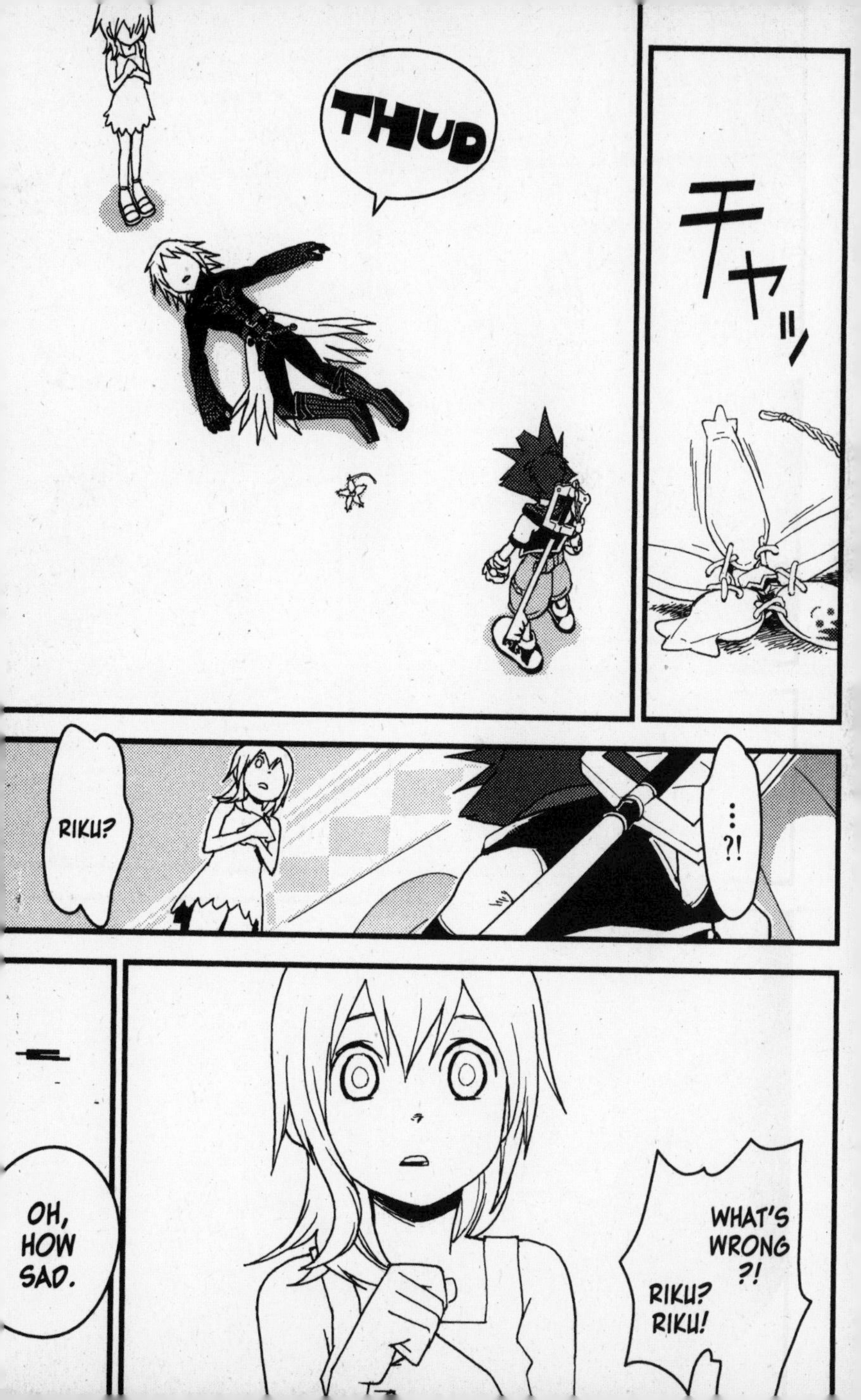
チャッ
THUD
...?!
RIKU?
WHAT'S WRONG?!
RIKU? RIKU!
OH, HOW SAD.

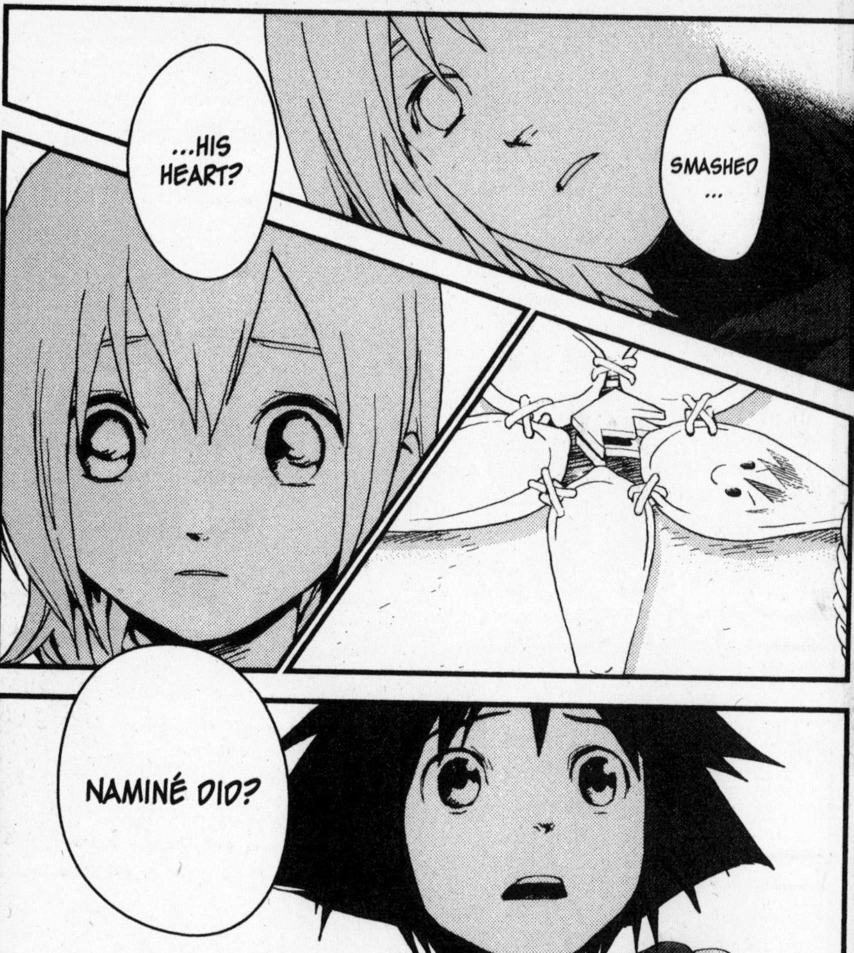
SMASHED ...
...HIS HEART?
NAMINÉ DID?

Card 11 SHOCK!!!

ACTUALLY...

...OUR PLAN IS STILL INTACT EVEN IF WE TELL HIM THE TRUTH.

...IF YOU THINK ABOUT IT...

ALL WE HAVE TO DO IS REWRITE HIS MEMORY AGAIN, RIGHT?

WITH YOUR POWERS, NAMINÉ.

OH, DON'T STAND THERE LOOKING ALL INNOCENT, GIRL.

...?

AND YOU KNOW WHAT ELSE?

THAT RIKU LYING THERE IS A PUPPET VEXEN MADE.

?!

BUT NAMINÉ BROKE HIS HEART, SO NOW HE'S JUST A DOLL AGAIN.

ITS MEMORIES WITH NAMINÉ WERE PLANTED, NOT REAL. ALL THIS TIME IT'S BEEN PICKING FIGHTS WITH YOU OVER BOGUS MEMORIES.

IT'S BEEN SO MUCH FUN TO WATCH!

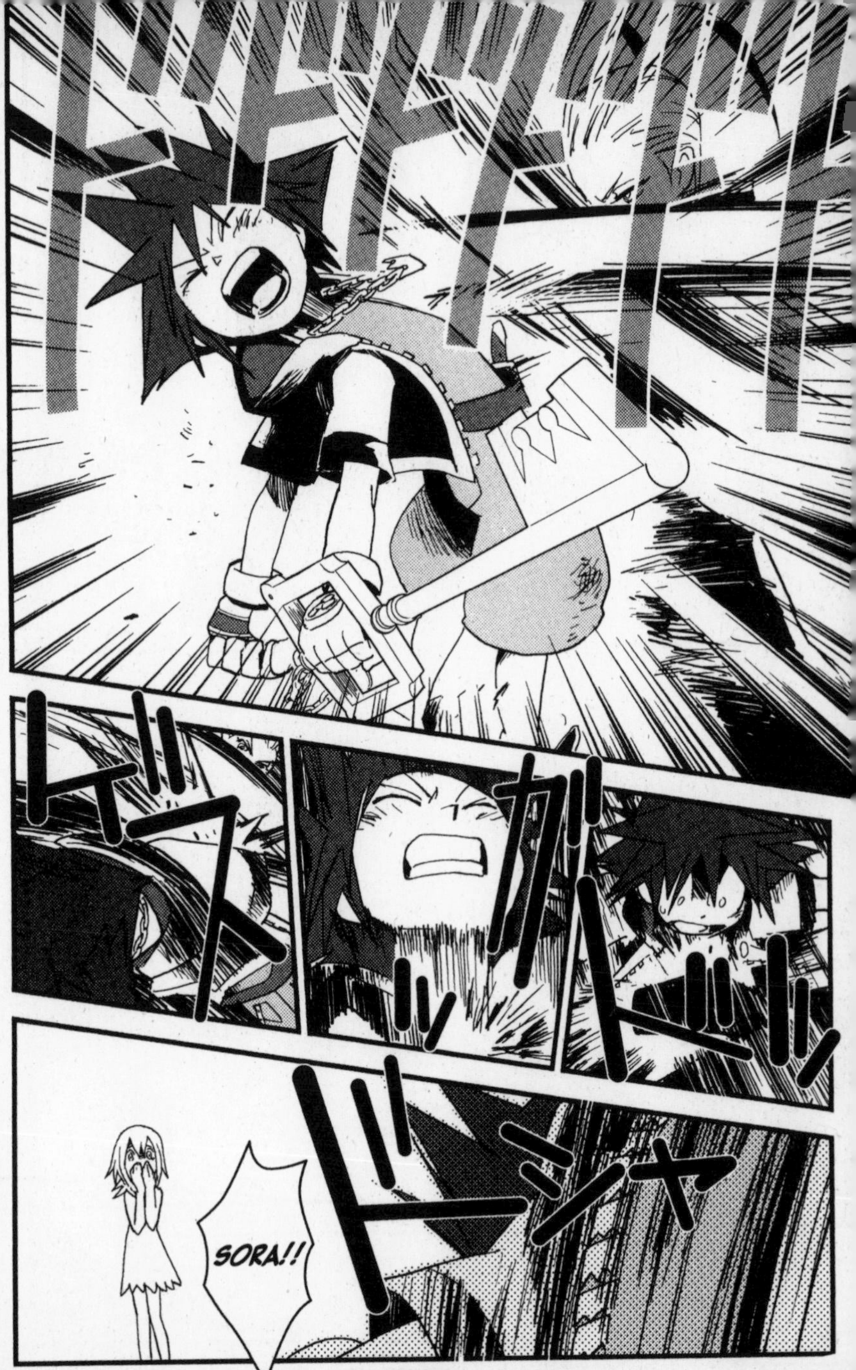
SORA!!

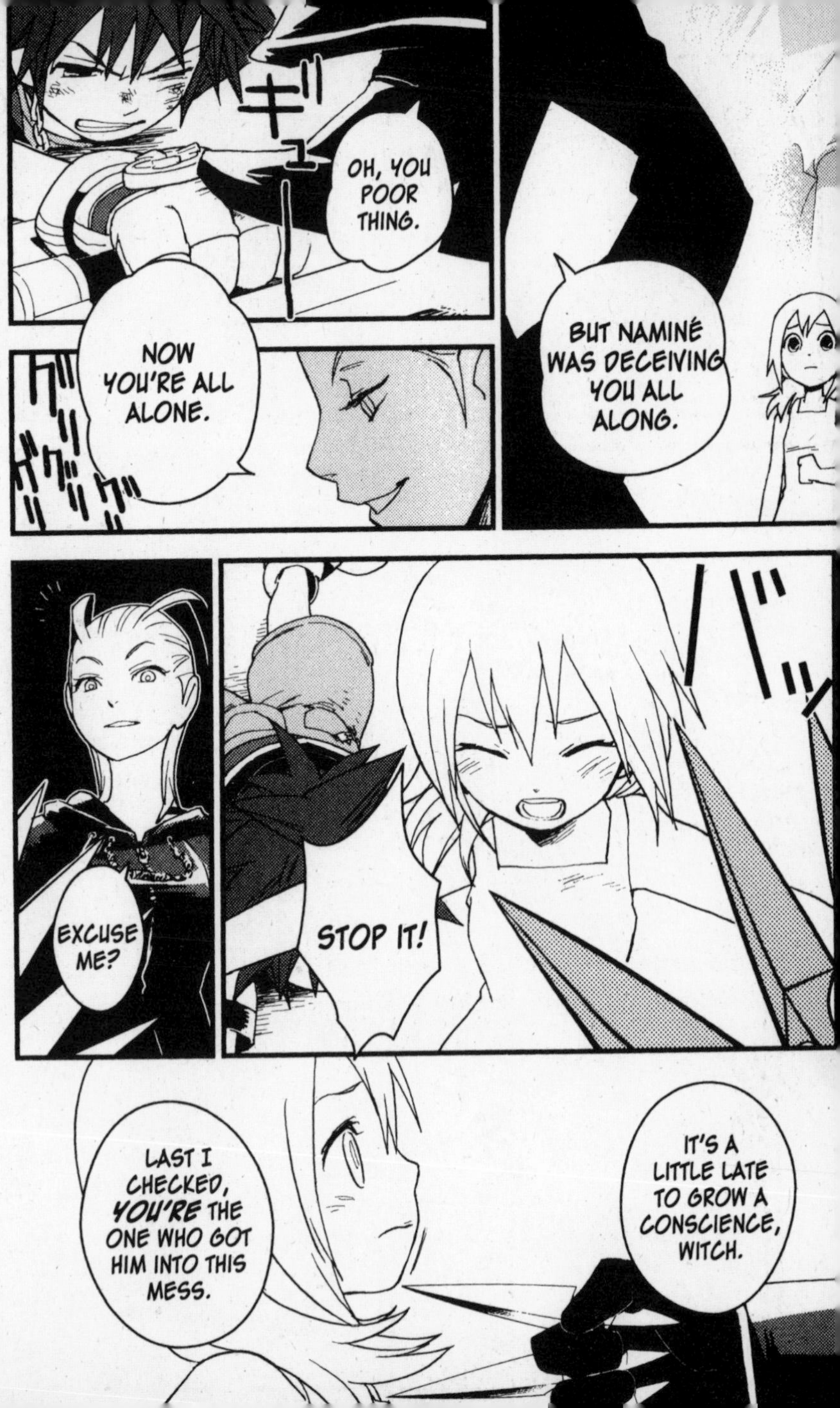
BUT NAMINÉ WAS DECEIVING YOU ALL ALONG.
ギュー
OH, YOU POOR THING.
NOW YOU'RE ALL ALONE.
バッ
STOP IT!
EXCUSE ME?
IT'S A LITTLE LATE TO GROW A CONSCIENCE, WITCH.
LAST I CHECKED, *YOU'RE* THE ONE WHO GOT HIM INTO THIS MESS.

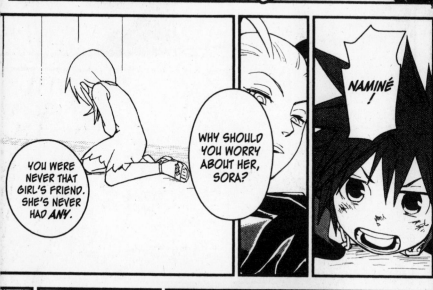

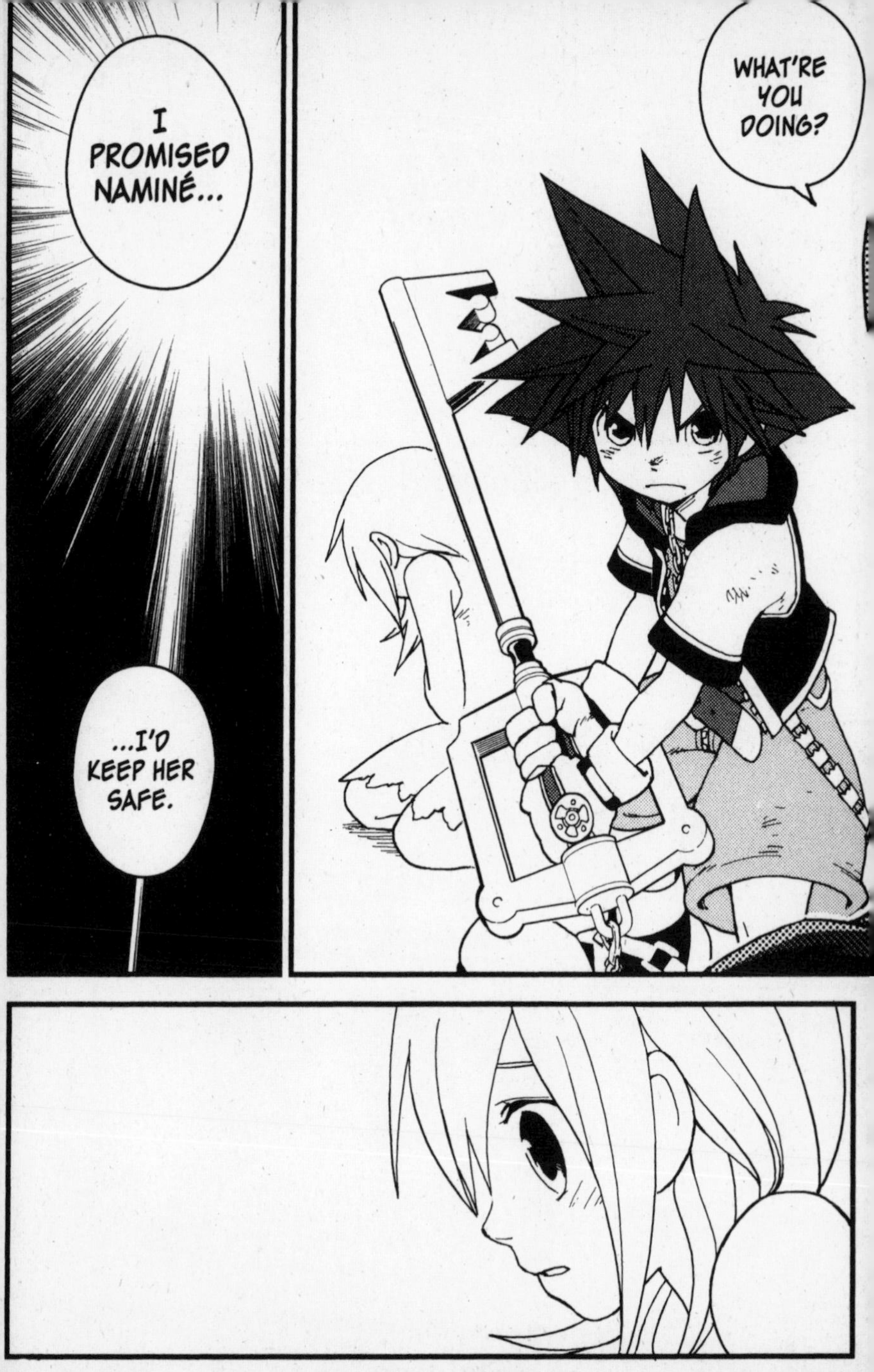
WHAT'RE YOU DOING?
I PROMISED NAMINÉ...
...I'D KEEP HER SAFE.

WHAT AN IDIOT!

WEREN'T YOU LISTENING?

HUH?!

BUT THEY'RE STILL MINE...

MAYBE MY MEMORIES *ARE* FAKE.

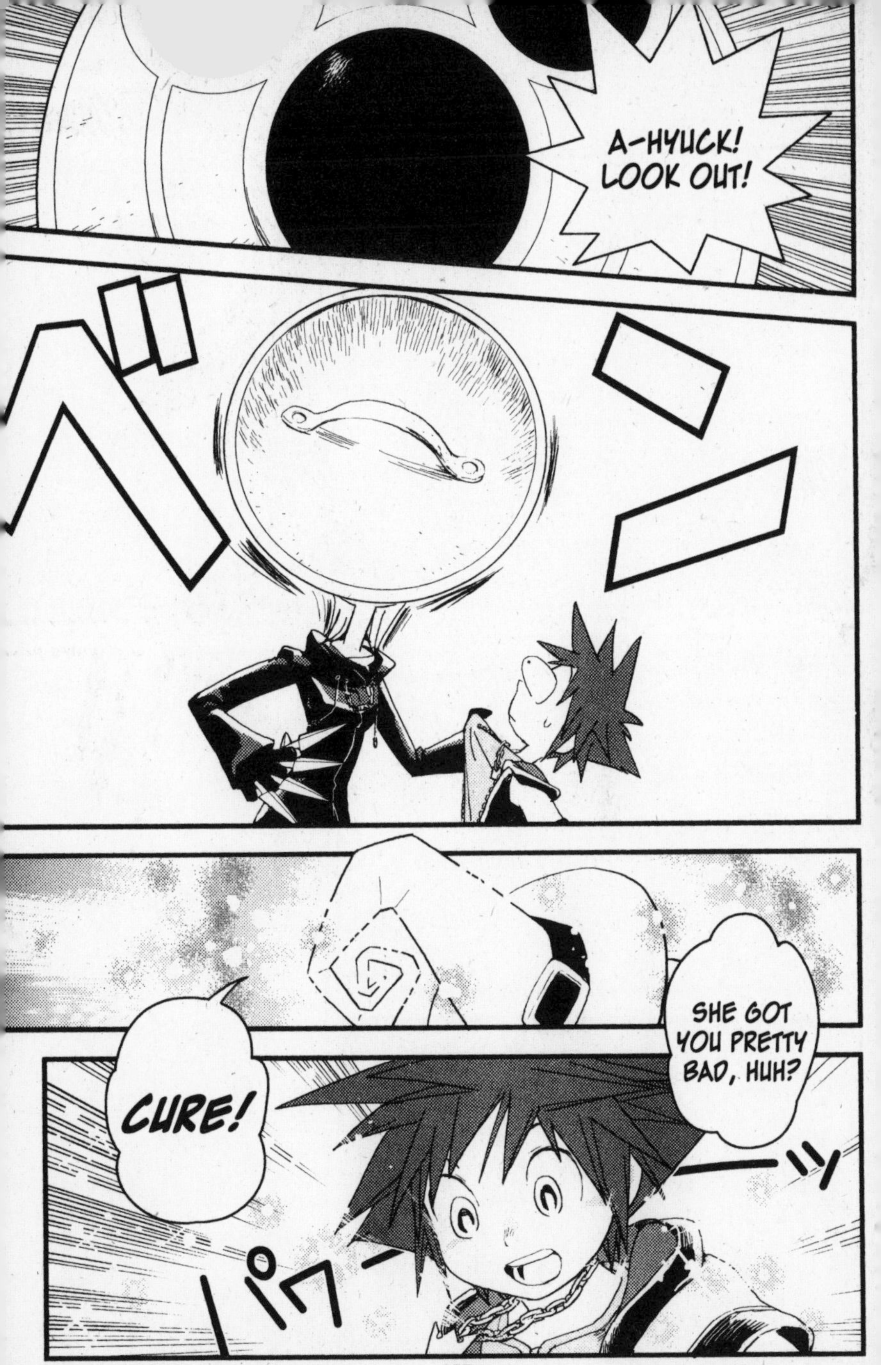
A-HYUCK! LOOK OUT!
SHE GOT YOU PRETTY BAD, HUH?
CURE!

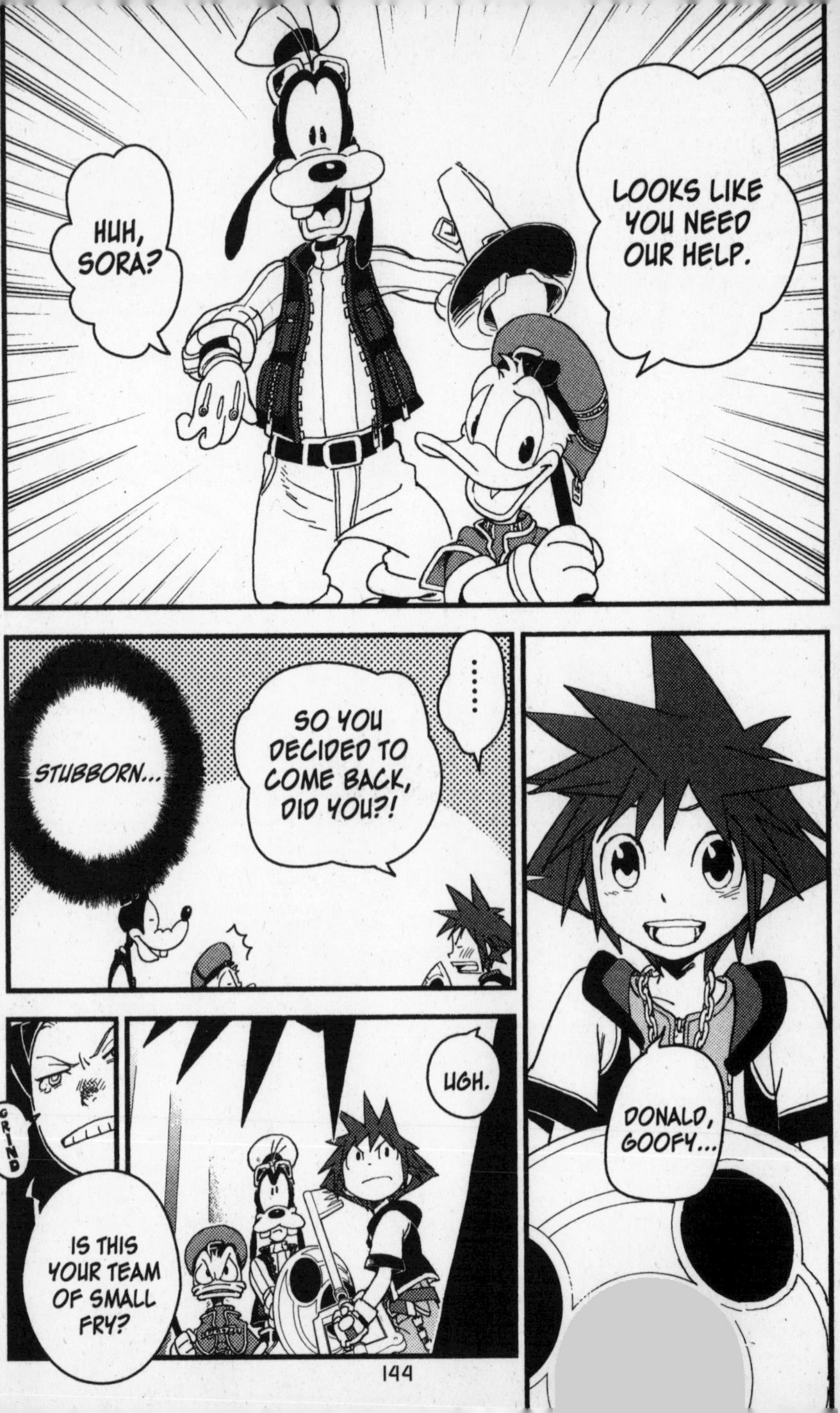
LOOKS LIKE YOU NEED OUR HELP.
HUH, SORA?
DONALD, GOOFY...
......
SO YOU DECIDED TO COME BACK, DID YOU?!
STUBBORN...
UGH.
GRIND
IS THIS YOUR TEAM OF SMALL FRY?

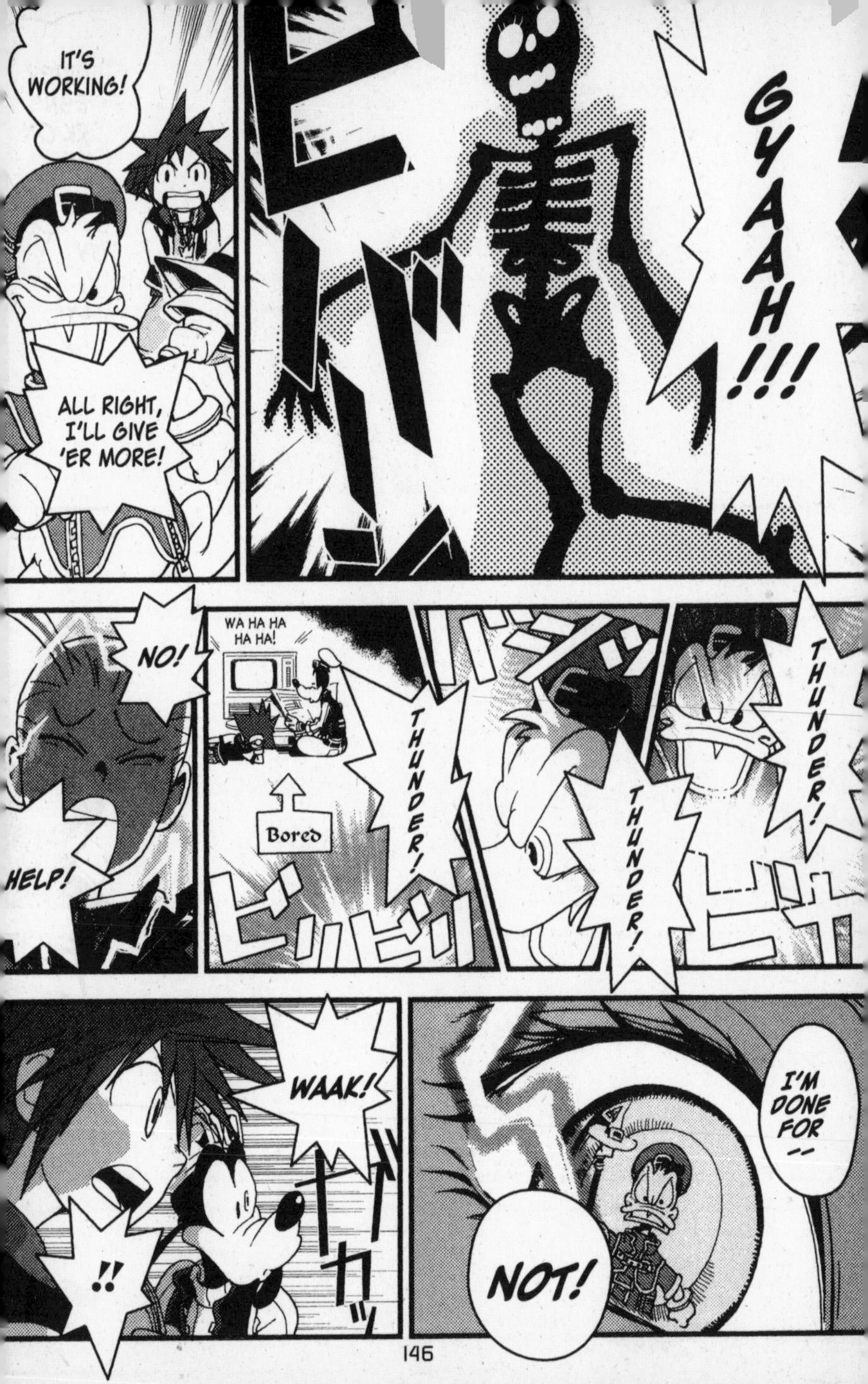
GYAAH!!!
IT'S WORKING!
ALL RIGHT, I'LL GIVE 'ER MORE!
THUNDER!
THUNDER!
THUNDER!
WA HA HA HA HA!
Bored
NO!
HELP!
I'M DONE FOR--
NOT!
WAAK!
!!

YOU COULD POWER THE AIR CONDITIONER, HAIR DRYER AND MICROWAVE AT THE SAME TIME!

WHAT A JERK...

OOPS, WAS THAT TOO MUCH OF A CHARGE?

YOU GUYS LOOK LIKE THE ELECTRICAL PARADE.

OUCH... UGH...

HO HO HO!

Trinity is a special weapon that can only be activated using the combined friendship power of Sora, Donald and Goofy.

BLIZZARD
!!!

FIRE!!!

DOUBLE
MAGIC
SPRINKLER!!!

TRINITY
LIMIT--

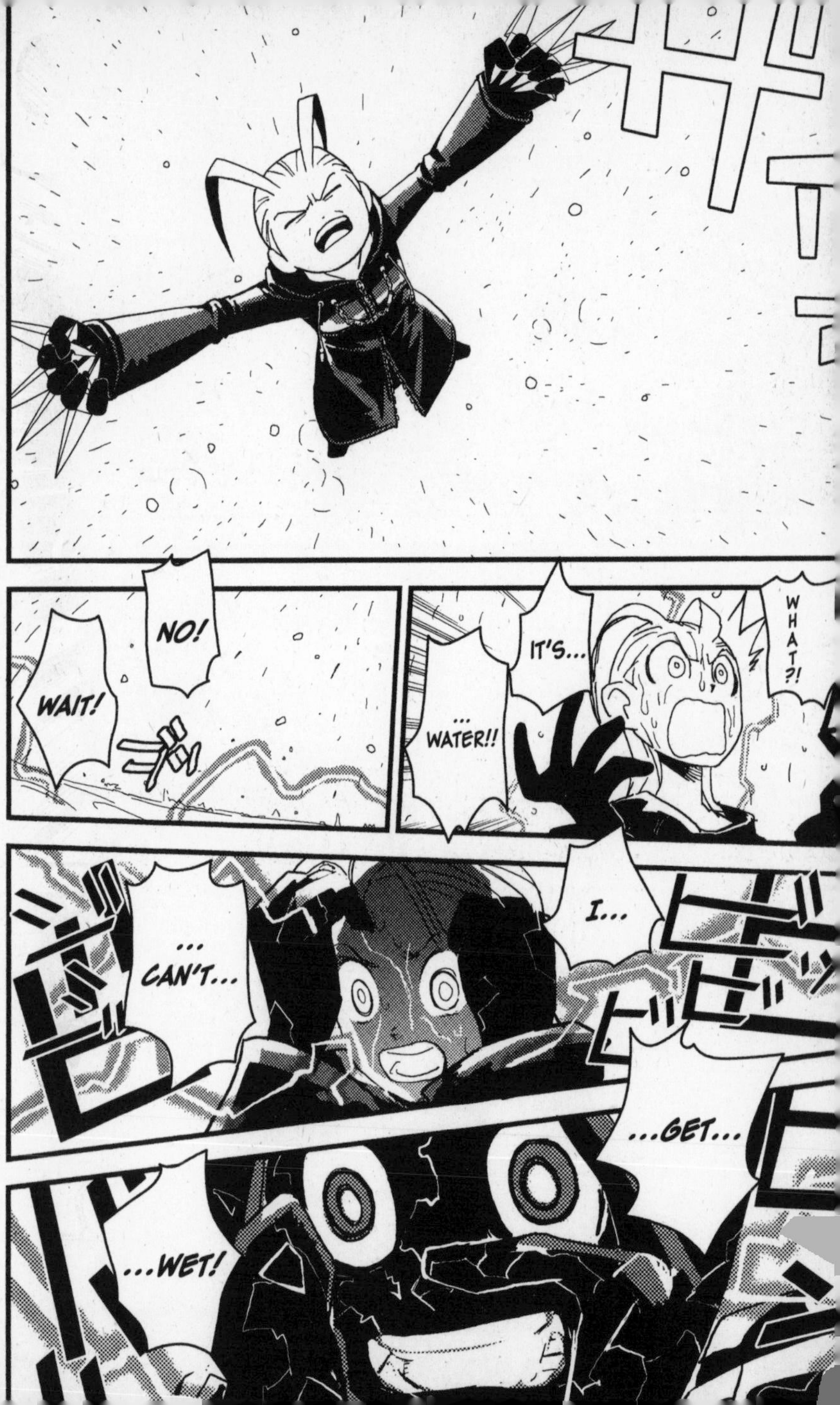
WHAT?!
IT'S...
...WATER!!
NO!
WAIT!
I...
...CAN'T...
...GET...
...WET!

ARE YOU SERIOUS ?!

WHAT ?!

OH NO!!

...WE CAN'T GET OUR MEMORIES BACK?

DOES THAT MEAN...

...YOU SHOULD BE ABLE TO GET YOUR MEMORIES BACK.

IF YOU GO TO THE TOP FLOOR...

WE SHOULD BE ABLE TO ESCAPE IF WE DEFEAT THAT MARL... SOMETHING.

NAMINÉ'S BEEN TRAPPED IN HERE...

LET'S GET THIS OVER WITH!

...ALL ALONE.

THANKS!

FOR COMING TO HELP!

WHAT ?!

A-HYUCK.

CAN'T LEAVE YOU ALONE, NOW, CAN WE?

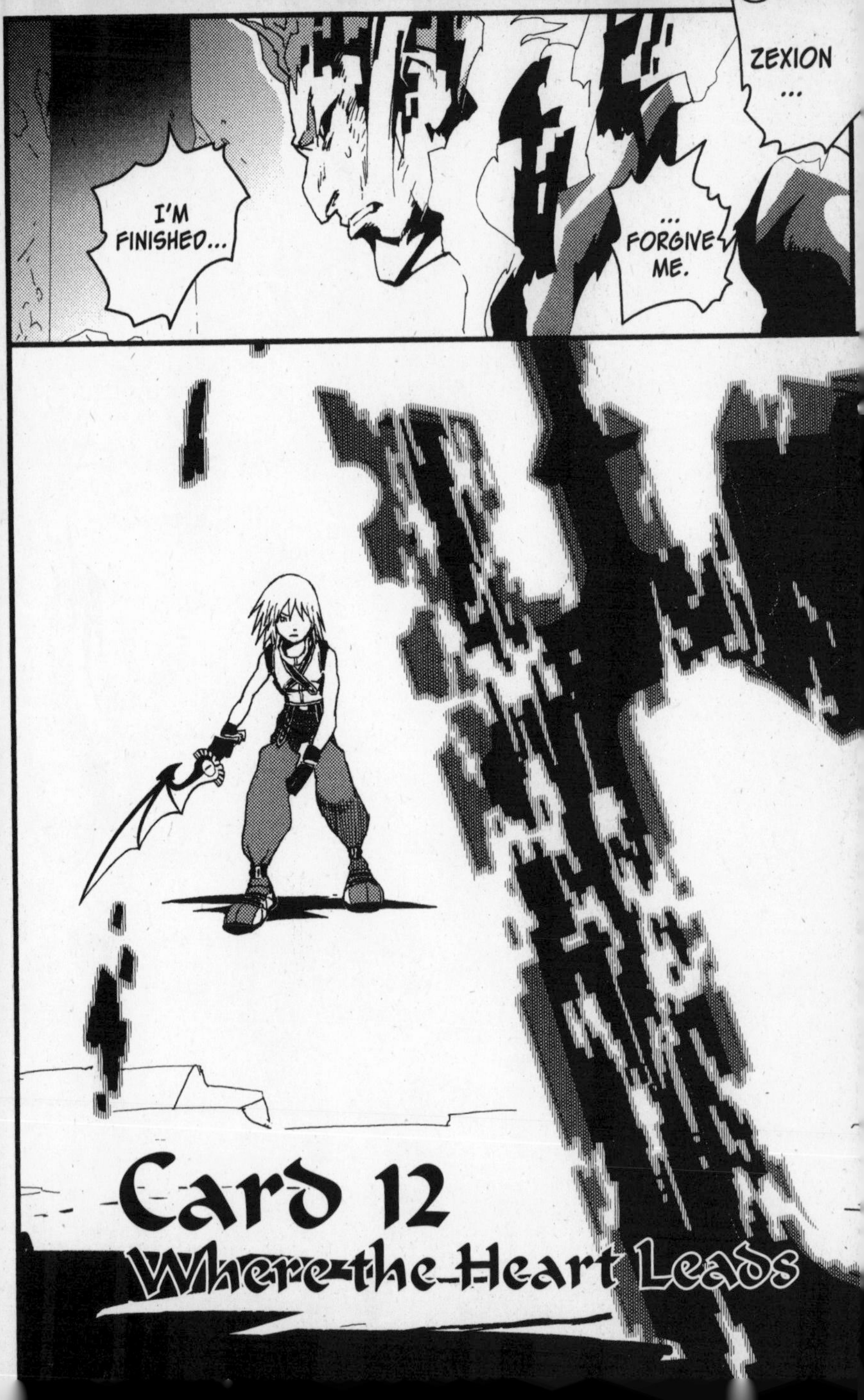
ZEXION ...
... FORGIVE ME.
I'M FINISHED...
Card 12
Where the Heart Leads

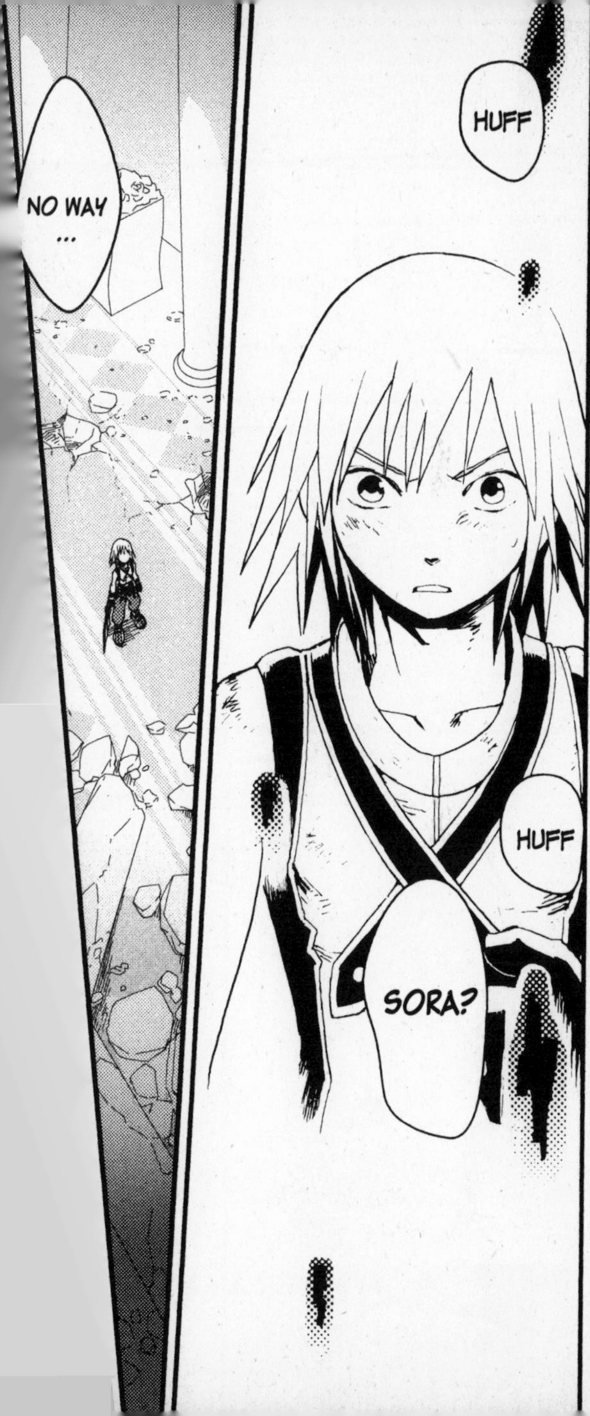
HUFF
HUFF
SORA?
NO WAY ...

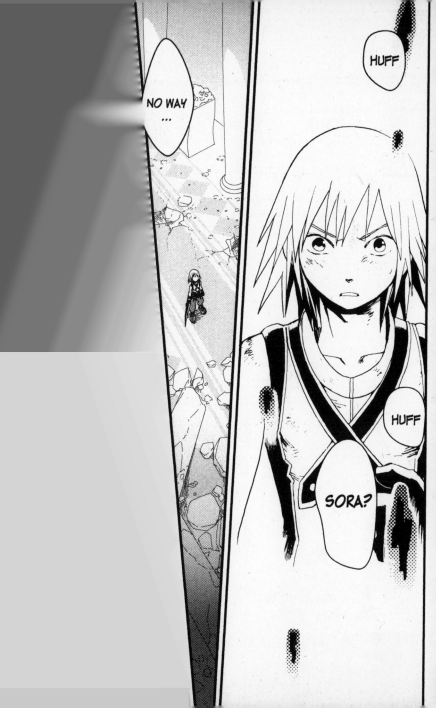

WE NEED TO DEVISE A STRATEGY.

WE HAVE NO IDEA WHAT THIS MARL-WHOEVER IS LIKE!

YOU CALL THAT A STRATEGY?

OKAY THEN. WE CAN'T WASTE OUR ITEMS.

EXACTLY!!!

WE HAVE BEEN GOING THROUGH OUR ITEMS RATHER QUICKLY...

IT MAY NOT BE THAT EASY TO DEFEAT HIM.

WELL, HE'S THE BOSS OF THIS CASTLE, RIGHT?

200 meters ahead!

Are you well equipp

WARM

Potion

Elixi

ER, IS THIS THE PUNCH LINE?

IT'S THE PRELUDE TO THE FINAL BOSS...

THIS IS ONE LONG HALLWAY.

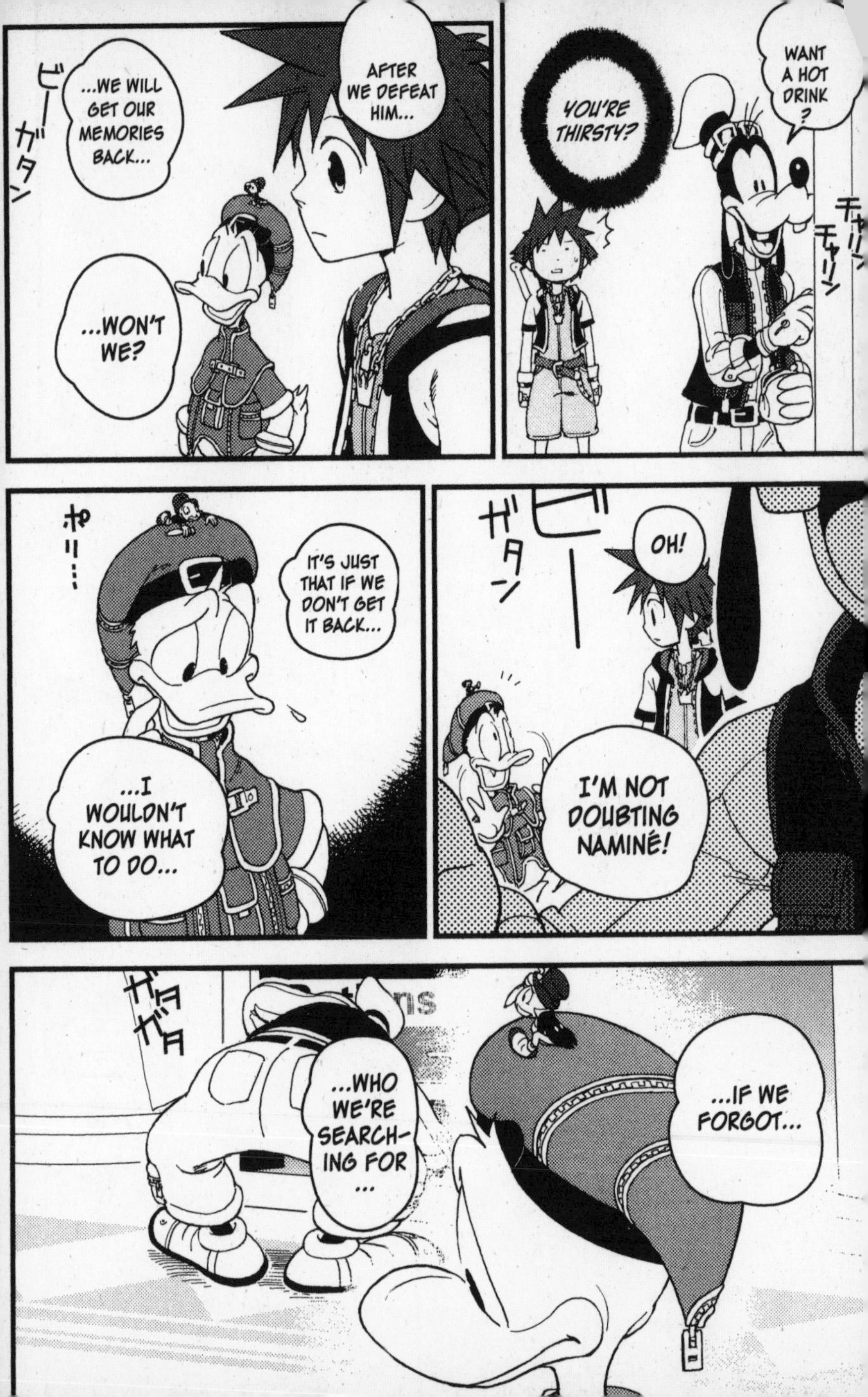
WANT A HOT DRINK?
YOU'RE THIRSTY?
チャリン チャリン
AFTER WE DEFEAT HIM...
...WE WILL GET OUR MEMORIES BACK...
...WON'T WE?
ビーガタン
ビー
ガタン
OH!
I'M NOT DOUBTING NAMINÉ!
ポリ…
IT'S JUST THAT IF WE DON'T GET IT BACK...
...I WOULDN'T KNOW WHAT TO DO...
...IF WE FORGOT...
...WHO WE'RE SEARCH-ING FOR...
ガタガタ

WHEN I THINK ABOUT HIM, IT WARMS MY HEART.

BUT I'M HAVING TROUBLE REMEMBERING WHAT KIND OF PERSON HE IS.

...AND THERE'S A BIG HOLE IN YOUR HEART.

IT'S REALLY TOUGH WHEN YOU LOSE SOMETHING PRECIOUS...

I REMEMBER HE'S WITH RIKU...

I...

I THINK I FINALLY KNOW HOW YOU FELT, SORA.

LOOK, LOOK! I WON A FREE DRINK!

A-HYUCK!

...and to lose is to find.

...where to find is to lose...

...Castle Oblivion...

This is...

UH, THAT'S GOOD TO KNOW.

WARM
Potions
Elixirs

But rest assured that you won't lose anything just because you won this free drink.

BEFORE WE LEAVE THIS CASTLE WE'RE GOING TO FIND...

WARM
Potions
Elixirs

...THE REASON WE CAME HERE.

WE'RE NOT GOING TO LOSE ANYTHING.

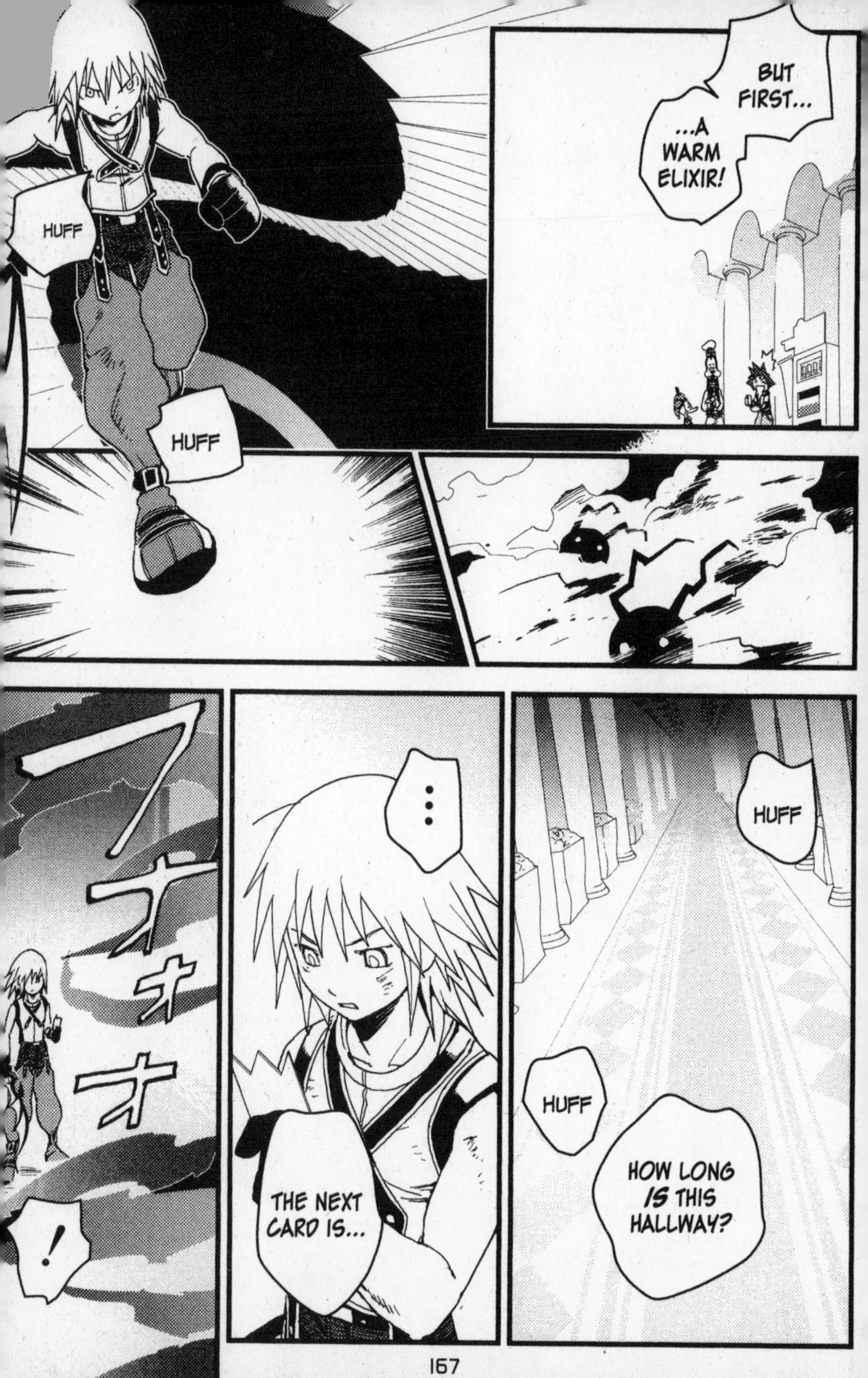
BUT FIRST...
...A WARM ELIXIR!
HUFF
HUFF
HUFF
HUFF
HOW LONG IS THIS HALLWAY?
...
THE NEXT CARD IS...
フォオ
!

ANSEM!

TALKING TO YOURSELF?

GO AWAY!

HOW STUBBORN...

YOU'RE NOT USING THE GIFT I GAVE YOU.

I WON'T LET YOU CONTROL ME!

OPEN YOUR HEART TO DARKNESS.

THE POWER OF DARKNESS WILL HELP YOU, RIKU.

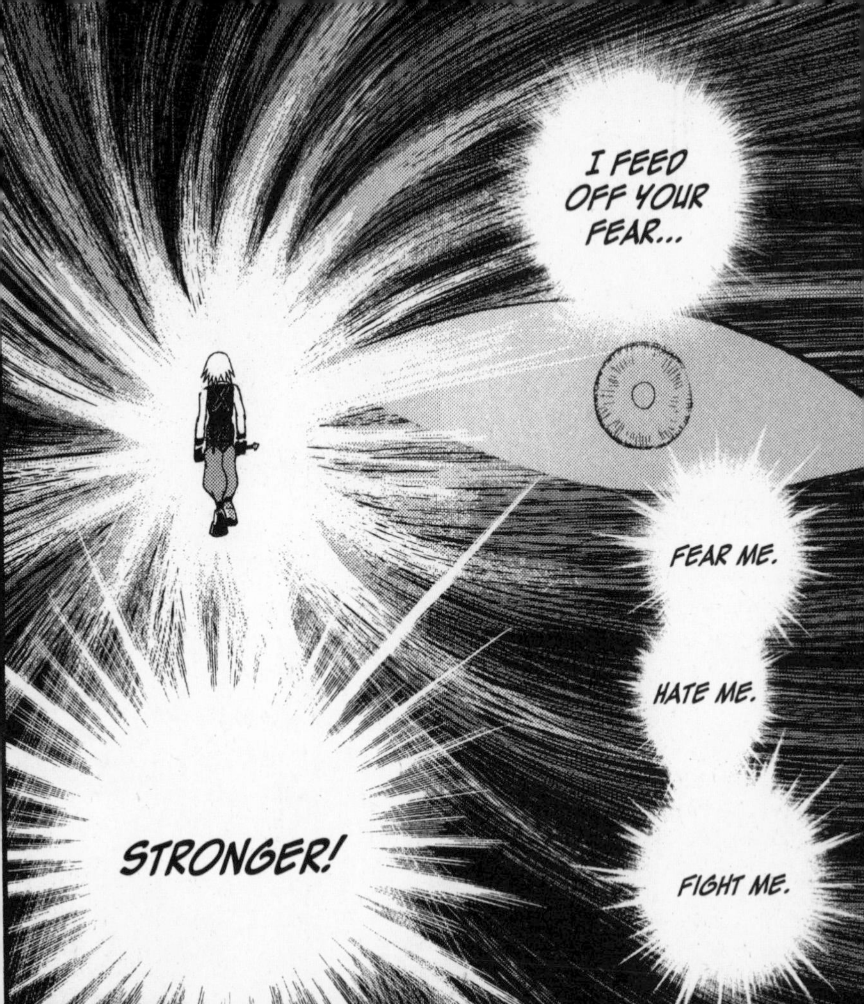
I FEED OFF YOUR FEAR...
FEAR ME.
HATE ME.
FIGHT ME.
STRONGER!
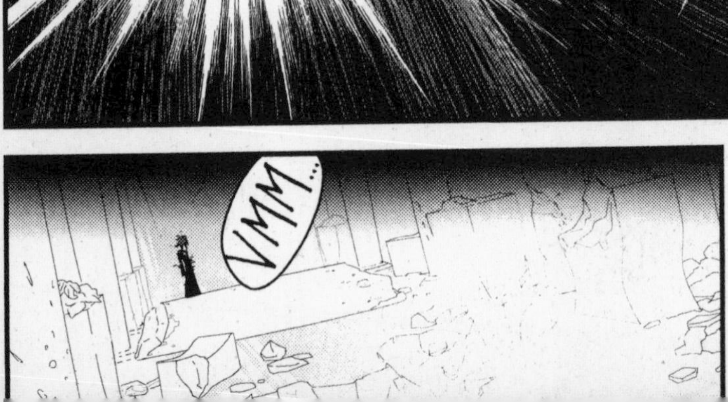
VMM...

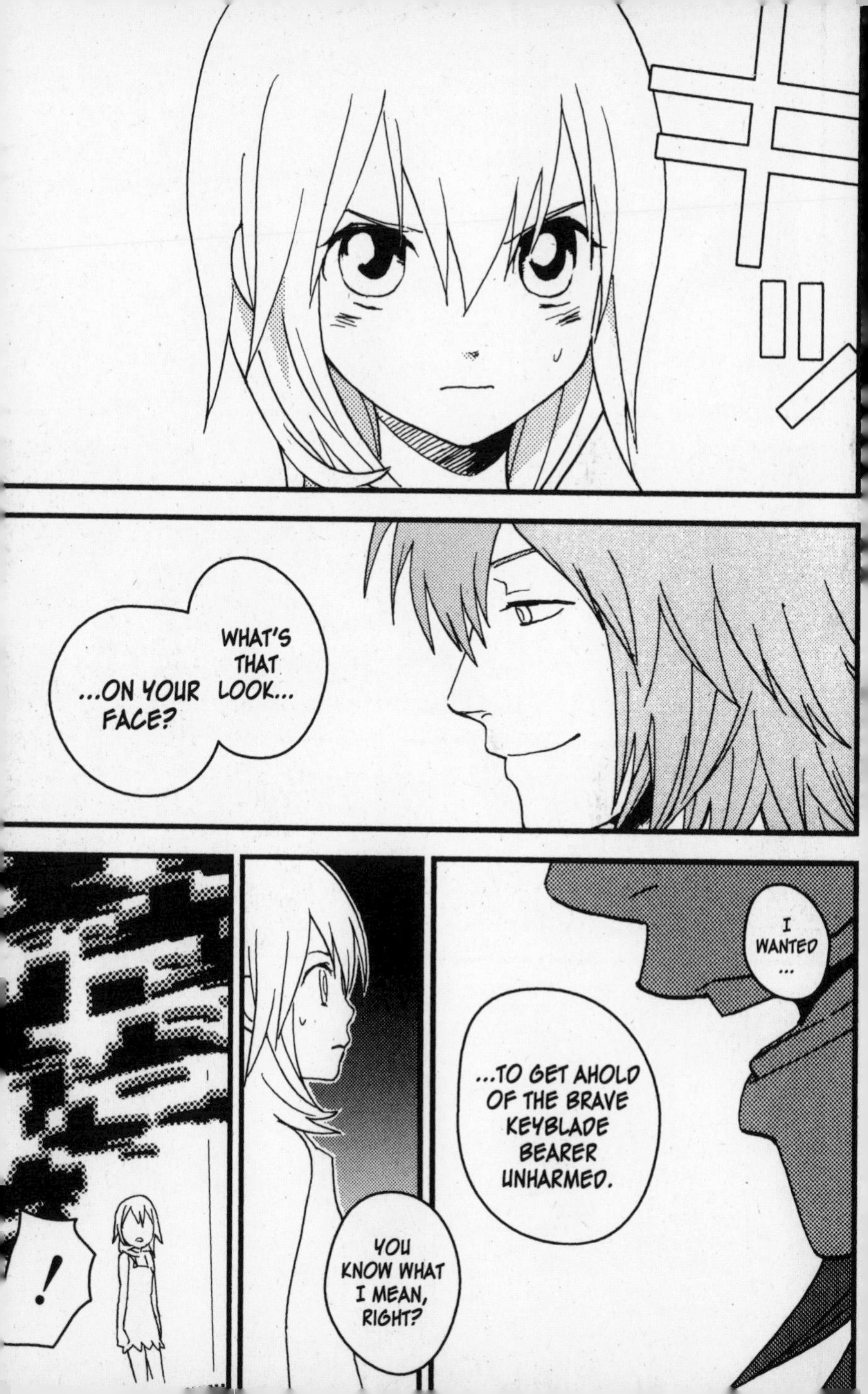
WHAT'S THAT LOOK...
...ON YOUR FACE?
I WANTED ...
...TO GET AHOLD OF THE BRAVE KEYBLADE BEARER UNHARMED.
YOU KNOW WHAT I MEAN, RIGHT?
!

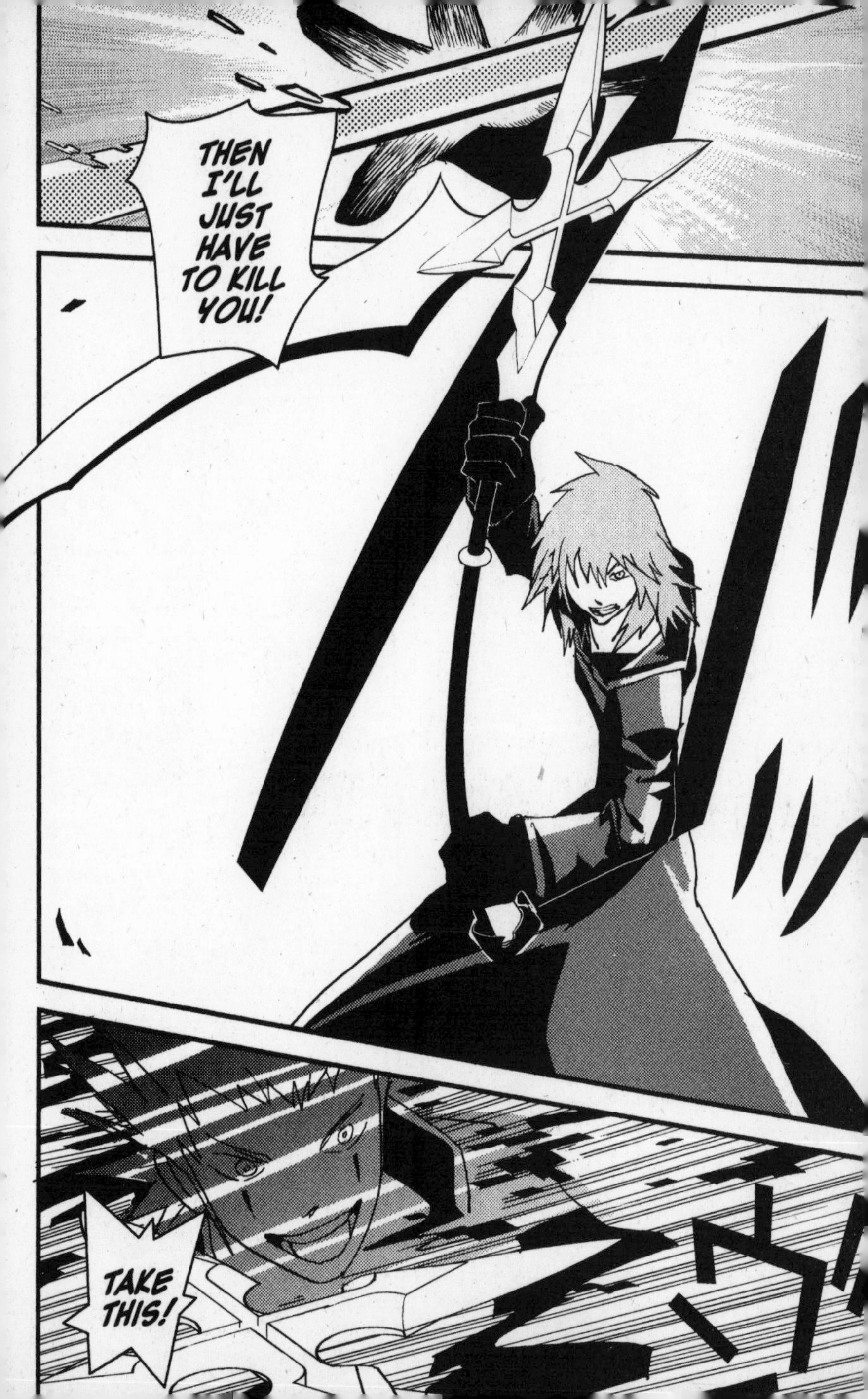
THEN I'LL JUST HAVE TO KILL YOU!
TAKE THIS!

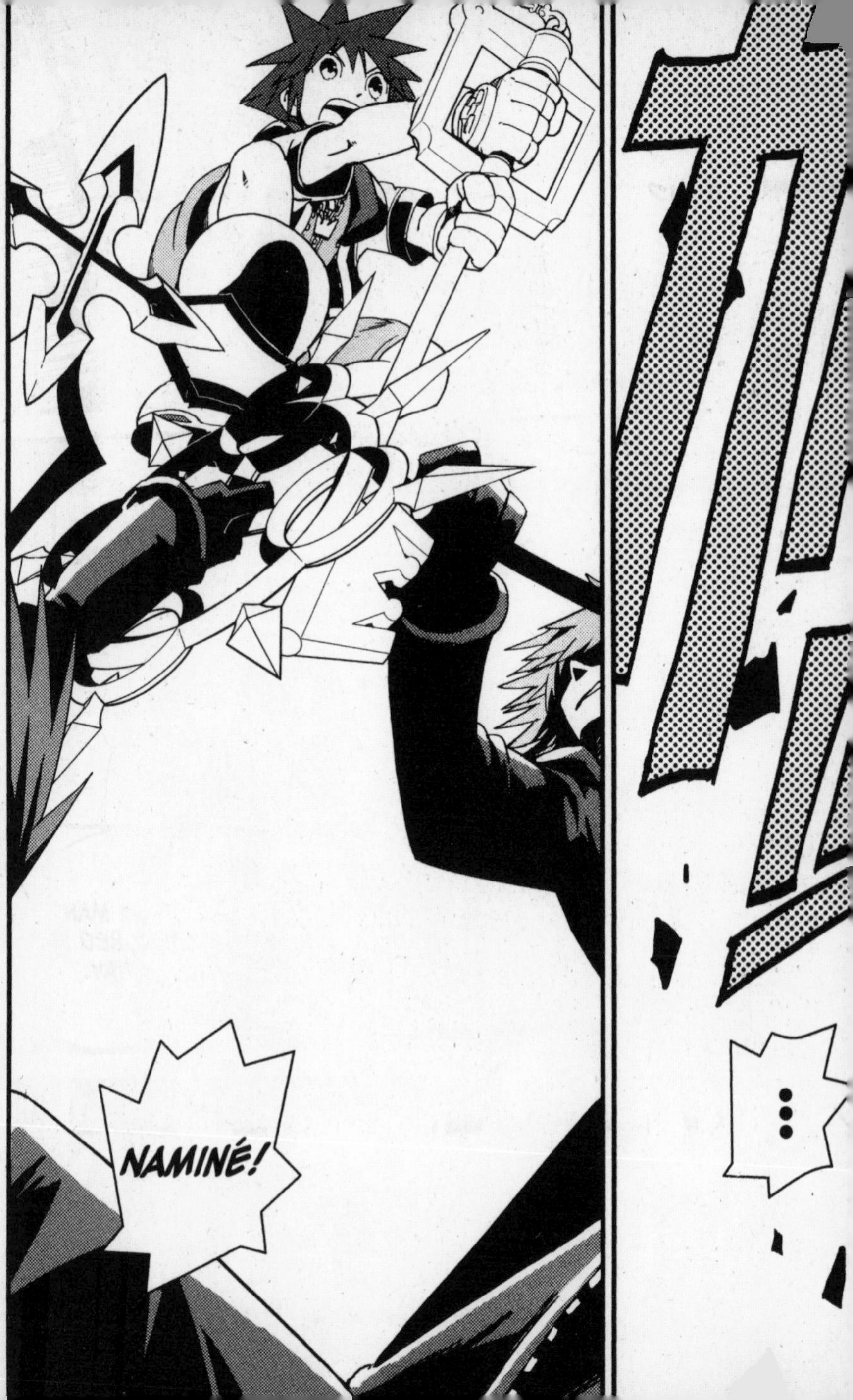
…
NAMINÉ!

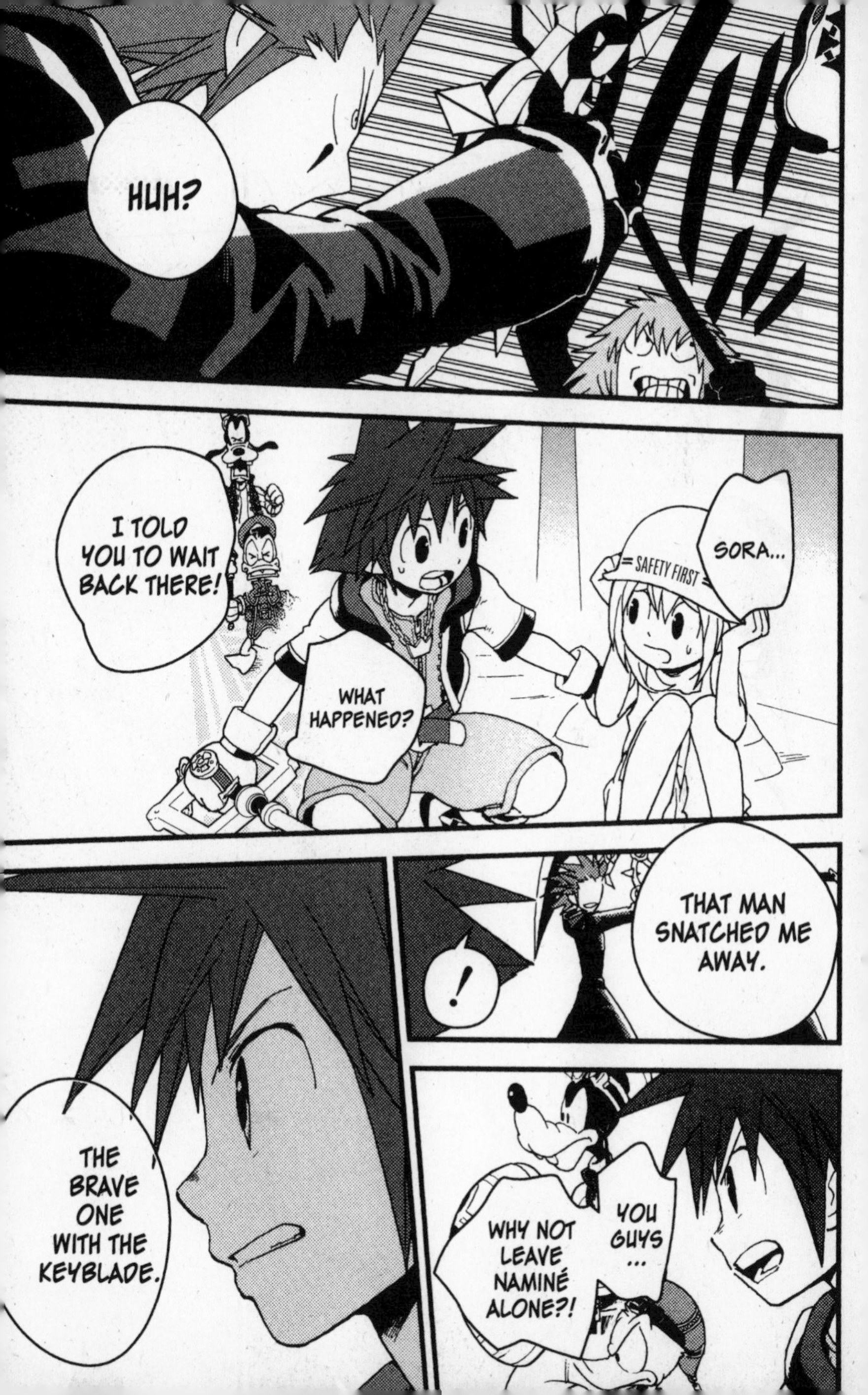
HUH?
SORA...
SAFETY FIRST
WHAT HAPPENED?
I TOLD YOU TO WAIT BACK THERE!
THAT MAN SNATCHED ME AWAY.
!
YOU GUYS ...
WHY NOT LEAVE NAMINÉ ALONE?!
THE BRAVE ONE WITH THE KEYBLADE.

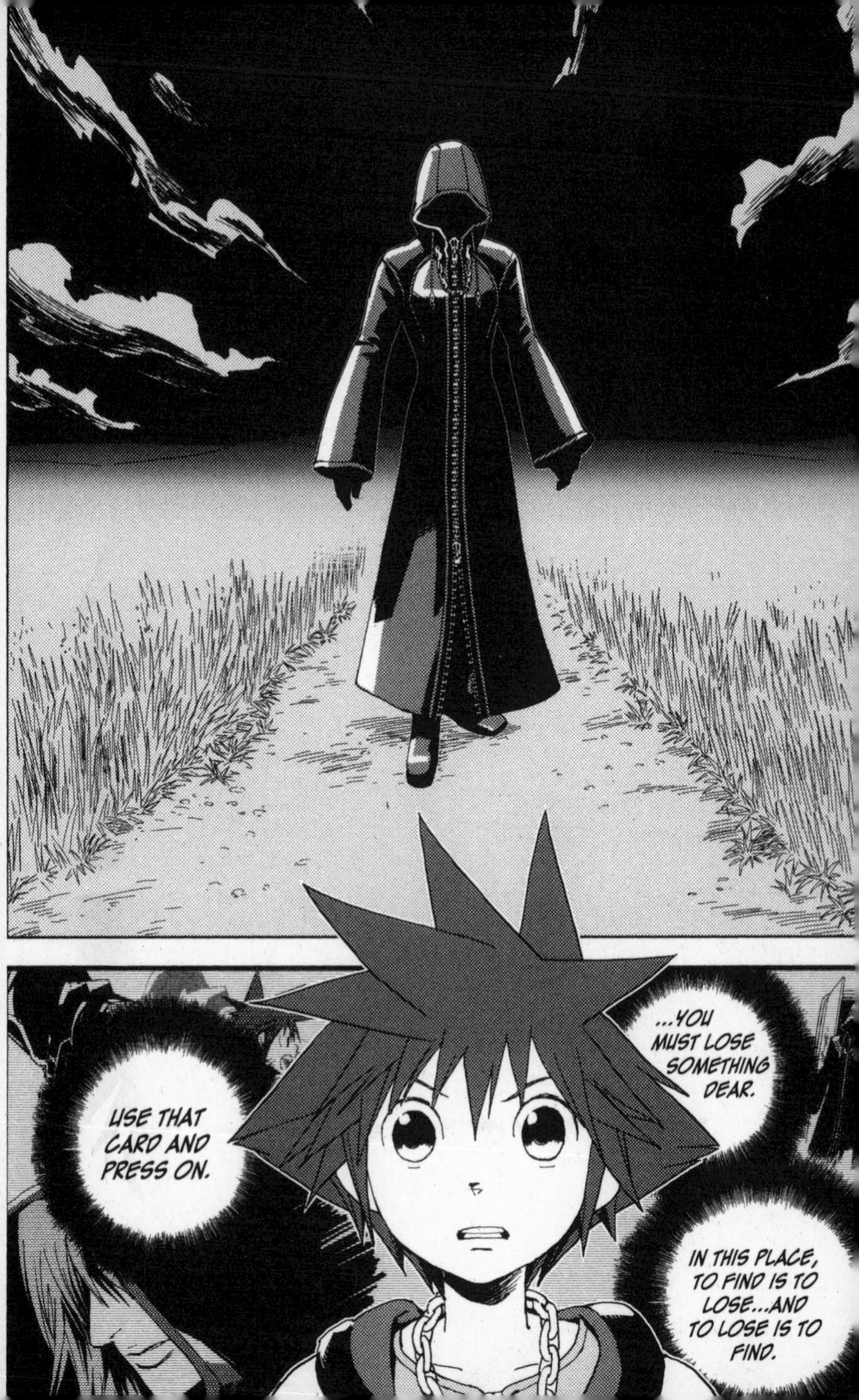
...YOU MUST LOSE SOMETHING DEAR.
USE THAT CARD AND PRESS ON.
IN THIS PLACE, TO FIND IS TO LOSE...AND TO LOSE IS TO FIND.

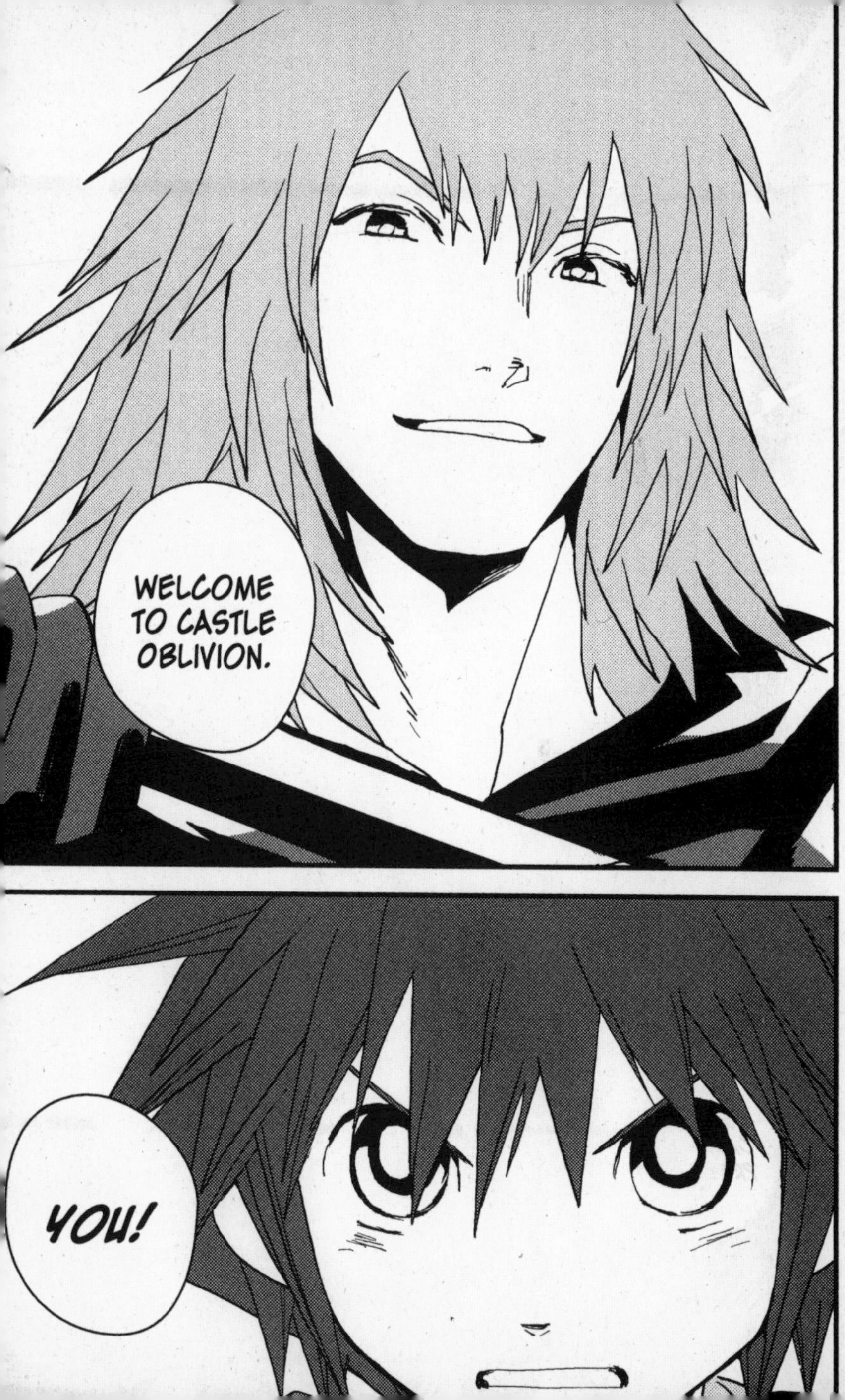
WELCOME TO CASTLE OBLIVION.
YOU!

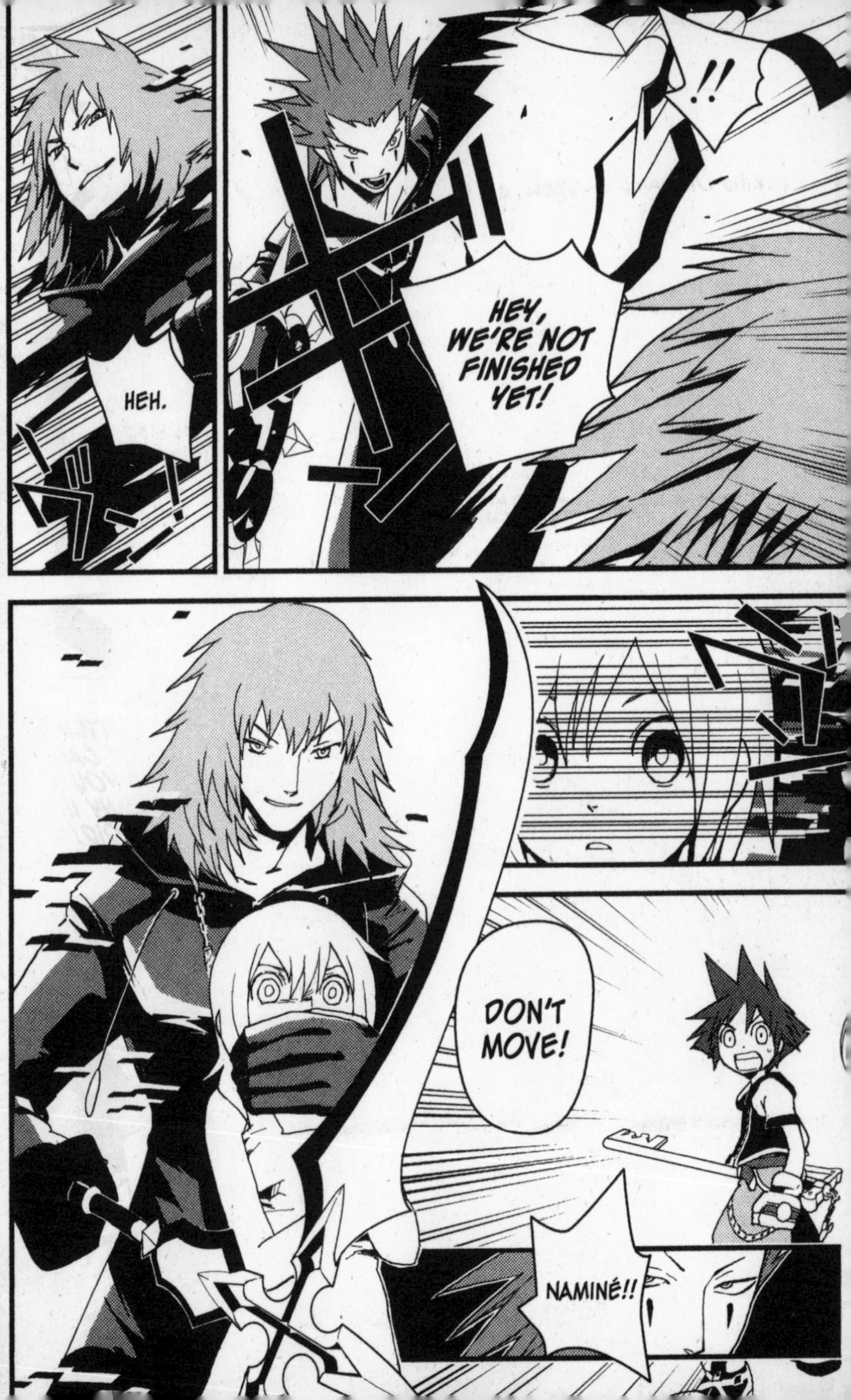
!!
HEY, WE'RE NOT FINISHED YET!
HEH.
DON'T MOVE!
NAMINÉ!!

THAT'S A GREAT JOKE.

IF *YOU'RE* GOING TO DO IT, BE MY GUEST.

GO.

HEY, I JUST WANTED TO KILL MARLUXIA.

?!

QUAACK!

WHAT'S WITH HIM?

......

GAWRSH! ARE WE BACK IN THE PICTURE?

SORA, LOOK!

I'M GLAD I'M BACK IN THE PICTURE, TOO.

HURRY INSIDE!

!!

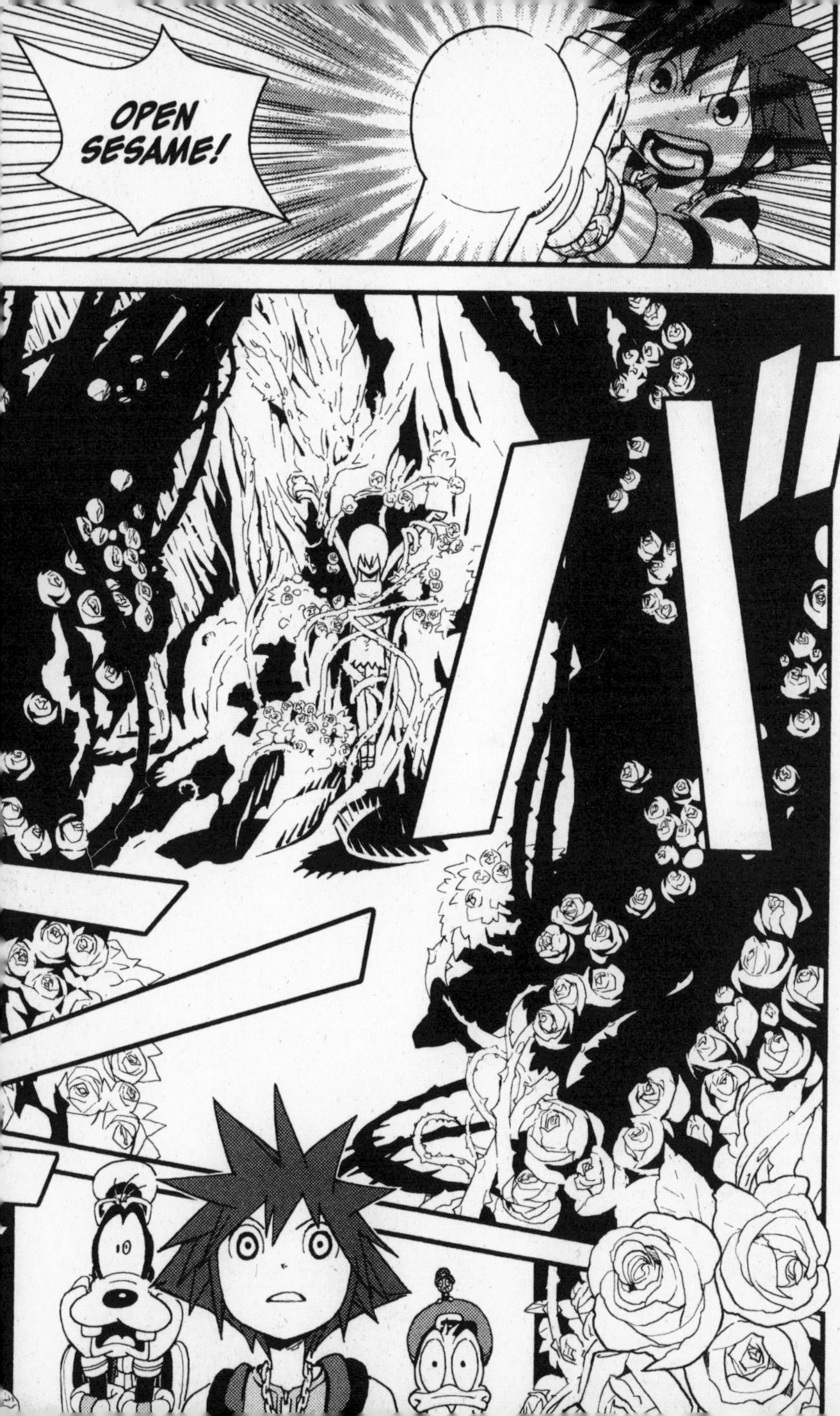
OPEN SESAME!

THAT WAS QUICK.

WELCOME TO MY FLOWER GARDEN.

THE ROSES HERE REPRESENT NAMINÉ'S FEELINGS.

THIS IS WHAT SHE WANTED.

SHE DIDN'T WANT TO HURT YOU ANYMORE.

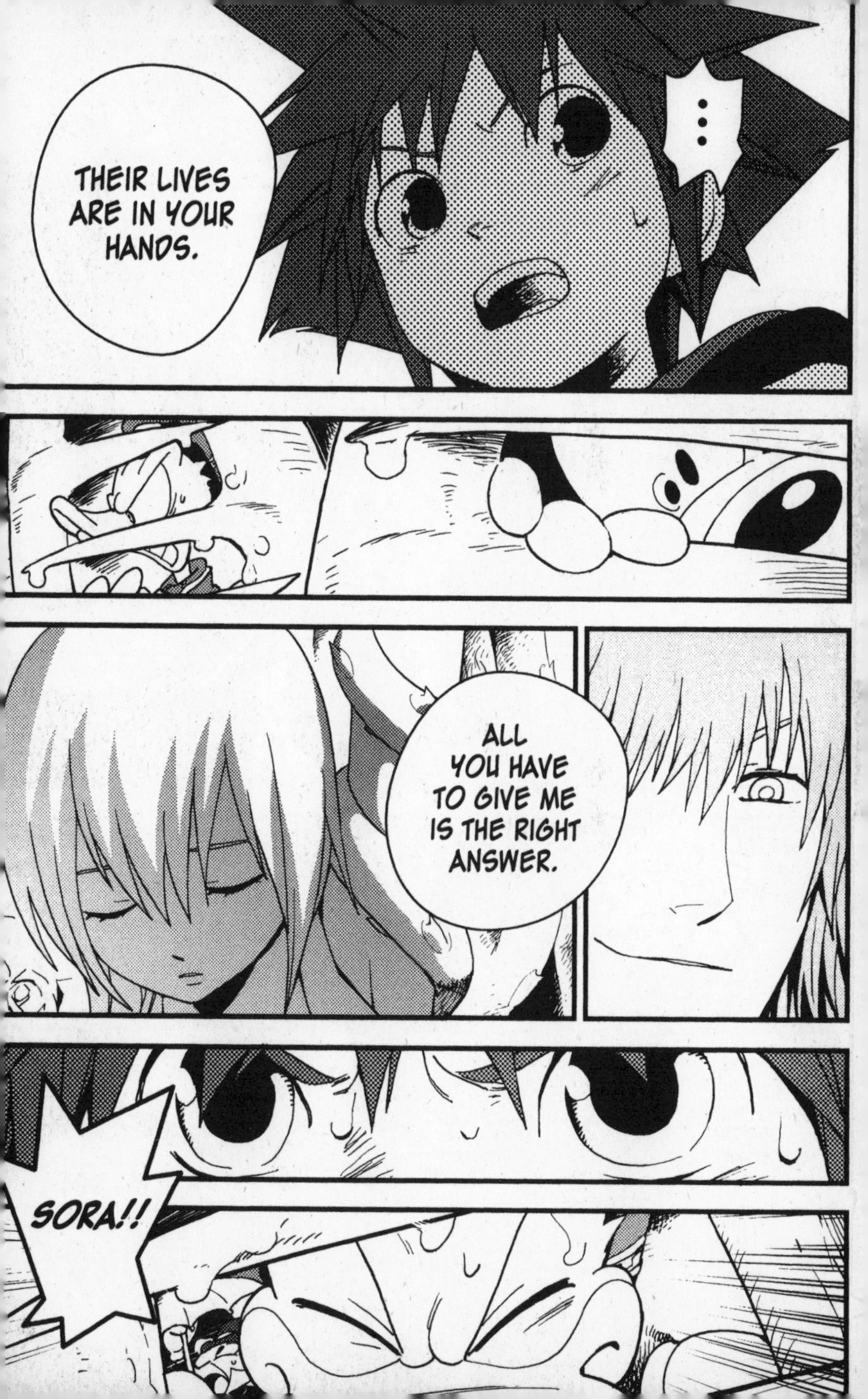
THEIR LIVES ARE IN YOUR HANDS.
...
ALL YOU HAVE TO GIVE ME IS THE RIGHT ANSWER.
SORA!!

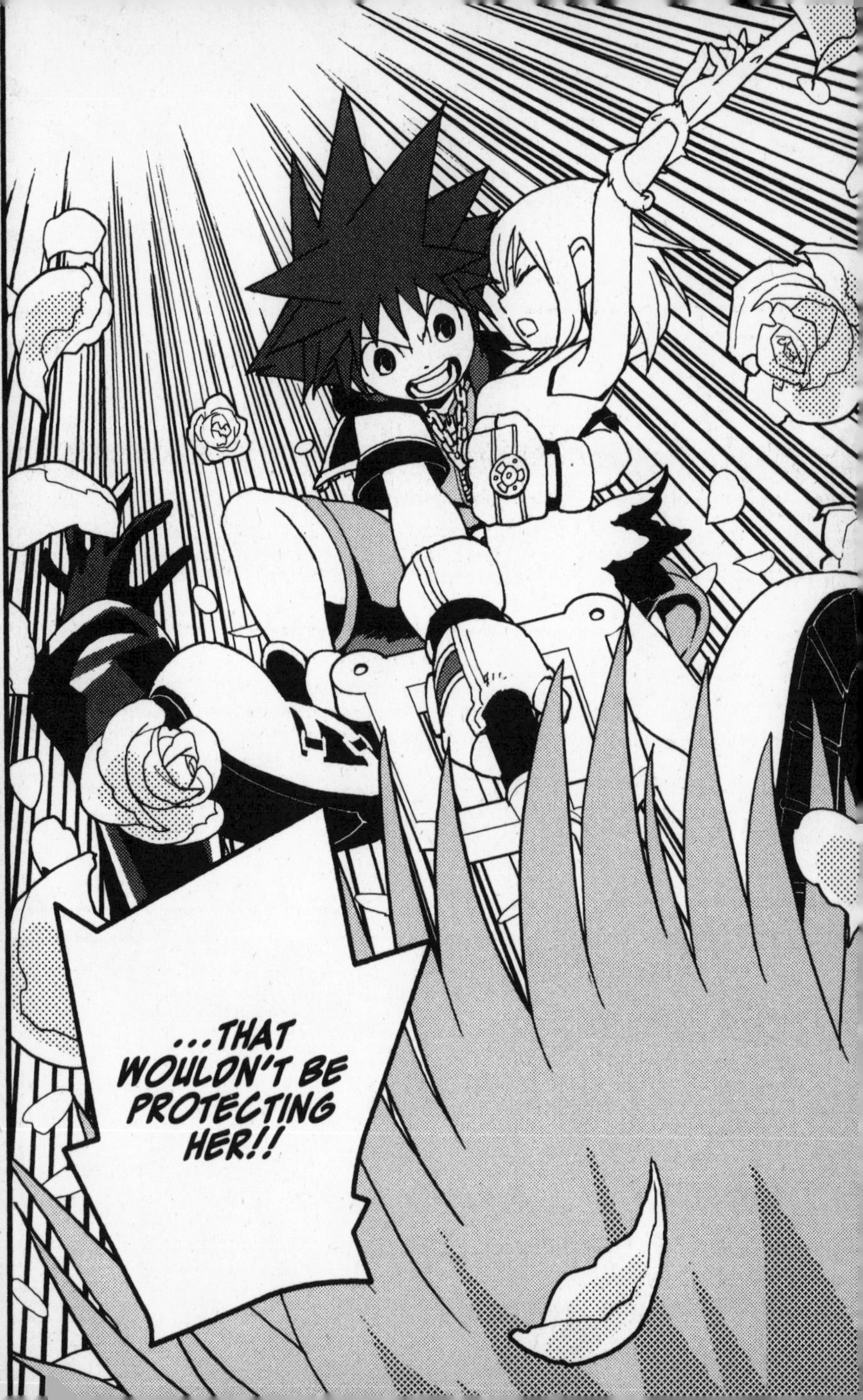
...THAT WOULDN'T BE PROTECTING HER!!

DON'T CRY.

I PROMISE.

I'LL COME BACK TO YOU.

THE SMELL OF THE WIND...

AH HA HA!

RIKU!

RIKU!

MAN, I MISS THEM...

SORA... KAIRI...

205

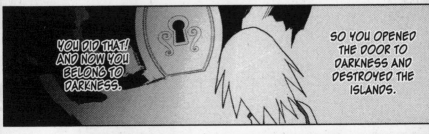

RECOGNIZE THE POSITION YOU'RE IN.

THAT'S RIGHT, RIKU.

WE'RE PREPARED TO WELCOME YOU WITH OPEN ARMS.

I'M... FADING?

CONSUMED BY THE LIGHT?

YOU CAN'T FADE.

MAYBE THAT'S NOT SO BAD...

NO POWER CAN DEFEAT YOU.

WHO'S THAT?

NOT THE LIGHT, NOT THE DARK. SO DON'T RUN FROM THE LIGHT--AND DON'T FEAR THE DARKNESS.

NOT THE KING?

KNOW THAT THE DARKNESS IS THERE AND DON'T GIVE IN.

THE DARKNESS IN YOUR HEART IS VAST AND DEEP...BUT IF YOU CAN STARE INTO IT UNFLINCHINGLY, YOU'LL NEVER KNOW FEAR AGAIN.

!

DO THAT, AND YOU'LL GAIN STRENGTH UNLIKE ANY OTHER.

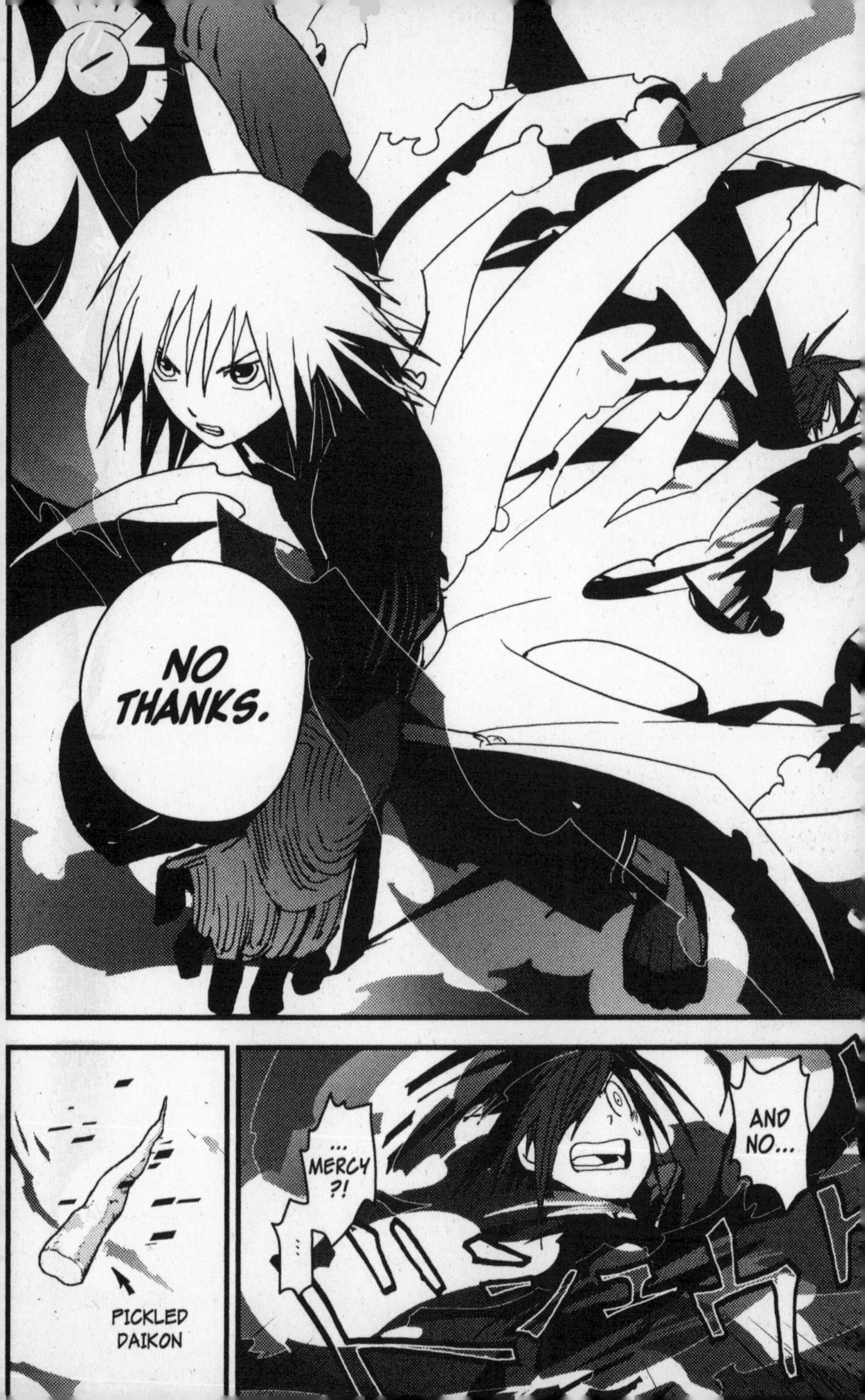
NO THANKS.
AND NO...
...MERCY?!
PICKLED DAIKON

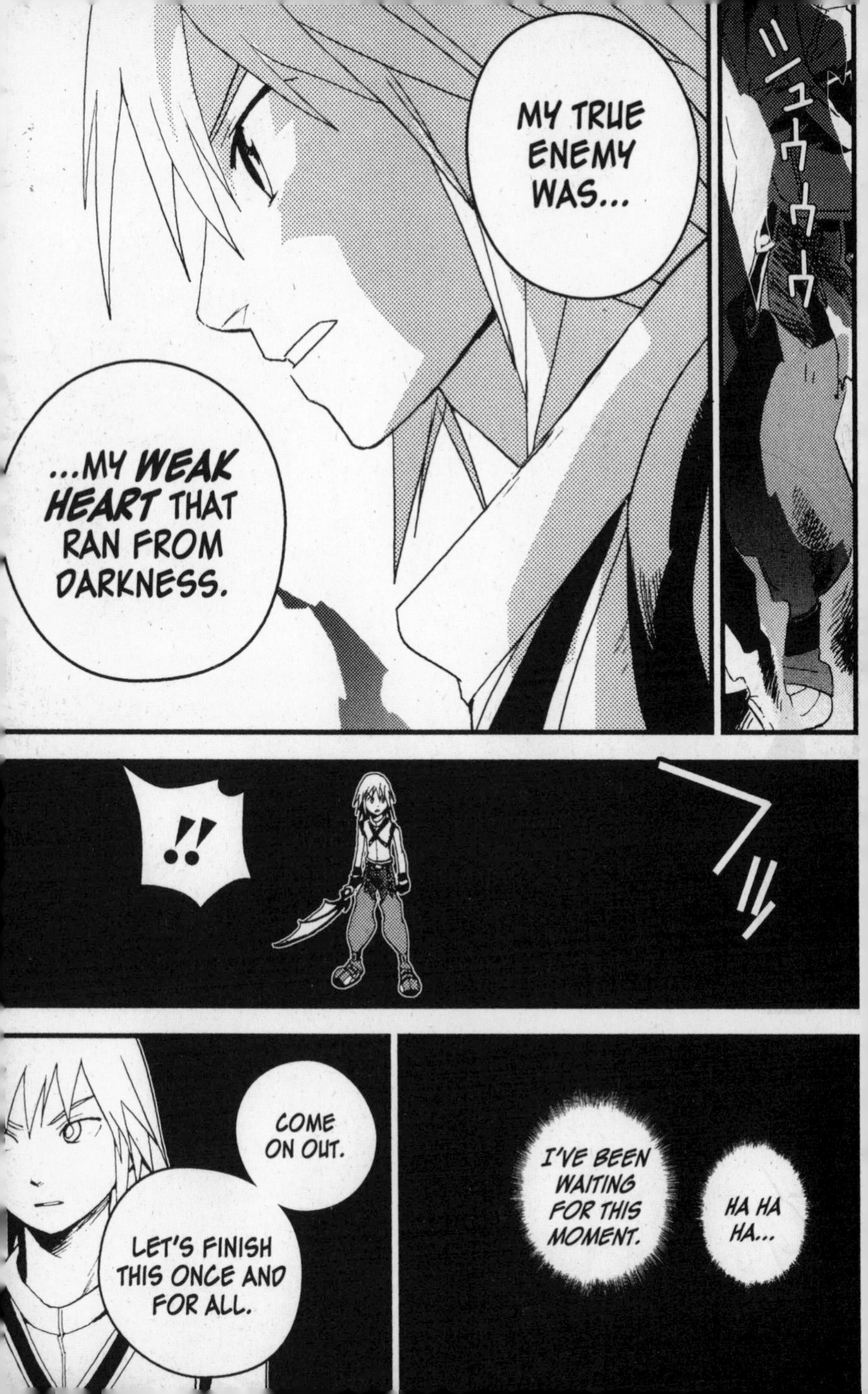
MY TRUE ENEMY WAS...
...MY **WEAK HEART** THAT RAN FROM DARKNESS.
!!
I'VE BEEN WAITING FOR THIS MOMENT.
HA HA HA...
COME ON OUT.
LET'S FINISH THIS ONCE AND FOR ALL.

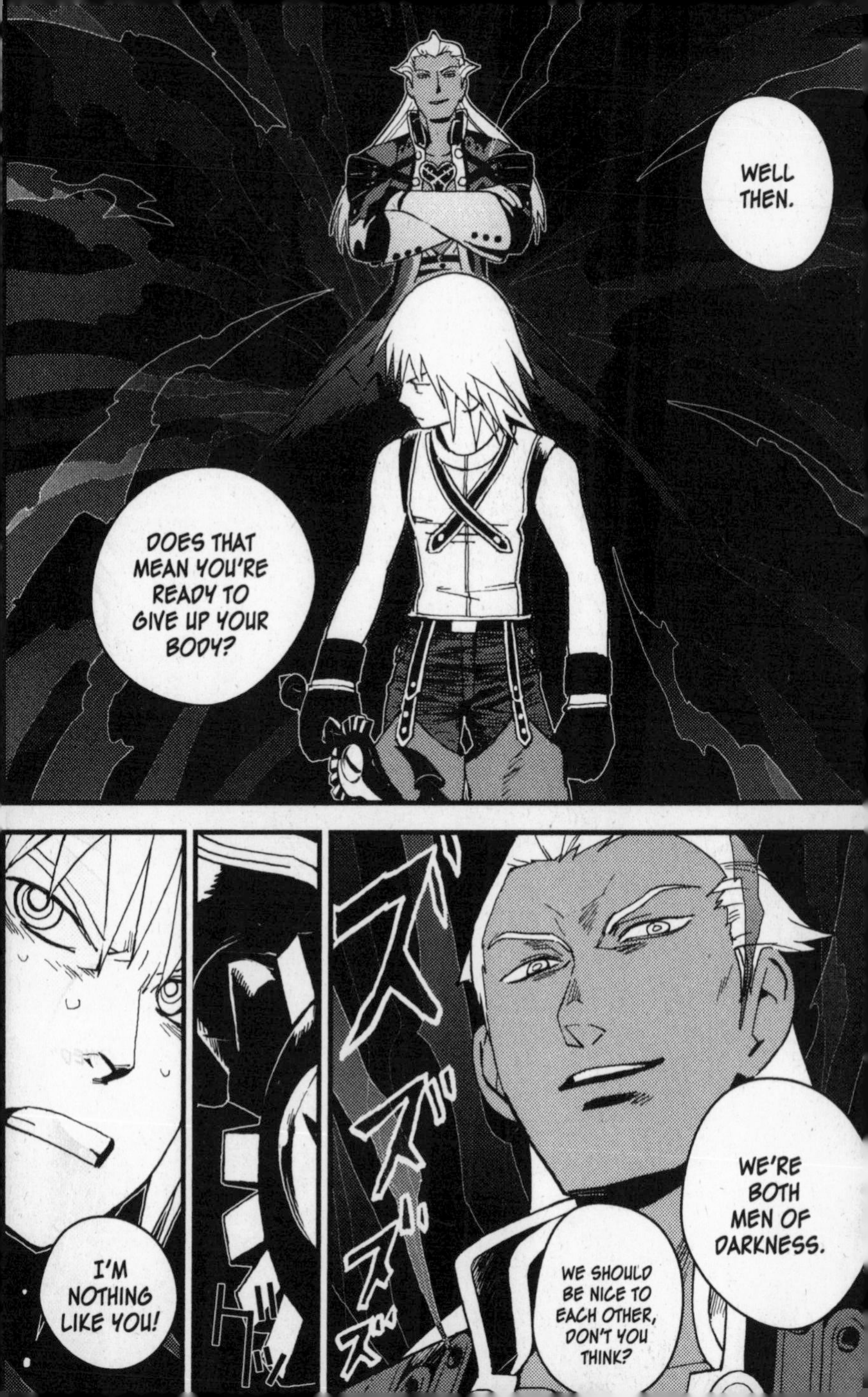
WELL THEN.
DOES THAT MEAN YOU'RE READY TO GIVE UP YOUR BODY?
WE'RE BOTH MEN OF DARKNESS.
WE SHOULD BE NICE TO EACH OTHER, DON'T YOU THINK?
I'M NOTHING LIKE YOU!

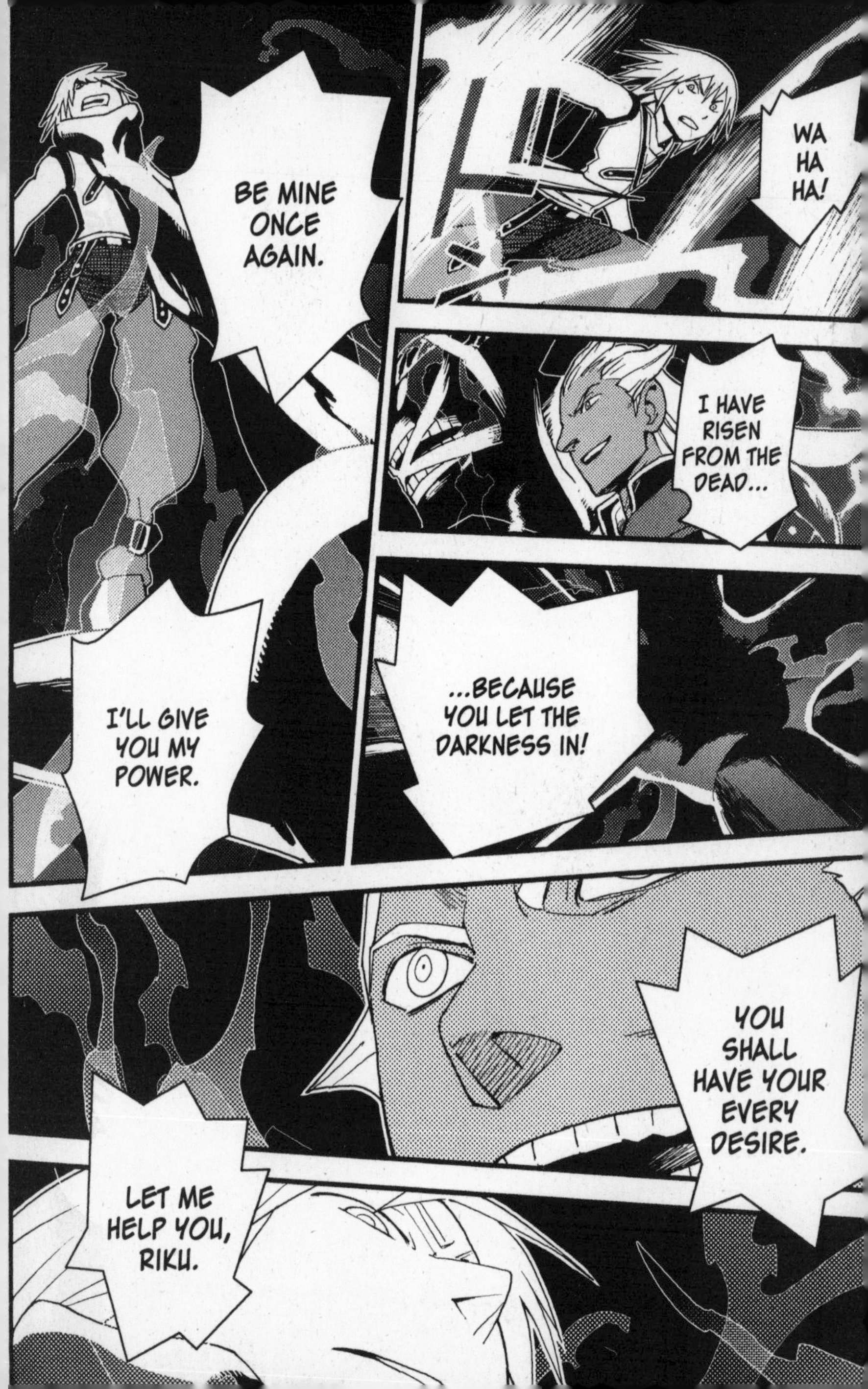
WA HA HA!
I HAVE RISEN FROM THE DEAD...
...BECAUSE YOU LET THE DARKNESS IN!
BE MINE ONCE AGAIN.
I'LL GIVE YOU MY POWER.
YOU SHALL HAVE YOUR EVERY DESIRE.
LET ME HELP YOU, RIKU.

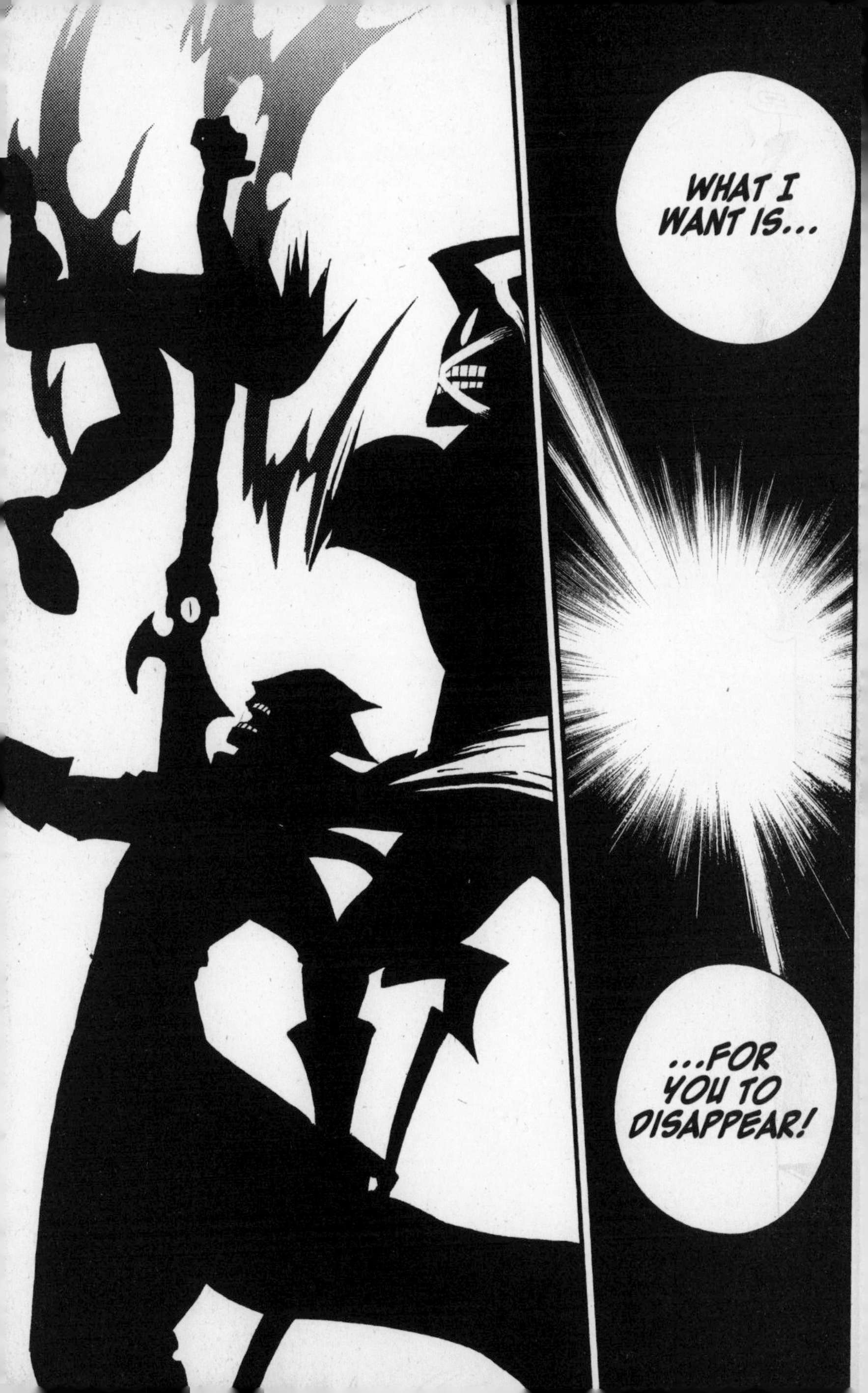
WHAT I WANT IS...
...FOR YOU TO DISAPPEAR!

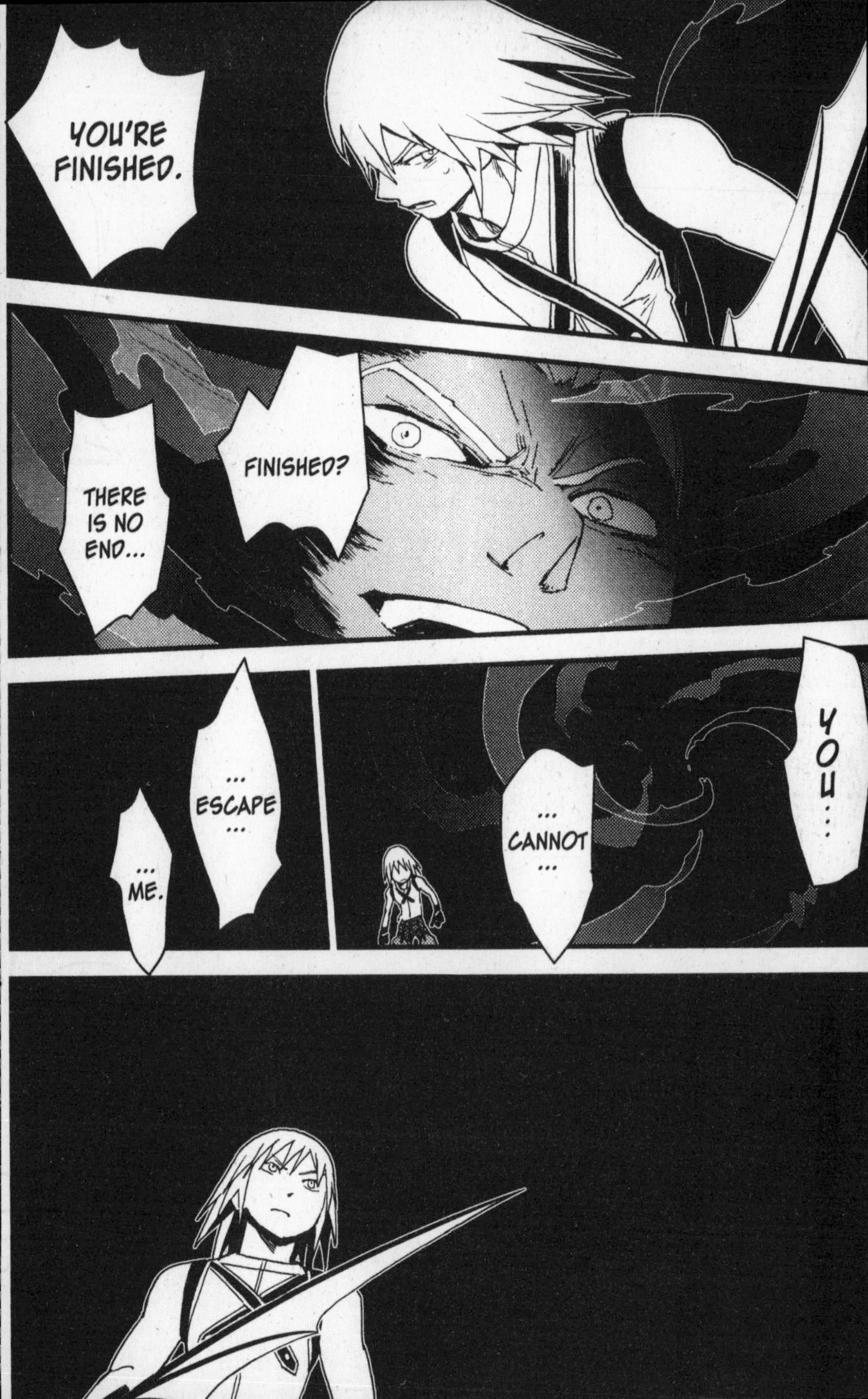
YOU'RE FINISHED.
FINISHED?
THERE IS NO END...
YOU...
...CANNOT...
...ESCAPE...
...ME.

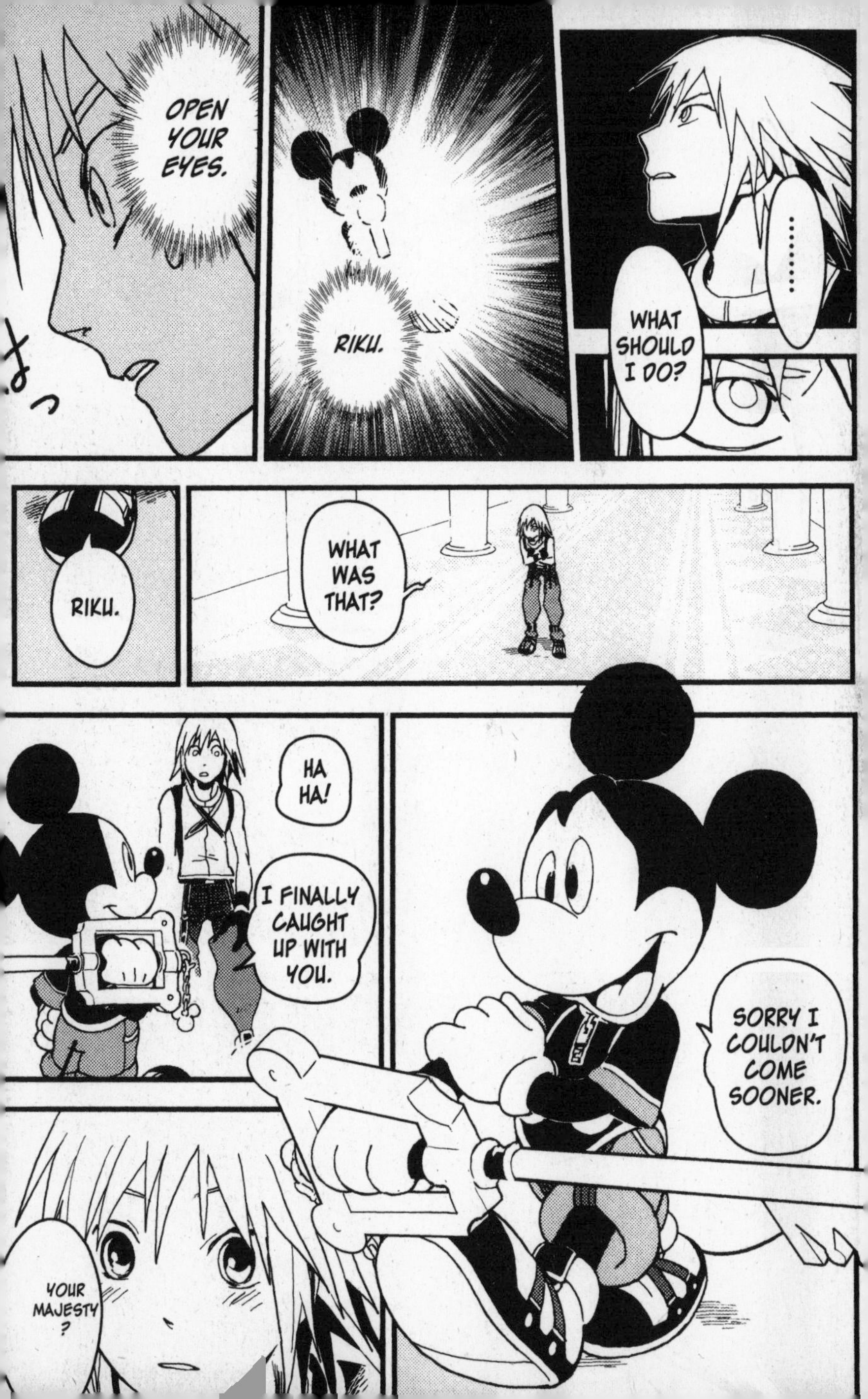
......
WHAT SHOULD I DO?
RIKU.
OPEN YOUR EYES.
はっ
WHAT WAS THAT?
RIKU.
SORRY I COULDN'T COME SOONER.
HA HA!
I FINALLY CAUGHT UP WITH YOU.
YOUR MAJESTY?

CORRECT. I WANTED TO FLUSH OUT THE ANSEM WHO WAS HIDING INSIDE OF YOU.

I CAN FEEL HIM.

RIKU...

HE'S STILL THERE.

THERE'S SOMEONE I WANT YOU TO MEET.

...IF I SEAL THE DARKNESS IN YOUR HEART ALONG WITH YOUR MEMORY.

...AND I CAN MAKE IT SO ANSEM NEVER ESCAPES...

SORA WAS ALWAYS SLACKING OFF WHEN WE WERE BUILDING OUR RAFT...

...BUT *I* CAN'T AFFORD TO SLACK OFF. *KEEP* YOUR LOCK.

I'D RATHER JUST FINISH ANSEM OFF ONCE AND FOR ALL.

THAT VOICE...

IT *WAS* YOU.

I HOPED YOU WOULD SAY THAT.

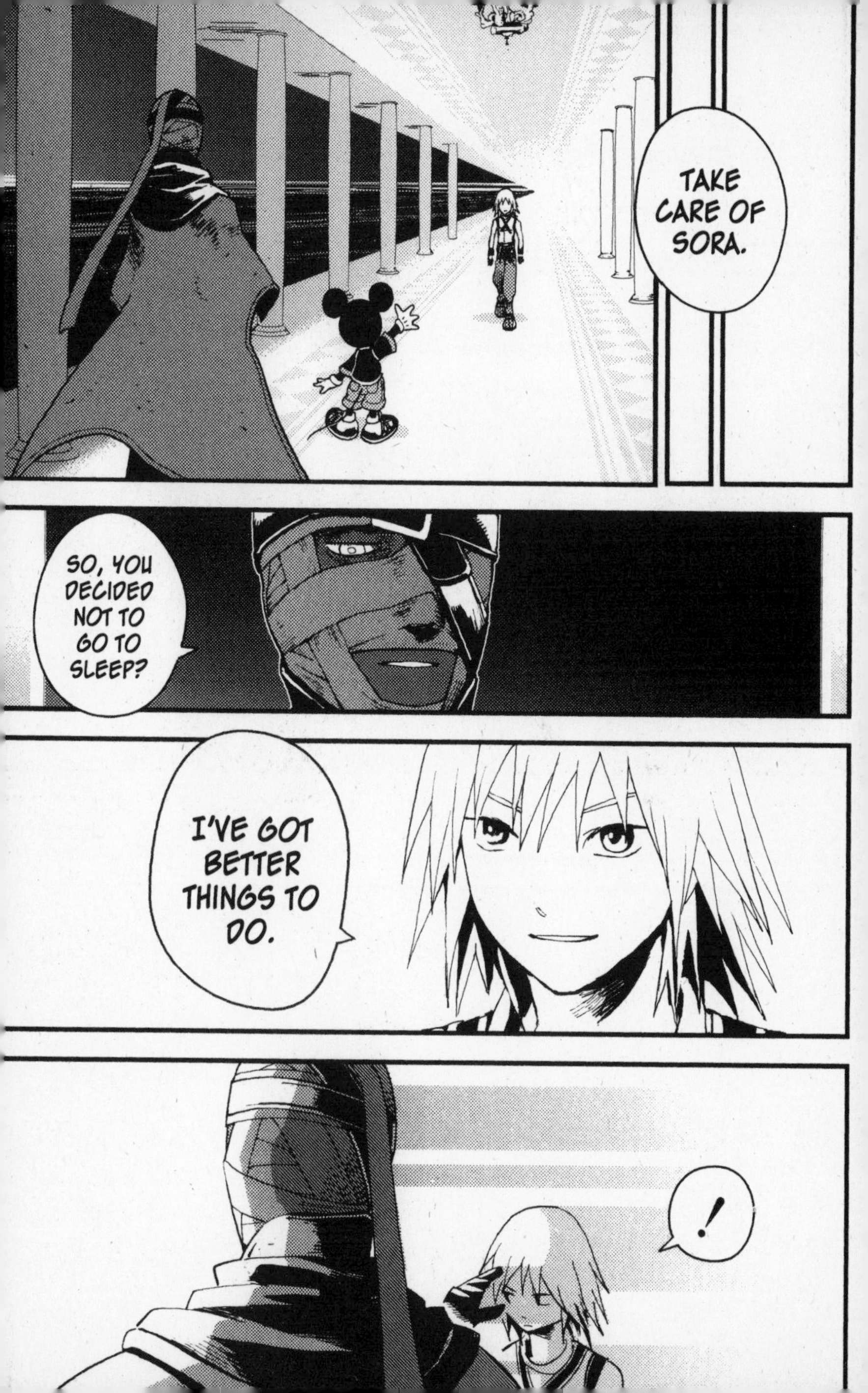
TAKE CARE OF SORA.
SO, YOU DECIDED NOT TO GO TO SLEEP?
I'VE GOT BETTER THINGS TO DO.
!

IT'S A NEW DAWN...

FOR NOW...

WHAT ABOUT THAT GIRL?

...LET'S JUST LEAVE HER ALONE.

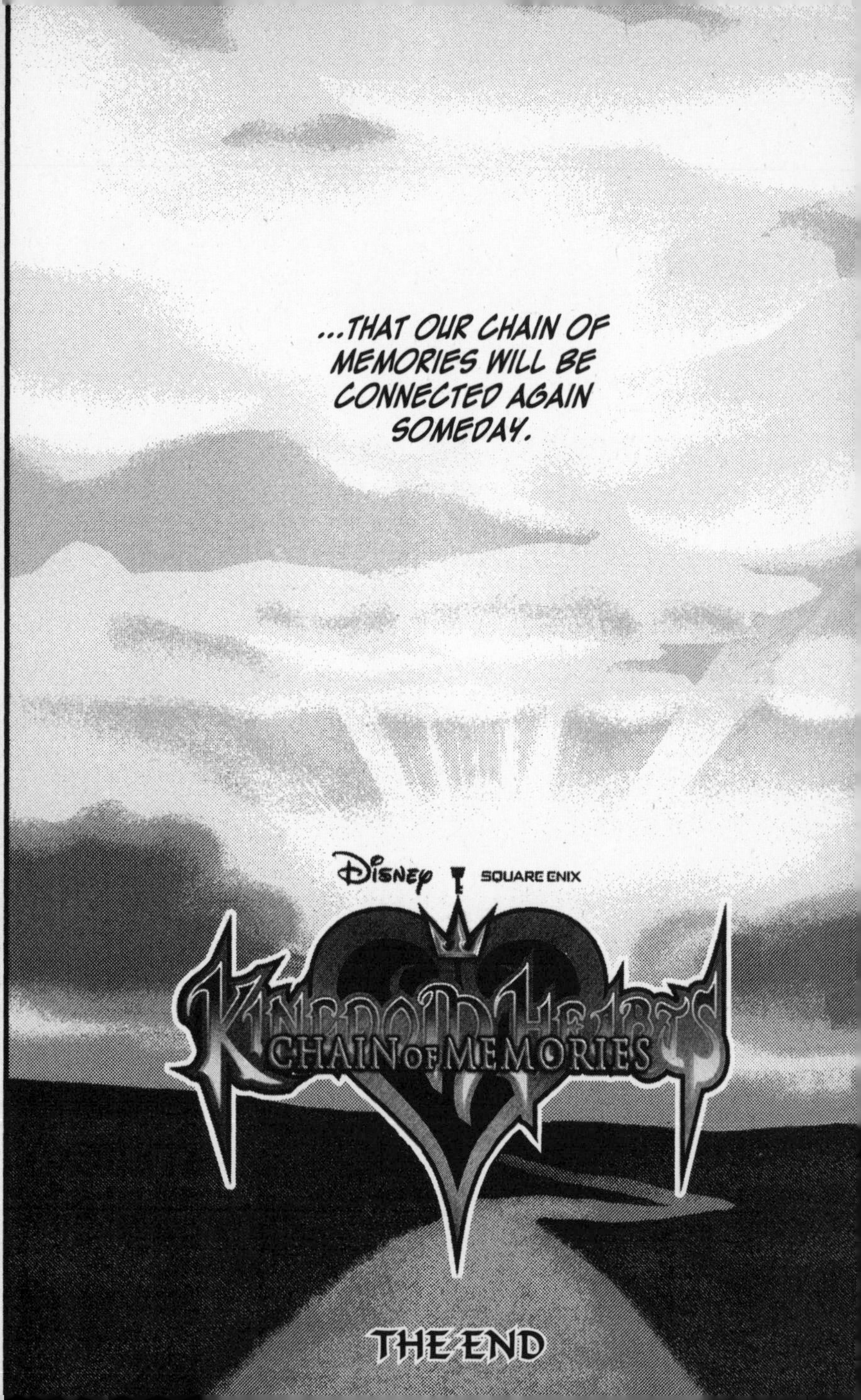
...THAT OUR CHAIN OF MEMORIES WILL BE CONNECTED AGAIN SOMEDAY.
DISNEY SQUARE ENIX
KINGDOM HEARTS CHAIN OF MEMORIES
THE END

SHE'S GONE!

AH!

WHERE'S NAMINÉ?

WHAT'S THIS?

NAMINÉ TOOK A BITE OUT OF IT!

I'LL PROTECT NAMINÉ!

I'LL KEEP THIS AS A LUCKY CHARM.

(MEAT)

NAMINÉ!!

230

...TO FIND MYSELF.

I'M HITTIN' THE ROAD...

VEXEN!

WHY DID YOU CREATE ME?

TAKE CARE OF NAMINÉ.

SORA!

FARE-WELL.

PAT

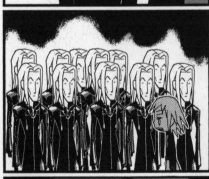

QUIT FOLLOW-ING ME!

We...are...all...failed...replicas.

VEXEN!!

Disney ! SQUARE ENIX

KINGDOM HEARTS
CHAIN OF MEMORIES

As Sora slumbers we can only hope he
will regain the precious memories of his
friends. But at what cost? Will he in turn
forget all about his new friend, Naminé?
And what about Kairi? How long will she
wait for Sora's return?
Meanwhile, Riku remains awake in a
quest to help Sora regain his memory
and to defeat the darkness within himself
once and for all...

The adventure continues in the next
installment of the blockbuster series
KINGDOM HEARTS II
Coming Soon!!

Disney SQUARE ENIX

KINGDOM HEARTS CHAIN OF MEMORIES

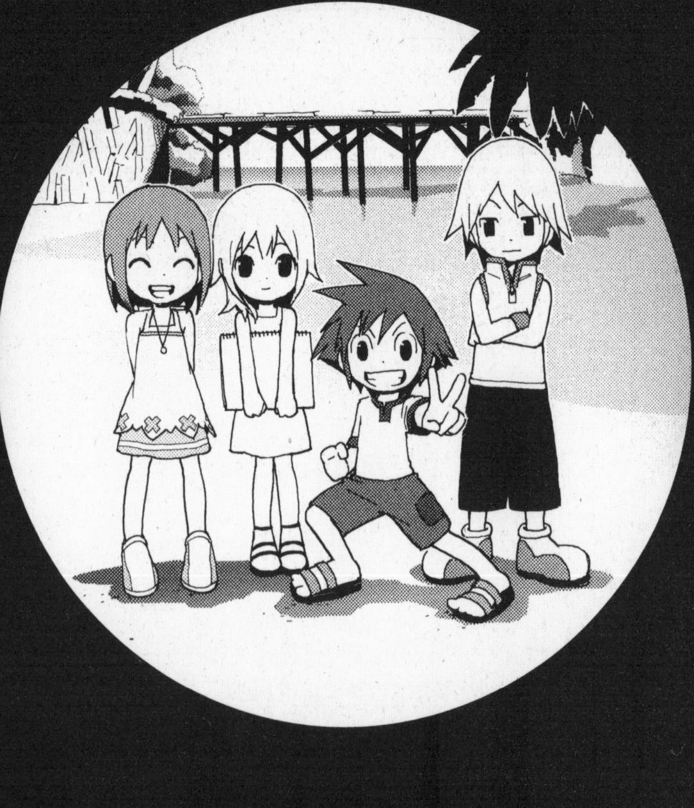

Disney SQUARE ENIX

Kingdom Hearts
Chain of Memories

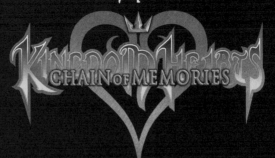

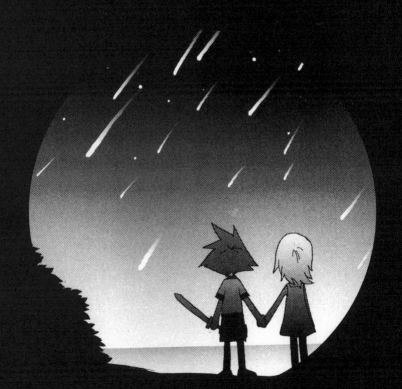

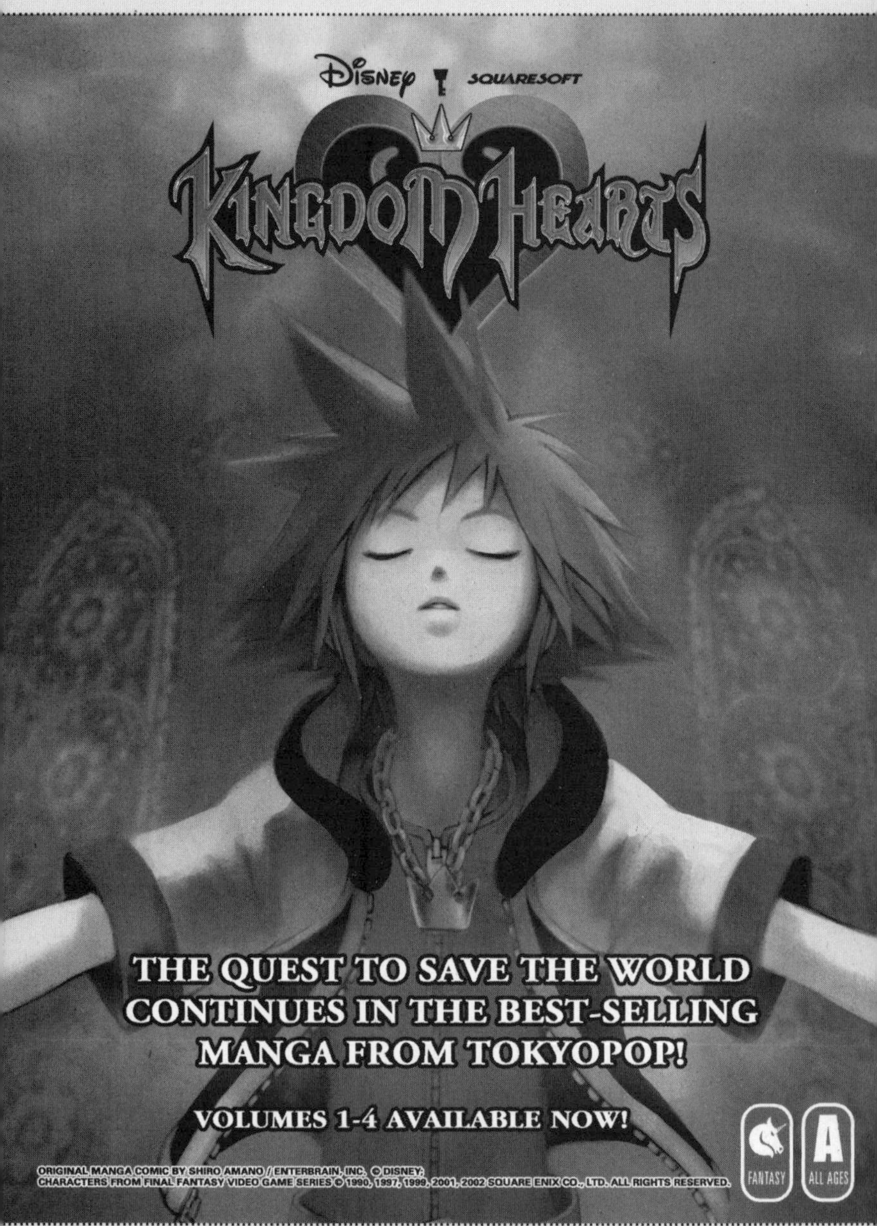
DISNEY SQUARESOFT
KINGDOM HEARTS
THE QUEST TO SAVE THE WORLD CONTINUES IN THE BEST-SELLING MANGA FROM TOKYOPOP!
VOLUMES 1-4 AVAILABLE NOW!
ORIGINAL MANGA COMIC BY SHIRO AMANO / ENTERBRAIN, INC. © DISNEY; CHARACTERS FROM FINAL FANTASY VIDEO GAME SERIES © 1990, 1997, 1999, 2001, 2002 SQUARE ENIX CO., LTD. ALL RIGHTS RESERVED.
FANTASY
A
ALL AGES

SPOTLIGHT TOKYOPOP MANGA SUPPLEMENT

THE DREAMING

BY QUEENIE CHAN

T
TEEN
AGE 13+

THE DORMS ARE ON THE SECOND FLOOR.
THIS WAY!
BATH-ROOM'S THAT WAY...
LIGHTS OUT AT TEN - BUT YOU CAN READ IN BED.
EVERY DORM DOOR HAS A NUMBER, AND 87--
IS YOUR DORM NUMBER!
TOKYOPOP
the dreaming
I
Queenie Chan
MAYBE IF I —
SU...
...AND WHAT'S BEHIND THAT DOOR ANYWAY?
!
WHAT THE--

ALL OF THEM VANISHED...WITHOUT A TRACE.

When twin sisters Amber and Jeanie enroll in an Australian boarding school, they soon uncover a dark, unexplained secret: Students have been known to walk off into the surrounding bushlands, where they have vanished completely! Few know how the girls disappeared...fewer yet know why. Amber and Jeanie soon realize that the key to unlocking a secret that has been hidden for years may lie in the world of their dreams!

SUSPENSE-HORROR SHOJO FROM THE CREATOR OF THE HIT WEB COMIC *BLOCK 6.*

FOR MORE INFORMATION VISIT: WWW.TOKYOPOP.COM/THEDREAMING

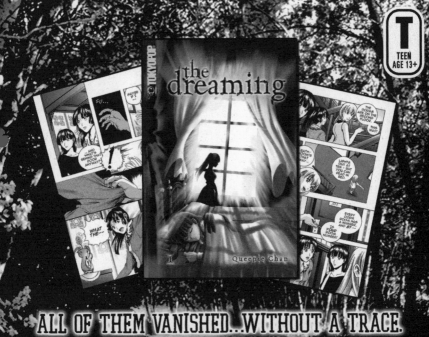

WARCRAFT
THE SUNWELL TRILOGY

RICHARD A. KNAAK · KIM JAE-HWAN

From the artist of the
best-selling *King of Hell* series!

It's an epic quest to save the entire High Elven Kingdom from the forces of the Undead Scourge! Set in the mystical world of Azeroth, *Warcraft: The Sunwell Trilogy* chronicles the adventures of Kalec, a blue dragon who has taken human form to escape deadly forces, and Anveena, a beautiful young maiden with a mysterious power.

EXPERIENCE THE MANGA

TEEN
AGE 13+

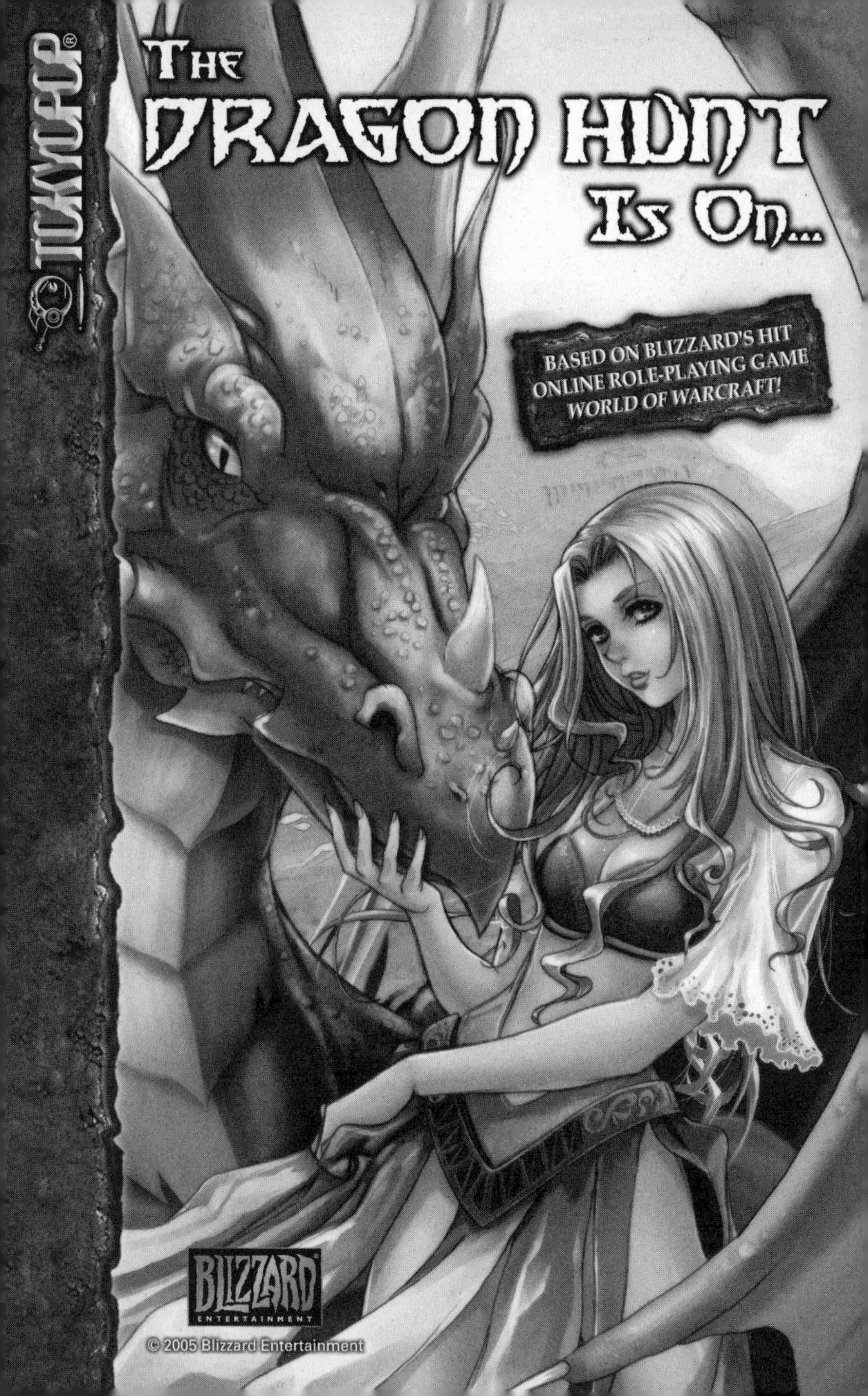
TOKYOPOP
The Dragon Hunt Is On...
BASED ON BLIZZARD'S HIT ONLINE ROLE-PLAYING GAME WORLD OF WARCRAFT!
BLIZZARD ENTERTAINMENT
© 2005 Blizzard Entertainment

STOP!

This is the back of the book.
You wouldn't want to spoil a great ending!

This book is printed "manga-style," in the authentic Japanese right-to-left format. Since none of the artwork has been flipped or altered, readers get to experience the story just as the creator intended. You've been asking for it, so TOKYOPOP® delivered: authentic, hot-off-the-press, and far more fun!

DIRECTIONS

If this is your first time reading manga-style, here's a quick guide to help you understand how it works.

It's easy... just start in the top right panel and follow the numbers. Have fun, and look for more 100% authentic manga from TOKYOPOP®!